India's Changing Borderland

Disputes the Fault Lines

India's Changing Borderland
Disputes the Fault Lines

Col. Puneet Raina (Retd.)

Gaurav Book Centre Pvt Ltd
Delhi

Publisher
GAURAV BOOK CENTRE PVT LTD
4832/24,Prahlad Lane,S-207 Ansari
Road, Daryaganj, Delhi-110002
Ph.: 43570976, 23278261
Email: gauravbookcentre@gmail.com

Edition: 2015

ISBN: 978-93-83316-31-1

Laser Typesetting
JEE-VEE Graphics, Delhi

Price: 1295/-

Printed
Vikas Computers, Delhi

Preface

Boundaries are manifestations of national identity. They can be trip-wires of war. This is all the more important if the involved parties are nuclear powers. It threatens to inflame long-standing boundary disputes that India has with China, Pakistan, Nepal and Bangladesh.

The India-Bangladesh boundary is no ordinary one. Hastily constructed in the dying days of British colonialism, it was the longest international boundary created during the age of decolonisation.

The recent detonation of a series of nuclear devices by India and Pakistan has increased tension in South Asia and threatens to inflame long-standing boundary disputes that India has with China, Nepal, and Pakistan. The disputes with China and Pakistan have already triggered several wars. The new Hindu-nationalist government in New Delhi has reversed movement toward détente with Beijing and Islamabad. The areas in contention with China and Pakistan are among the largest land-boundary disputes in the world. The Indo-Nepali dispute over Kalapani is more recent and involves a small area.

The 2014–15 India–Pakistan border skirmishes are a series of ongoing armed skirmishes and firing exchange between the Border Security Force and Pakistan Army along the Line of Control (LoC) in the disputed Kashmir area and Punjab. Started from mid-July 2014, military officials and media reports of both countries gave different accounts of the incident, each accusing the other of initiating the hostilities. The incident sparked outrage both in Pakistan and India and harsh reactions by the Indian army and Pakistan armed forces and governments.

The book examine the deeper history of environmental change and political conflict in a region that is now particularly vulnerable to climate change, and at the fault-lines of strategic conflict between India and neighbour.

—Editor

Contents

1

Introduction

INDO-BHUTAN BORDER

India and Bhutan share a 669 km long boundary. The boundary is demarcated except along the tri-junction with China. The process of demarcation of the India-Bhutan border started in 1961 and was completed in 2006. Like with Nepal, India's boundary with Bhutan is also an open boundary. The border was peaceful till Indian insurgent groups such as the Kamtapur Liberation Organisation (KLO), United Liberation Front of Asom (ULFA) and National Democratic Front of Bodoland (NDFB) established camps in the southern districts of Bhutan. Taking advantage of the open border, these insurgents would sneak into Bhutan after carrying out extortions, killings and bomb blasts. This problem has been effectively dealt with during the Bhutanese government's 'Operation All Clear', which saw the destruction and uprooting of all insurgent camps in Bhutanese territory. However, stray insurgent incidents such as extortion and killings are still carried out by the surviving members of ULFA along the border areas. Smuggling and trafficking are also rampant along the border. Chinese made goods, Bhutanese cannabis, liquor and forest products are major items smuggled into India. Livestock, grocery items and fruits are smuggled out of India to Bhutan.

INDIA BHUTAN CHINA STRATEGIC TRIANGLE

India Bhutan and China are part of a strategic triangle in the Eastern Himalayas with the inverted apex jutting in the form of the all important Chumbi Valley in Yadong (Yatung) county of Tibetan Autonomous Region (TAR). Given proximity of the Chumbi Valley to India's jugular to the North East the 20 kms wide Siliguri corridor, the two arms of the triangle resting on Indian state of Sikkim in the West and Bhutan in the East assume importance. Chinese plans to extend the Qinghai Tibet railway to Xigaze and Yadong close to the Sino Indian border have added to concerns in India with tardy communication links on the Eastern frontier. Given the strategic significance, India has been able to maintain balance primarily through the Indo Bhutan Treaty of Friendship first signed in 1949 and revised on mutually agreed terms in 2007.

Thus two arms of the triangle could be said under Indian control and influence, even as China holds the base. This equation may be upset in case China is able to gain greater access to the Bhutanese arm of the triangle with a reset of the Sino Bhutan boundary, negotiations for which are underway. Given the difficult terrain on the Western arm of the Chumbi Valley and scope for expansion is primarily in the East. These fears were attenuated with the first ever summit held between the prime ministers of Bhutan and China in Rio recently. An over view of the relationships would therefore be in order and is covered as per succeeding paragraphs.

Indo Bhutan Treaty of Friendship in 2007 has led to greater diplomatic freedom to Thimpu opening prospects of engagement across the board. The most significant change in 2007 was mutual reaffirmation of sovereignty and territorial integrity in the preamble of the Treaty which was not there in the 1949 text. More over Article 2 of the 1949 Treaty stated that Bhutan will be guided by the advice of India on external relations.

The Article read, "The Government of India undertakes to exercise no interference in the internal administration of Bhutan. On its part, the Government of Bhutan agrees to be guided by the advice of the Government of India in regard to its external relations". This has been reviewed of the 2007 Treaty reads, "__the Government of the Kingdom of Bhutan and the Government of the Republic of India shall cooperate closely with each other on issues relating to their national interests. Neither Government shall allow the use of its territory for activities harmful to the national security and interest of the other". The sum total of implications of the change is greater freedom of choice to Bhutan in management of sovereignty and external relations.

This background is essential to understand the nuances of the first ever bilateral held between the Chinese Prime Minister Wen Jiabao and Bhutan's Prime Minister, Jigmi Y. Thinley on the side lines of the Rio Conference on Sustainable Development in June 2012. While Bhutan has been expanding foreign relations over the years and in 2011 chaired South Asian Association of Regional Cooperation (SAARC), there was no formal diplomatic relations or summit level contact with Beijing.

Having greater autonomy post 2007 Treaty, it is inevitable that there would be greater traction for Bhutan to establish diplomatic relations with China the only nation other than India with which it shares a land border. Proposal for diplomatic relations was first discussed between the two countries in 1998 during the 12th Round of border talks.

Significantly, Bhutan and India are the only two countries with which China has not resolved land borders. There are two areas of dispute, one falling in North West Bhutan covering 269 sq km and the other Central Bhutan covering 495 sq km. The North West area comprises Doklam (89 sq km), Sinchulumpa (42 Sq km), and Shakhatoe (138 Sq km) in Samste, Haa and Paro districts and Central parts the Pasamlung and the Jakarlung valley in the Wangdue Phodrang district. The 1998 agreement between Bhutan and China entitled, "Maintain Peace and Tranquility on the Bhutan-China Border Areas," provides the framework for stability on the border. However despite this there have been reports of intrusions by Chinese troops in Bhutanese territory. In November 2007 some reports indicate dismantling of unmanned posts in the Dolam Valley..Bhutan's media reported a number of intrusions in 2009.

At the same time Bhutan and China have held 19 rounds of talks on the boundary dispute so far the last one being held in January 2010 after a gap of four years where a joint field survey was agreed upon. This was to be carried out of disputed areas in Doklam, Charithang, Sinchulumpa and Dramana in Bhutan's North

West and Pasamlung and the Jakarlung valley in the Wangdue Phodrang district in Central Bhutan. It is reasonably well established by now that China is looking for a package deal with Bhutan seeking areas in the North West while establishing Bhutan's claims in the Central region. This offer was first made in the sixth round of talks held in August 1990. Chinese quid pro quo does not take into account that the territory is a part of the sovereign state of Bhutan and strategic interests seem to be pushing Beijing to offer a package to the southern neighbor. Herein lies the rub where India's interests come in given proximity of the North West areas to the Chumbi Valley. In case Bhutan seeks to appease China to move the trajectory of relations forward, it would most certainly cause concern in Delhi and may even be objected to.

In the light of this legacy the Wen Jiabao – Thinley meet seems to be an opening gambit by both sides to test the waters on how far they can push the envelope without India blocking the package deal altogether. Premier Wen Jiabao as per a report by the AFP stated, "China is willing... to establish formal relations with Bhutan, resolve the border issue between the two nations at an early date, strengthen exchanges in all areas and advance Sino-Bhutanese relations to a new stage." A report in the Hindu of 27 June also quoted Mr. Wen saying that China was "willing to complete border demarcation with Bhutan at an early date." Mr. Thinley was quoted by Xinhua the official Chinese news agency to have expressed that Bhutan wishes to forge formal diplomatic ties with China as soon as possible. Bhutan has also sought China's support in elections to the non permanent seat in the United Nations Security Council being vacated by India in 2013.

South Asia experts from Chinese think tanks, China Institutes of Contemporary International Relations (CICIR) and Chinese Academy of Social Sciences (CASS) as quoted by the Hindu in a report on 26 June 2012 have been quick to speculate that Bhutan would not have taken these initiatives without India's express, "approval or agreement."

The official web site of the Cabinet Secretariat of the Royal Government of Bhutan however makes muted remarks on the bilateral summit and states, "The meeting [Wen Jiabao-Thinley] carries great historic significance as it marks the first meeting between the heads of the two governments. They discussed bilateral issues of mutual interest and multilateral cooperation including Bhutan's bid for a non permanent seat on UN Security Council for the term 2013-2014, elections for which are to be held in fall this year". No mention was made of either diplomatic relations or boundary issue.

Bhutanese writer, Kuenzang Choden writing in web site The Bhutanese on 22 June 2012, quotes Media Attache of Bhutan Prime Minister's office to refute any initiative by Prime Minister Thinley to propose establishment of diplomatic relations with China. He states, "local Chinese media had misreported that Bhutan and China will establish diplomatic ties." Kuenzang further goes on to quote a Foreign Ministry official who sought to remain anonymous indicating, "It is unlikely that Bhutan and China will have diplomatic relations soon. There are certain policies when it comes to the Permanent five of the United Nations Security Council."

There are obviously different versions being floated of deliberation during the summit. Has the Chinese media gone overboard in flagging the initiative for bilateral relations and resolution of boundary issue will not be clear but without a push from the officials accompanying the Prime Minister these reports are unlikely to have been published. Has Bhutan gone ahead with the move after approval from New Delhi as some Indian media reports and Chinese scholars seem to suggest or the Prime Minister of Bhutan has been misquoted by the Chinese media as Bhutanese authorities are indicating or this is an unilateral initiative by Thimpu, hence the foreign office cover up is not clear so far.

Suffice to say that first summit level contact between Bhutan and China has been established and the engagement will be taken forward to establish diplomatic relations and possibly even resolve the boundary issue in times to come. The trajectory may not be easy to determine at this juncture nor the time frame predictable. Settlement of boundary however is unlikely to happen soon. Given importance of the Chumbi Valley India is unlikely to agree to any concessions by Bhutan that leads to exchange of territory in this area providing further elbow room to China. Fears expressed by reports in the Indian media may therefore may be unfounded.

On the other hand Chinese keenness to extend the railway line to Yadung and secure the Bhutanese arm of the Chumbi Valley triangle may be as much due to fears of India cutting off the salient jutting threateningly towards the Siliguri corridor. This will overcome the vulnerability of the Siliguri Corridor providing it additional depth. This could be one explanation for given the operational challenges of launching a major thrust through the Chumbi Valley to cut off the Siliguri corridor and India's build up of forces on the Eastern front, Chinese offensive in the area will be posed major operational challenges.

What ever it be, given mutual apprehensions, strategic stability in the India Bhutan China triangle would require statesmanship of a high order. This will depend on how the political and military leadership of the three countries and especially New Delhi and Beijing are able to manage the same ensuring Thimpu's sovereignty and autonomy. The Indian government has done well not to over react to media reports and would be seeking full details of Chinese interaction from Bhutan to chart out a future course of action. This will no doubt be done keeping in view larger national interests of managing relations with China amicably yet not compromising on basic national security interests, thus implying any attempt to extend the Eastern arm of the inverted apex of the Chumbi Valley will be fiercely resisted by New Delhi.

INDO-MYANMAR BORDER

India-Myanmar boundary stretches for 1643 km. The boundary was demarcated in 1967 under an agreement signed by both countries. However, numerous earlier treaties and acts had affected the alignment of portions of the boundary and formed much of the basis of the new agreement. To begin with, the Treaty of Yandaboo of 1826 negated Myamarese influence on Assam, Cachar, Jaintia and Manipur and pronounced the Arakan mountain range as the boundary between British India and Myanmar. An Agreement was negotiated in 1834, which returned Kubaw valley to Myanmar. In 1837, the Paktai Range was accepted as the boundary between

Assam and Myanmar. In 1894, the Manipur - Chin Hills boundary was demarcated, and in 1896 Col. Maxwell redemarcated the Pemberton - Johnstone line, placing thirty-eight pillars on the ground. These pillars were referred to in the 1967 agreement. The Lushai Hills-Chin Hills boundary was demarcated in 1901 with minor alterations in 1921 and 1922. Under the Government of India Act of 1935, Myanmar was separated from India, but the resolution of the border between them was left to the newly independent governments. At the time of independence, the boundary between India and Myanmar was partially disputed, particularly the position of Moreh along with a few villages. Since relations between the two countries were extremely cordial, the disputed nature of the boundary did not cause major concern to either of them. However, the rise of insurgency and subsequent violation of the boundary by both insurgents and security forces of both countries forced India and Myanmar to negotiate a settlement of the boundary on 10 March 1967.

The location of the Indo-Myanmar boundary throws up many challenges for the effective management of the boundary. Though the boundary is properly demarcated, there are a few pockets that are disputed. The rugged terrain makes movement and the overall development of the area difficult. The internal dynamics of the region in terms of the clan loyalties of the tribal people, inter-tribal clashes, insurgency, transborder ethnic ties also adversely affect the security of the border areas.

There is practically no physical barrier along the border either in the form of fences or border outposts and roads to ensure strict vigil. Insurgents make use of the poorly guarded border and flee across when pursued by Indian security forces.

Close ethnic ties among the tribes such as Nagas, Kukis, Chin, etc., who live astride the border help these insurgents in finding safe haven in Myanmar. These cross-border ethnic ties have facilitated in creation of safe havens for various Northeast insurgent groups in Myanmar. As a result, various insurgent groups such as the National Socialist Council of Nagaland (NSCN), the United National Liberation Front (UNLF), the Peoples Liberation Army (PLA), and others have established bases in Myanmar. When pursued by the Indian security forces, these insurgents cross the poorly guarded border and take shelter in these bases. The Indian government has been requesting the Myanmar government to take action against the Indian insurgents, but the Myanmar government appears either unwilling or incapable of flushing them out of its territory.

The location of the boundary at the edge of the "golden triangle" facilitates the unrestricted illegal flows of drugs into Indian territory. Heroin is the main item of drug trafficking. The bulk of heroin enters India through the border town of Moreh in Manipur. It is reported that the local insurgent groups are actively involved in drugs and arms trafficking. The smuggling of arms and ammunition, precious stones and Chinese made consumer items finds its way into India illegally. Red Sanders, ATS (amphetamine type stimulant), grocery items, bicycle parts, etc. are smuggled from India. Human trafficking is also rampant along the border. The provision of allowing the tribal communities of both countries to travel up to 40 km across the border without any passport or visa has also contributed to increased smuggling in the region.

India-Myanmar Relations

High level visits have been a regular feature of India-Myanmar relations for several years. After the formation of the new government led by President U Thein Sein on March 30, 2011, Shri S.M. Krishna, Minister of External Affairs, was the first high level dignitary to visit Myanmar on June 20-22, 2011. Smt Nirupama Rao, Foreign Secretary, accompanied EAM during the visit. During this visit, MoU on Setting up of Indo-Myanmar Industrial Training Centre at Myingyan in Myanmar was signed by EAM and H.E. U Soe Thane, Minister of Industry-II of Myanmar. Documents pertaining to the construction of ten 500-tonne rice silos with Indian assistance of US$ 2 million in Yangon and Ayeyarwaddy Divisions were also handed over.

President U Thein Sein paid a State visit to India on October 12-15, 2011. The visit represented the first State visit from Myanmar to India following the swearing in of a new Government in

Myanmar in March 2011. President Thein Sein had a meeting with the Prime Minister of India, Dr. Manmohan Singh, which was followed by delegation level talks. He was accompanied by Chief of General Staff Lt Gen. Hla Htay Win, Minister for Border Affairs and Myanmar Industrial Development Lt. Gen Thein Htay, Minister for Foreign Affairs U. Wunna Maung Lwin, Minister for Agriculture and Irrigation U Myint Hlaing, Minister for Religious Affairs Thura U Myint Maung, Minister for Industry (1) and (2) U Soe Thane, Minister for Electric Power (1) U Zaw Min, Minister for National Planning and Economic Development and Livestock and Fisheries U Tin Naing Thein, Minister for Transport U Nyan Tun Aung, Minister for Energy U Than Htay, Minister for Science and Technology U Aye Myint, Minister of Commerce U Win Myint, Deputy Minister for Health Dr. Win Myint, and other senior officials.

During the visit, two documents were signed, namely, the Memorandum of Understanding for the Upgradation of the Yangon Children's Hospital and Sittwe General Hospital; and the Programme of Cooperation in Science & Technology for the period of 2012-2015. Pyithu Hluttaw (Lower House) Speaker Thura U Shwe Mann led a high level parliamentary delegation to India from December 11-17, 2011. The visit was in response to a joint invitation extended by Shri M. Hamid Ansari, Vice President of India/Chairman, Rajya Sabha and Smt. Meira Kumar, Speaker of the Lok Sabha. The objective of the visit was to share India's experience in parliamentary practices and procedures with the visiting Myanmar delegation. Myanmar Foreign Minister U Wunna Maung Lwin paid an official visit to India from January 22-26, 2012. During the visit, he called on Prime Minister and held bilateral discussions with EAM. During his visit, he delivered a lecture at the Indian Council for World Affairs on the topic "Myanmar: A Country in Transition to Democracy". Prime Minister of India Dr. Manmohan Singh paid a state visit to Myanmar from may 27-29 2012.

During the Visit Prime Minister several new initiatives were announced and singed 12 MoUs and agreements including extension of a new line of credit (LOC) for US$500 million to

Myanmar, support for setting up an Advance Centre for Agriculture Research and Education in Yezin, a Rice Bio-park in the integrated Demonstration Park in Nay Pyi Taw, and an Information Technology Institute in Mandalay. In addition important agreements such as Air Service Agreement, Establishment of Joint Trade and Investment Forum, MoU on Border Areas Development, and establishment of Border Haats and Cultural Exchange Programme.

Major Indian Projects in Myanmar

The Government of India is actively involved in over a dozen projects in Myanmar, both in infrastructural and non-infrastructural areas. These include upgradation and resurfacing of the 160 km. long Tamu-Kalewa-Kalemyo road; construction and upgradation of the Rhi-Tiddim Road in Myanmar; the Kaladan Multimodal Transport Project; etc.

An ADSL project for high speed data link in 32 Myanmar cities has been completed by TCIL. ONGC Videsh Ltd. (OVL), GAIL and ESSAR are participants in the energy sector in Myanmar. M/s RITES is involved in development of the rail transportation system and in supply of railway coaches, locos and parts. In September 2008, Ministry of Electric Power-1 (MoEP-1) and NHPC signed an agreement for development of the Tamanthi and Shwezaye Hydro-Electric Power project in Chindwin River valley and NHPC submitted the updated DPR on Tamanthi and is working on the DPR on the Shwezaye project.

A heavy turbo-truck assembly plant set up in Myanmar by TATA Motors with GOI financial assistance was inaugurated on December 31, 2010. An India-Myanmar Industrial Training Centre has been set up by HMT(I) in Myanmar with the assistance of GOI in Pakokku, a second centre is being set up in Myingyan, while the Myanmar-India Centre for English Language (MICELT), a Myanmar-India Entrepreneurship Development Centre (MIEDC) and an India-Myanmar Centre for Enhancement of IT Skills (IMCEITS) are all operational. Other projects include revamp of the Ananda Temple in Bagan, upgradation of the Yangon Children's Hospital and Sittwe General Hospital, erection of disaster proof rice silos etc. India has also assisted in the reconstruction of 1 high school and 6 primary schools in Tarlay township, the area worst affected by the severe earthquake that struck north-eastern Myanmar in March 2011.

Commercial and Economic Relations

Bilateral trade has expanded significantly from US$ 12.4 million in 1980-81 to US$ 1070.88 million in 2010-11. India's imports from Myanmar are dominated by agricultural items (beans, pulses and forest based products form 90% of our imports). India's main exports to Myanmar are primary and semi-finished steel and pharmaceuticals. At the institutional level, the Confederation of Indian Industry and the Union of Myanmar Federation of Chambers of Commerce and Industry (UMFCCI) entered into an MoU in February, 2000.

An MoU was also signed between CII and the Myanmar Computer Federation (MCF) in 2001. In 2004, an Agreement on setting up of a Joint Task Force between Union of Myanmar Federation of Chambers of Commerce and Industry (UMFCCI) and Confederation of India Industry was signed, as was an MoU between Myanmar-India Business Club (MIBC) and Federation of Industries and Commerce of North-Eastern Region.

The mechanism of the Joint Trade Committee (JTC), chaired by the respective Commerce Ministers, has been effective in reviewing and setting policy objectives for bilateral trade between the two countries.

Set up in 2003, the Joint Trade Committee has met four times so far (the last being in September 2011) and has successfully directed the rapid growth of commercial relations between the two countries. During the 4th JTC meeting both sides reviewed bilateral trade and investment and agreed to double the bilateral trade to US$ 3 bn by 2015.

In 2008, during the 3rd Joint Trade Committee Meeting between India and Myanmar, United Bank of India signed an MoU with three Myanmar national banks (Myanma Foreign Trade Bank, Myanma Economic Bank and & Myanma Investment and Commercial Bank) to facilitate trade. However, this channel is being mostly utilized for border trade only. In addition to this, a Bilateral Investment Promotion Agreement (BIPA) and a Double Taxation Avoidance Agreement (DTAA) were also signed in 2008. India and Myanmar are both signatory to the India-ASEAN Trade in Goods Agreement, which was signed in August 2009. Myanmar is also a beneficiary country under India's Duty Free Tariff Preference Scheme for LDCs.

FACTS BEHIND CHINA-INDIA BORDER DISPUTE

If a general of the Chinese imperial government representing the Manchu dynasty had, by force of arms, pillage and plunder, succeeded in subjugating the North American continent and on that basis had artificially created a border line between the United States and Canada called, let us say, The Manchu Line, would a sovereign U.S. government abide by thus border line?

Let us suppose further that the boundary line demarcated by this general included, for the Canadian side, parts of Buffalo, Detroit, Seattle and Duluth. Let us suppose again that the treaty between Canada and the U.S. dictated by this general had never been accepted by any government of the United States, and that in truth the people of the U.S. regarded this treaty and its boundary line as illegal, null and void, and as the imposition of a foreign power at a time when the U.S. was weak, divided and under the domination of a foreign imperialist power.

All we have to do with this analogy is to just change the name — Canada to India, United States to China and China to Great Britain — and the picture becomes immeasurably clearer than it is represented in the U.S. press.

The Mcmahon Line

It is the position of the Chinese People's Republic that the so-called McMahon Line — named after the British General McMahon — is illegal, null and void, and the result of a predatory, imperialist imposition of the British government in the year 1914.

No Chinese government ever accepted the McMahon Line. Neither did the Imperial Government of China in 1914, nor the Chiang Kai-Shek government ever agree to it. The very fact that even the Chiang Kai-Shek clique, which is nothing but a tool of U.S. imperialism, has not dared to dispute the Chinese People's Republic's position of the China-India border dispute, it in itself the most eloquent testimony to the correctness of the Chinese position.

Nevertheless, the Chinese People's Republic has made every effort to achieve a reasonable and just settlement of the territory in dispute. It has consistently shunned the use of arms.

Proposals For Negotiations

Although the border dispute is almost three years old now, and the Chinese have made innumerable other approaches to the Indian government to settle it on some amicable and acceptable basis the Nehru government has invariably turned them down. In the past two months alone the Chinese government made several proposals for negotiations.

It made a notable effort on August 4, and another one on September 13. In neither of these proposals did the Chinese government lay down any preconditions for the negotiations. Nor did the Chinese government resort to the type of language which could in any way be construed as a threat to India.

On the contrary, the diplomatic notes directed to the Indian government were couched in the most conciliatory language, and were calculated to effectuate a reasonable settlement which would safeguard the territorial integrity of China as well as India.

As a matter of fact, the London Times, certainly no friend of the Chinese revolutionary government, had to publicly admit on October 8 that if military operations were resumed on the Sino-Indian border, "onlookers will have to note that it was New Dehli.., that declined to embark upon them (talks)..."

The position of the London Times is of exceptional importance because it has always sided with India as against China. The London Times was obliged to make the above statement only after the Indian paper, Tribune, had reported that at a cabinet meeting the Indian government had decided to use armed force to deal with China.

Nehru's "Limited Offensive"

It was also reported in the world press on October 8, that Nehru had authorized India's new commander-in chief of the eastern border area to "fight a limited offensive operation."

These are the incontrovertible facts. As to what lies behind the aggressive attitude of the Nehru government, it must be borne in mind first of all that the imperialist world, particularly the U.S. would like nothing better than to see the two principal Asiatic powers, the two powers which hold the greatest revolutionary promise for mankind in the east, locked in military combat, shedding the blood of thousands, absorbing the resources and energies of millions of people, which should be used to construct a revolutionary way of life. The efforts of the U.S. government, it must be noted, have been directed, insofar as India is concerned, not only to make it economically and financially dependent upon U.S. monopoly interests, but also to inflame the Indian bourgeoisie, particularly its right-wing extremist elements, against the Chinese People's Republic.

Four Billion U.S. Aid

According to The New York Times of October 22(1969), the U.S. has poured into India more than four billion dollars. A substantial section of this money has gone to line the pockets of Indian businessmen, government officials, and especially the extremist elements who are interested in diverting the mass discontent of the Indian peasants and workers into other channels. U.S. diplomats, State Department planners, and military figures in the Pentagon have for a long time felt that the biggest diversionary tactic that imperialism could employ to disrupt the revolutionary anti-imperialist front was to continually stir up, bribe and corrupt as many of the representatives of the Indian bourgeoisie as it could to fan the flames of an India-China war.

Nehru himself was subjected to unremitting pressure when he was in the U.S. More U.S. aid was used as bait to lure Nehru into the trap of a protracted India-China war, which can only result in further detriment to India, China and the cause of all oppressed people.

Since Nehru's Visit

Since the Indian Prime Minister left the shores of the U.S. there have been only rare intervals in which there has been a let up in the war fever fanned by the Indian bourgeoisie and its agent Nehru. For a long time Nehru played the role of moderator between left and right in the Indian-China border dispute, cautioning the extremist elements of the bourgeoisie in Parliament, and repudiating suggestions for offensive operations by his military advisers.

But his October 4 decision, taken after a cabinet meeting, made it clear beyond any shadow of a doubt that he had completely capitulated to the right wing on this issue and was kowtowing to U.S. imperialist interests. The present military efforts of the Chinese are merely a response to the offensive action taken after the Indian cabinet session.

A Defensive Battle

The Chinese government is fighting a defensive battle. It is only too well aware that U.S. imperialism is ready at all times to take advantage of any preoccupation that China may have with India to open another front against China wherever and whenever it finds it feasible, whether it be in the Pescadores, the Taiwan strait or new harassments over the air space of China. There are those who say China should give in — give up what belongs to China in the interest of peace. These are the people who are always ready to give, especially things that do not belong to them.

When to give — or whether to give — is a question which only the Chinese can decide, as it as *their* territory. Surely the Chinese, who have gone through hell and fire in the course of 22 years of civil war, in which they have had to trade many times — space for time — and in fact have endured many retreats, need no reminders on this score.

Solidarity of Asian People

The workers of the world and the progressive anti-imperialist countries in particular, are most deeply concerned in a speedy, reasonable and honorable settlement on the part of China and

India. Such a settlement can only be arrived at if the ruling group in New Delhi accepts China's offer for the resumption of talks on a high level between the two governments without any pre conditions. A border settlement would remove a tremendous obstacle to the solidarity of the Asian people who are struggling for a new life, and would be a tremendous rebuff to imperialism and its servants and underlings.

NEPAL-INDIA-CHINA TRI-JUNCTION POINTS, YET TO BE FIXED

But the tri-junction points (zero serial numbers) on both the western and eastern ends of the borderline have not yet been fixed, where Nepalese, Chinese and Indian territories meet. This is due to the fact that the Indian representative was not present during boundary demarcation, though Nepal had intimated and invited India formally. But there was no response from India, as it is reported.......... But nobody knows even the approximate period of the finalization of these triple-points, because it needs the consent of India, as an inevitable fact.

Boundary Protocols

After the completion of the joint boundary demarcation physically on the ground, Boundary Protocol was signed on 20 January 1963 by Chinese Vice-Premier and Foreign Minister Chen Yi and Vice-Chairman of the Nepalese Council of Ministers and Foreign Minister Dr. Tulasi Giri.

Now it is high time to make the fourth protocol, because twelve years have elapsed since the third protocol was signed. Some of the main boundary pillars might have been damaged and disappeared and same is the case with reference pillars or markers due to landslide, flood and snow. So it is necessary to formulate a joint inspection committee to erect the missing pillars and repair the damaged ones. Nepal-China friendship will be further consolidated as good neighbour with the inspection and maintenance of Nepal-China borderline at an interval of a decade. This is the common interest of both the nations. Next, it is expected that Nepal will undertake positively to open two more trade routes at Kimathanka (Dingri) and Mustang (Liji) in the very near future as already agreed by both nations. It will help to promote not only the trade and economic activities but also to strengthen furthermore the cordial friendship between the people of Nepal and China.

SECTORS OF SINO-INDIAN BORDER: WESTERN SECTOR, MIDDLE SECTOR AND EASTERN SECTOR

The Sino-Indian border is generally divided into three sectors namely: (i) the Western sector, (ii) the Middle sector, and (iii) the Eastern sector.

The Western Sector

This 2,152 km long sector of the Sino-Indian border separates Jammu and Kashmir State of India from the Sinkiang province of China. The frontier between Sinkiang and Pakistan occupied Kashmir (PoK) is about 480 km long. The rest is boundary between Ladakh and Tibet.

The boundary in the western sector runs along the Muztagh Ata Range and the Aghil Mountain across the Karakoram Pass via Quara Tagh pass and along the main Kunlun Range to a point east of 80°E longitude and 40 km north of Hajit Langer.

It forms a physical boundary between Gilgit area and Sinkiang following the main Karakoram watershed separating the streams flowing into the Indus basin from those flowing into the Tarin basin. Farther south-east the boundary runs along the watershed across Lanak La, Kone La and Kepsang La, then follows the Chemesang River across Pergyon Lake and the Kailash Range. Here the boundary constitutes the watershed between the Indus system in India and the Khotan system in China.

The western sector boundary is the outcome of the British policy towards the state of Jammu and Kashmir. These boundaries were defined by the treaties of 1665 and 1686 (known as Ladakh-Tibet agreements) and were confirmed by 1842 Dogra-Ladakh agreement among Kashmir, Tibet and China. However, this boundary was never delimited precisely on maps and has led to several boundary disputes between China and India. The Chinese claim rests mainly on ethnic grounds, and on the assertion that the wastelands of the Aksai Chin in disputed territory were always linked more with Tibet and Sinkiang.

The Chinese claim that Aksai Chin is just an extension of Tibet with regard to language, religion and culture. But in Chinese documentation regarding the actual occupation of the area by Tibet in inconclusive. The Indians, on the other hand, claim that the area has been historically administered by the state of Jammu and Kashmir since 1849, and that the Indo-Tibet Treaties of 1665, 1684 and 1842 confirmed the boundary between Tibet and Ladakh.

China claims the Aksai Chin district, the Changmo valley, Pangong Tso and the Sponggar Tso area of north-east Ladakh as well as a strip of about 5,000 sq km down the entire length of eastern Ladakh. China also claims a part of Huza-Gilgit area in North Kashmir (ceded to it in 1963 by Pakistan), although the whole territory has been effectively under the British sovereignty since 1895.

Since 1954, the Chinese have repeatedly violated the international border between India and China and penetrated deep into the Indian Territory in the western sector. China renewed aggression in 1959 and the Line of Actual Control (LoAC) become of series of positions occupied by the Chinese forces rather than a well defined border between the two countries. In 1962, China waged a full scale war and its forces intruded far deeper into the Indian Territory. Currently the Chinese occupation line runs 16 to 240 km west of traditional line. China is in actual possession of about 54,000 sq km of the Indian Territory of which 37,555 sq km is in Ladakh area alone.

The Middle Sector

The middle sector boundary between China and India is 625 km long and runs along the watershed from Ladakh to Nepal. Two Indian states of Himachal Pradesh and Uttaranchal touch this border. The boundary of Himachal Pradesh follows the water parting between the Spiti and Para Chu rivers and continues along the watershed between the eastern and western tributaries of the Satluj.

The Uttaranchal boundary is demarcated by the watershed between the Satluj on one hand and the Kali, the Alaknanda, and the Bhagirathi on the other. This boundary crosses the Satluj near the Shipki La on the Himachal-Tibet border.

Thereafter, it runs along the watershed passes of Mana, Niti, Kungri-Bingri, Dharma and Lipu Ladakh. It finally joins trijunction of China, India and Nepal. This part of the border was approved by the Tibetan and the British governments under the 1890 and 1919 treaties. Although there are not much serious territorial problems between the two countries, the Chinese lay claim on nearly 2,000 sq km area in this sector.

The Eastern Sector

The 1,140 km long boundary between India and China runs from the eastern limit of Bhutan to a point near Talu-Pass at the trijunction of India, Tibet and Myanmar. This line is usually referred to as the Me Mahon Line after Henry Me Mahon, a British representative who signed the 1913-14 Shimla Convention. This line normally runs along the crest of the Himalayas between Bhutan and Myanmar.

India has stressed that the Me Mahon Line is the international boundary between Tibet and India as was agreed to between the governments of India, China and Tibet. On the other hand China considers the Me Mahon line as illegal and unacceptable, claiming that Tibet had no right to sign the 1913-14 convention held in Shimla which delineated the Me Mahon Line on the map. India challenges such a position, maintaining that Tibet was independent and in fact concluded several independent treaties which were considered valid by all parties, and were in operation for decades.

China declined the validity of the Me Mahon Line as an international boundary and laid claims to areas south of this line up to the foot of the Himalayan range in the Brahmaputra valley. The whole of Arunachal Pradesh, measuring over 88 thousand sq km has been claimed by China as the Chinese territory. This area has been administered by India since 1947.

Chinese government never formally questioned the validity of 1913-14 Shimla convention until 1959. India has been striking at the two crucial points. First, Britain and India had been exercising jurisdiction over the area since 1914 and 1947 respectively and second China never disputed the Indian control over the area until 1959. Even in 1956 when the Chinese attention was drawn to certain maps drawn by China which showed these areas to be parts of China, the Chinese government promised to look into the 'cartographic errors' in their maps.

China's relations with India started taking a bad turn in 1950s when China started consolidating its position in Tibet and then in Ladakh. By 1956, China started intensifying its intrusions into the Indian Territory. India wishfully hoped that the insurmountable barrier of the Himalayas would prevent Chinese to attack Indian Territory.

Indian apprehensions grew in 1956 when China built a road through Ladakh linking West Tibet with Sinkiang and quickly moved into Aksai Chin and eastern Ladakh. China also moved its forces into the North-East Frontier Agency (NEFA), the present Arunachal Pradesh.

Reported small-scale armed clashes between 1959 and 1962 escalated into a full-scale war in October, 1962 when China launched a major offensive in Ladakh in the western sector and NEFA in the eastern sector. Indian armed forces were not well trained to fight a modern war in a rough and rugged mountainous terrain. They were outnumbered and outgunned by the Chinese forces.

Following lessons have been learnt from Chinese aggression over India:

(i) The myth that the Himalayas were an effective defense barrier was exploded.

(ii) India's naive confidence in China's friendliness had dulled its perception regarding effective security measures in the Indo-China borderlands.

(iii) The prompt and positive response of western countries in rushing military supplies to the war zone helped improve the image of the West in Indian eyes.

(iv) India realised that posture of "non-alignment" was no substitute for defense preparedness.

Surprisingly, Chinese forces pulled back without annexing the disputed territory in the eastern sector. In the western sector, however, they did not pull out of most of Aksai Chin. Perhaps they did so due to the fear that their advance troops would have been cut off from supply bases in Tibet in winter of 1962 when the high passes in the Himalayas would have been closed by snow. The Chinese justified their withdrawal by stating that they had no further territorial ambitions.

The primary aim of Chinese invasion was to deprive India of its moral leadership in the world especially among the Afro-Asian countries, and to put pressure on it to join the socialist camp. China's collusion with Pakistan is a clear indication of this political ambition.

Perhaps China miscalculated its political power strategy. The support of the Western countries to India compelled China to rethink its strategy. India's unity in the face of Chinese aggression was another deterrent for China to achieve political mileage.

An uneasy truce had been prevailing for a long time since the October, 1962 war. Neither side made a serious effort to normalise the situation on the border. The Colombo powers, spearheaded by Ceylon (now Sri Lanka) and the erstwhile Soviet Union failed to bring about a respectable agreement between the two countries. Several countries condemned China as an aggressor. However, Cuba, Albania and Portugal supported the Chinese.

Of late, leaders of both the countries have engaged themselves in improving the bilateral relations. Several meetings have been held to resolve the problem of border issues. A major development took place in October, 2003 when China made a significant change in its official website. It removed the mention of Sikkim from its list of nations.

In May, 2004, China recognised Sikkim as a part of India for the first time. The world map in World Affairs Year Book 2003/2004 does not show Sikkim as separate country in Asia. It also does not mention Sikkim in its index of countries.

The move was significant since it involves recognition of Sikkim-China border which is a part of the Me Mahon Line. If things go as planned, the two nations should be able to work out the guide lines for transforming the Line of Actual Control (LoAC) into a mutually acceptable and internationally recognised boundary. However, China still insists that Arunachal Pradesh is a disputed territory.

China has also suggested a 'package deal'. It asked India to accept Chinese domination over Aksai Chin in return of China's acceptance of Me Mahon Line as the international boundary.

India, however, has advocated 'sector-by-sector' approach. Indian side is hopeful because China has settled border disputes with Russia and Vietnam.

2

India's Boundary Disputes with China, Nepal, and Pakistan

The recent detonation of a series of nuclear devices by India and Pakistan has increased tension in South Asia and threatens to inflame long-standing boundary disputes that India has with China, Nepal, and Pakistan. The disputes with China and Pakistan have already triggered several wars. The new Hindu-nationalist government in New Delhi has reversed movement toward détente with Beijing and Islamabad. The areas in contention with China and Pakistan are among the largest land-boundary disputes in the world. The Indo-Nepali dispute over Kalapani is more recent and involves a small area.

INDIA-CHINA (AKSAI CHIN AND ARUNACHAL PRADESH)

In the 1962 Sino-Indian War, China seized a Switzerland-sized area, Aksai Chin (Aksayqin), and overran Arunachal Pradesh (an Indian state the size of Austria). There are also other, smaller pockets of disputed area. The PRC withdrew from virtually all of Arunachal Pradesh to the Line of Actual Control (LAC), which approximates the McMahon Line that is found in a 1914 agreement initialed by British, Tibetan, and Chinese representatives. Chinese and Indian forces clashed in the Sumdorong Chu valley of Arunachal Pradesh in 1986-87. Relations began to thaw in 1988.

On 7 September 1993, China and India signed an accord to reduce tensions along their border and to respect the LAC. During

November 1996, China and India agreed to delimit the LAC and institute confidence-building measures (CBMs) along the frontier. The agreement pledged nonaggression, prior notification of large troop movements, a 10-km no-fly zone for combat aircraft, and exchange of maps to resolve disagreements about the precise location of the LAC. In August 1997 the sides ratified the CBM agreement. There seems to have been little substantive progress, except for a series of high-level visits. The most recent, on 27 April, was the first visit by a PRC Chief of Staff to India. However, two weeks before the visit the new Indian Defense Minister, George Fernandes, accused the PRC of repeated violations of Indian territory, including the construction of a helipad on "Indian" territory in the disputed zone, and of aiding Pakistan's nuclear and missile programs. On 3 May he publicly labeled China as India's number one threat and alleged that the PRC was stockpiling nuclear weapons in Tibet, expanding naval activity off the Burmese coast, and conducting surveillance against India from Burma's Coco Islands. After the visit of General Fu Quanyou and PRC protests, Fernandes said that his characterization of China as India's principal threat was a personal view, but he went on to pledge that the number of Indian troops along the frontier with China would not be reduced. Such a statement calls into question part of the agreed CBMs. (To view a map of this area click here.)

China and India have yet to address their fundamental and very large land boundary disputes. Moreover, their bilateral relations are complicated by the issues of Tibet (Xizang), Sikkim, and Kashmir. India plays host to the Dalai Lama and a large number of Tibetan refugees. They present an implicit threat to Chinese control of Tibet, which it invaded in 1950. On its maps, the PRC continues to portray Sikkim, which was absorbed by India in 1974, as an independent country. In addition to the Aksai Chin, China and India dispute another section of Kashmir (the area west of Aksai Chin).

RESOLVING THE BOUNDARY DISPUTE: CHINA'S REASONS AND INDIA'S CHOICES

The final settlement of the Sino-Indian territorial and boundary dispute is not a question of 'if' but 'when'. Four pertinent reasons suggest that China can be ultimately trusted to settle the dispute. On its part, India can take certain steps to ensure that China's reasons do not alter and that 'compromise' is seen as mutually beneficial.

One, China has steadily resolved its territorial disputes with almost all of its 15 land neighbours. Negotiations with the Soviet Union and Vietnam began in 1964 and 1977 respectively. However, it was not until much later that the negotiation processes fructified; it was only in October 2004 that the eastern sector of the Sino-Russian border was finally resolved with the signing of the Supplementary Agreement. With Vietnam, China signed a land boundary agreement in 1999, although they continue to meet regularly at the governmental level to thrash out details pertaining to the Beibu Gulf and the placement of border markers. Therefore, boundary negotiations between China and its other neighbours have been long and arduous affairs. The slowness of the boundary negotiations between India and China needs to be seen in this context.

Two, China has settled 17 of its 23 territorial disputes since 1949, according to M. Taylor Fravel, Assistant Professor of Political Science at MIT. Fravel suggests that regime insecurity and legitimacy crises in peripheral border regions best explain why China not only made concessions but also favoured the peaceful resolution of its territorial disputes. Despite a significant rise in China's economic and military strength vis-a-vis weaker neighbours, China received less than 50 per cent of the contested land. China's 'peaceful development' and 'new security concept' are directly responsible for the gradual stabilization of its borders-both concepts demand peaceful and stable borders for sustained economic growth.

Three, the absence of territorial disputes on China's western flank is a consequence of its 'western development' strategy. Starting with Myanmar and Nepal in the 1960s, a flurry of diplomatic activity saw the resolution of China's borders with Tajikistan and Kazakhstan (in 2002), Kyrgyzstan (in September 2004), Russia (in October 2004), and Mongolia (in November 2005). The pacification of China's western border is driven by the need to build cross-border linkages for economic development as well as the suppression of the three evils-separatism, extremism and terrorism. China's two westernmost provinces that border India, Xinjiang and Tibet, are important to China not least due to the fear that an economic imbalance can potentially fuel secessionist sentiments amongst the Uighurs and Tibetans.

Four, China is likely to reserve the use of force to settle heartland disputes. The hard component of China's comprehensive national strength will continue to dictate an inflexible stance on Taiwan's reunification as well as territorial conflicts of strategic value. Therefore, China is unlikely to make concessions on approximately 30,000 square kilometres of Aksai Chin, not least due to the fact that the Karakoram highway that traverses it provides a strategic link between Pakistan, and China and a shorter route between Tibet and Xinjiang. However, even in the case of disputes over territory of great economic value, such as the South China Sea, China has emphasized the joint development and exploitation of resources, albeit without making any concessions.

As emerging powers, India and China will continue to be pitted against each other. The sheer size and altitude of the disputed area is likely to make demarcation a difficult and lengthy process. However, India can take certain steps to ensure it remains in China's interest to settle the dispute. India must do its utmost to convince China that it is not the target of the newly sealed Indo-US strategic relationship. India must clarify that the support for Tibetans in India is humanitarian and cultural and not a challenge to China's sovereign territoriality. China's friendship with Pakistan cannot be wished away; however, India can make itself important to China by promising trade and joint border development projects that make good business sense. India's inclusion into the Shanghai Cooperation Organisation as an observer in July 2005 was an important recognition of India's commitment to curbing cross-border terrorism.

Even though there are reasons to believe that China is not a revisionist state determined to use force to uphold its territorial claims, proactive steps to create lobbies with vested interests in resolving the dispute must be taken. The seventh round of Sino-Indian border talks in March 2006 helped provide a 'constructive and friendly' atmosphere. It is time for India and China to carry that forward and focus on opening Nathu La for trade, reviving the Stilwell Road for trade across India's northeast, building border free trade zones similar to the Sino-Kazakh one and establishing independent inter-linkages between border regions through transport linkages akin to the Kashgar (Xinjiang, China)-Gilgit (Northern Areas, Pakistan) bus service. Discussion on the Sino-Indian boundary talks must therefore go beyond the rhetoric on China's 'concirclement' of India; it must emphasize the domestic constraints and foreign policy concerns of the Chinese government and the resolution of territorial disputes that such a study reveals.

CHINA'S BORDER SPAT WITH INDIA

The recent meeting between India's National Security Adviser MK Narayanan and China's Vice-Foreign Minister Dai Banggio at Coonoor in Tamil Nadu was the continuation of a series of such meetings in the context of the border dispute between the two countries. While this is a good thing to go by, the main point is: what has been the actual progress in the matter? After every meeting, a standard joint communiqué is issued to the effect that the téte-a-téte was fruitful and the dialogue is being maintained in an atmosphere of friendship and mutual cooperation. Diplomatic jargon cannot be limitless; it must end somewhere.

Again, from time to time one hears of Chinese intrusion into Arunachal Pradesh, especially in the area of Sumdorong Chu Valley and the northern range of the Mishmi Hills. There is also the occasional media report that China claims this Northeastern state of ours on the grounds of a combination of history as well as geography.

India's drawback is that our foreign policy has always been linked to the vote bank. In fact it was a vote bank issue that created the border dispute with China in the first place way back in the late '50s and early '60s. The origin of this problem is worth discussing as this itself suggests the solution. Soon after China secured Tibet, Beijing sent a delegation to New Delhi under then

Prime Minister Zhou en Lai with a proposal on Aksai Chin in northern Kashmir, adjacent to the Siachen Glacier. The delegation submitted to us that movement from Tibet to Sinkiang province was a huge problem because one had to traverse the inhospitable Kunlun Mountains en route. Hence it was suggested both countries could arrive at an understanding by which India could lease out Aksai Chin to China, as this would enable the latter to build an all-weather highway across this stretch of territory.

Thus movement from Tibet to Sinkiang would not then involve negotiating the Kunluns at all and India, too, could use this highway as a bonus. In any case, Aksai Chin was just an ice desert with an average height of 18,000-19,000 feet and nothing grew there, let alone having any human habitation. New Delhi reacted with its usual brash arrogance, thundering words to the effect that 'not an inch of our sacred motherland' would be given, et al. Zhou en Lai was shown the door gracelessly.

The Chinese delegation went back and decided to implement a tenet in Hindi conveying the meaning that if ghee cannot be taken out by a straight finger then a crooked finger would be used! China militarily attacked India and physically captured Aksai Chin by force in late 1962 and built the desired highway through it. China is still very much in occupation of this area, cocking a snook at India now and then! On our part we bemoaned our fate, blamed Beijing for gerrymandering into our territory and generally made a political nuisance of ourselves. Nothing helped, of course.

During its attack on India, China had also deeply transgressed into what was earlier known as the North East Frontier Agency that later became Arunachal Pradesh. However, after delivering a crushing military-cum-political defeat on India, China moved back to its own side of the border in this area. This apart, China disputes an area along the Uttarkhand-Tibet border named Barahoti.

China has a strong army garrison in this area at a place called Taklakot that keeps a watching brief over Barahoti. India, therefore, has been well and truly boxed in by China, courtesy New Delhi's folly of riding the high horse with Zhou en Lai's delegation of yore. Diplomacy has never been a strong point with us and the country has suffered badly as a consequence. The science and art of statecraft continue to be subservient to the omnipotent vote bank as far as our leaders are concerned.

New Delhi, for reasons best known to itself, brought out a Lok Sabha resolution in 1994 wherein it was categorically stated that we would retake Aksai Chin by force. Obviously this resolution was nothing but a vote bank gimmick that our näive citizens — including many members of our intelligentsia — swallowed all the way. While firmly occupying Aksai Chin, China periodically needles India over Arunachal Pradesh and Barahoti. Normally, Barahoti remains dormant but Arunachal Pradesh makes news, sometimes with alarm. This has been the state of affairs since 1962. No government at New Delhi since that year has tried to accept the reality and taken any pragmatic steps to reconcile the border situation with China, notwithstanding the fact that currently our relations with China are improving virtually by the day.

The question is, what needs to be done in order to resolve the ongoing impasse? There is only one solution: India must formally accept Zhou en Lai's suggestion of yesteryear but cede Aksai Chin to China. It is doubtful whether China will accept the lease aspect now. The Chinese are a very proud race and will never climb down. In any event, China holds the aces in this matter, never mind the McMahon Line's relevancy to us.

Truth to tell, this solution was hinted by China's previous regime under President Jiang Zemin through his then Foreign Minister Tang Jiaxuan during Prime Minister AB Vajpayee's tenure. While the Sikkim issue got reconciled, Aksai Chin could not be followed through due to the change of government in India in 2004.

China is not really interested in Barahoti and Arunachal Pradesh — Beijing uses these two as pressure points on New Delhi to see reason over the border dispute, a dispute that hinges purely on Aksai Chin. The sooner we come to terms with this, the better.

INDIA-PAKISTAN-CHINA (KASHMIR)

When India and Pakistan became independent of Great Britain in 1947, the various princely states, including that of Jammu and

Kashmir, could accede to either country. An armed revolt of Muslim peasantry against the Maharaja of Jammu and Kashmir prompted the Maharaja to accede to India in order to gain military aid. Pakistan objected and the countries went to war.

The matter was taken up by the UN Security Council in 1948, which adopted a resolution calling for the restoration of order, the withdrawal of Pakistani forces and reduction of Indian forces, and a UN plebiscite. India and Pakistan objected to various of these provisions.

They went to war over Kashmir again in 1965. In 1971 India intervened in Pakistan's civil war that led to the independence of Bangladesh. India and Pakistan came close to war over Kashmir in 1990. (To view a map of this area click here.)

UN observers monitor part of the Indo-Pakistani cease-fire line. The current line was established by the 1972 Simla accord and approximately follows the 1949 Cease-fire Line. The coordinates of the Simla line have not been published, and the line was never delimited in the forbidding Siachin Glacier, near the Chinese frontier, where India and Pakistan frequently trade artillery rounds. Firing incidents and allegations of infiltration are chronic along the entire cease-fire line.

The Indian-controlled part of Jammu and Kashmir became a state in 1974. The parts of Kashmir controlled by Pakistan, Azad Kashmir and the Northern Areas, have anomalous status as administered territories. In 1963 China and Pakistan delimited a boundary that India claims illegally gave part of Kashmir to China. In 1987 a Sino-Pakistani protocol formalized demarcation of their boundary. The termination of this boundary at the Karakoram Pass on the Chinese line of control suggests that Pakistan recognizes Chinese sovereignty over Aksai Chin, which is part of the former Princely State of Kashmir.

India and Pakistan have held sporadic talks. In June 1997, they agreed to eight issues for discussion, including the issue of Kashmir and their maritime boundary. Pakistan wants to set-up a separate task force on Kashmir; India has resisted the idea. Talks have made little progress due to changes in the respective governments. The recent efforts by US Ambassador Richardson to resolve the dispute seem to have been blown out of the water by Indian and Pakistani nuclear tests.

INDIA-NEPAL (KALAPANI)

The dispute between India and Nepal involves about 75 sq km of area in Kalapani, where China, India, and Nepal meet. Indian forces occupied the area in 1962 after China and India fought their border war. Three villages are located in the disputed zone: Kuti [Kuthi, 30°19'N, 80°46'E], Gunji, and Knabe. India and Nepal disagree about how to interpret the 1816 Sugauli treaty between the British East India Company and Nepal, which delimited the boundary along the Maha Kali River (Sarda River in India).

The dispute intensified in 1997 as the Nepali parliament considered a treaty on hydro-electric development of the river. India and Nepal differ as to which stream constitutes the source of the river. Nepal regards the Limpiyadhura as the source; India claims the Lipu Lekh. Nepal has reportedly tabled an 1856 map from the British India Office to support its position. The countries have held several meetings about the dispute and discussed jointly surveying to resolve the issue. Although the Indo-Nepali dispute appears to be minor, it was aggravated in 1962 by tensions between China and India. Because the disputed area lies near the Sino-Indian frontier, it gains strategic value.

Like most boundary dispute, those of India with its neighbors are symptomatic of wider bilateral relations. Boundaries are manifestations of national identity. They can be trip-wires of war. Recent developments in South Asia suggest that peaceful resolution of these disputes is receding from reach.

ISSUE OF KALAPANI / LIMPIYADHURA THE NORTH-WESTERN BORDER OF NEPAL

The Treaty of Sugauli of 4 March 1816 is the basis to delineate and demarcate the western/north-western border of Nepal, even though the Boundary Treaty of November 1, 1860 implied specially the south-western portion, as the restoration of Banke, Bardiya, Kailali and Kanchanpur districts as new territory.

Status of the river Kali and Kalapani

It is not yet demarcated the status and origination of the river Kali. The river is known as Kali at the upper reaches, Mahakali in the middle portion and Sarjoo or Gogra or western branch of Gogra when it comes down to plain area.

There is a controversial debate about the origin point of river Kali, whether it is originated from Limpiyadhura (5,532 meter) or Lipulek (5,029 mtr).

The second debate is over the location of Kalapani, whether it is located in the Nepalese territory or Indian side. In other words, the question is whether Kalapani belongs to Nepal or India. There has been an issue of national interest for everyone that raised much hue and cry since October 1996.

To reach into a concrete conclusion, one has to study the historical documents and old maps, which are inscribed and established on and around the time of the treaty. And the other is, on the spot findings with hydrological facts and some of the points are as follows:

- Maps as evidence ....
- Location of Kalapani ....
- Statements concerning Kalapani ....
- Nepal-India boundary joint working group ....
- India intends to study proofs from Nepal ....
- Kali / Kalapani itself as a proof ....

It is clearly engraved on above-menntioned maps that the river which has originated from Limpiyadhura is the Kali as delimitated by the Treaty of Sugauli, as the western borderline of Nepal. Based on the historical documents and various maps of the era of the treaty and scientifically enunciated hydrological principle, it is no difficult to reach the conclusion that the north-western border corner of Nepal is located at Limpiyadhura.

Nextly, Kalapani itself is a concrete and on the spot geographical proof, because Kalapani is located towards east of the river Kali, as the Treaty of Sugauli says that all those areas lying to the east of the river Kali is the territory of Nepal.

Status of Masonry *Junge* Pillar

The border demarcation work between Nepal and India was started after the Treaty of Sugauli (ratified on 4 March 1816). Surveying and demarcation of border with pillars had been started just after monsoon season of 1816.

The border line was divided into nine segments starting from point A to K. Point A was located at Phalelung of Panchthar district as the tri-junction of Sikkim, Bengal and Nepal whereas the last station K was established at Brahmadev Mandi of Kanchanpur district.

North of Phalelung to Jhinsang Chuli in eastern Nepal and north of Brahmadev Mandi to the origination point of the river Mahakali in western Nepal were not demarcated at that time. The demarcation of the eastern segment has been started recently, but it is yet to be started in the western segment up to the source of river Mahakali. The reason for not demarcating on these two segments in those days may be that it is the river course of Mahakali on the west and Singhalila mountain range is elongated on the eastern border adjoining Sikkim.

Issue of *Junge* Pillars

The Nepalese people believe that masonry *Junge* pillars are the main boundary monuments erected on the boundary line between Nepal and India. But recently field level Indo-Nepal joint border survey team regarded the *Junge* as the reference pillar (RP) while they were working on the Mechi riverine sector during November-December 1995.

Description of *Junge* Pillar

Junge pillars are the masonry pillars, the construction of which started was just after the Treaty of Sugauli-1816, with a view to demarcate the border between Nepal and India. It is regarded as the main boundary pillar with its shape and size. The dimension of *Junge* pillar is 2.2 metres in height and its diameter is 3 metres in round shape. Its foundation is 1 mtr deep under a rectangular platform of 2 mtr by 1 mtr.

Boundary pillar (BP) versus reference pillar (RP)

To resolve the status of *Junge* pillar whether it is the main boundary pillar or a reference pillar, one has to know the construction criteria of these pillars. In this respect, there may be a question as what is the difference between BP and RP or what are the ingredients to make it different from the other.

It is defined that "main boundary pillars have been erected at intervals of about five kilometres with intermediate or auxiliary pillars at interval of about 500 metres." These pillars will be established in the main chainage of the border line to create the line of sight between the two main pillars. To recognize its status, the main boundary pillars are automatically larger in shape and size in comparison to intermediate and reference pillars.

Junge is the Main Boundary Pillar (BP)

Followings are the points to honour the status of main boundary pillars (BP) to the masonry *Junge* pillars:

- On the map of 1818 (British Boundary on the Northern Frontier of Zillah of Poornneea in North Behar) PP is written on the *Junge* pillar and PP is mentioned as Masonry Permanent Pillar..........
- There is a technical fact that every BP should have its RPs. For example, BP number 35 along Mechi river has RPs as 35 A.B. on Nepal side and 35 C. on Indian side of the border...........

In the light of these points and technical facts, all 913 *Junge* pillars erected during the British regime in India belong to the same status of main boundary pillars (BPs), no matter whether these are located in land sector or riverine sector along the boundary between Nepal and India.

Locations of Violated Nepal-India Border

Altogether 26 out of 75 districts of Nepal have border linkages with India, of which 21 are undergoing the violation of their territory by India. There are 54 such border points within those 21 districts where Nepal's territory seems to be encroached upon.

The total area under encroachment is estimated at around 59,970 hectare, of which Kalapani-Limpiyadhura alone covers 37,840 ha, Susta area 14,860 ha, various places in Jhapa district cover around 1,630 ha, and other places in other districts occupy around 5,640 ha. Taken together, the following border areas of the Nepalese territory have frequently been reported as encroached upon by India:

1. Kalapani-Limpiyadhura:..........
2. Bramhadevmandi-Purnagiri: ....
3. Tanakpur Barrage and Inundated Area:..........
4. Banbasa-Gaddachauki:.........
5. Sharada Barrage Area:.........
6. Shuklaphanta:...........
7. Parasan-Khuddakankad:...........
8. Sati-Birnala-Bhadanala:..........
9. Manau, Khairi and Tapara:..........
10. Murtiya:...........
11. Manpur-Bhimapur:..........
12. Santalia:.........
13. Holia, Nainapur

MOUNT EVEREST WAS CLAIMED BY CHINA

Before the boundary treaty between Nepal and China was signed, there were debates, disputes and claims at several places of the frontier areas. Some of the disputes which dated back to the time of Bhimsen Thapa had remained unsettled. But the demarcation of the border formally solved and ended those historical debates.

Issue Raised

But at another press conference in Kathmandu on 3 April, B.P. Koirala disclosed, which is off the record, that Mt. Everest (Sagarmatha) also lies in the area claimed by China. In a somber tone, he said that China had made a claim on Sagarmatha. They argued that Sagarmatha belonged to them but Nepal had rejected their claim.

Presentation of Maps

When Prime Minister Bisheswore Prasad Koirala had visited Beijing, China had said that Sagarmatha lies within the frontier of China. At that time both sides had presented maps showing Sagarmatha within their respective boundaries.

Finding the Highest Mountain

Scientists had found Sagarmatha as the world's highest peak more than 150 years ago. The Survey of India has surveyed and measured the peaks of the Himalayas during 1849-50 from the Indian territory, 176 kilometers far away using the Great Triangulation Surveying technique.

That time the peaks had no specific names and the peaks were given the Roman numerical. Sagarmatha was given the number XV and was called Peak XV.......... Boston Museum of Science/ National Geographic Society measured its height and formally declared on 11 November 1999 as 8,850 metres, as this project was operated by Dr. Bradford Washburn, Honorary Director of Boston Museum of Science.

Naming and meaning of Sagarmatha

Sagarmatha was formed by the combination of two words *Sagar* and *Matha*. The word *Sagar* is the transformation of *swarga* (heaven) in Vedic and Sanskrit letters, and it is in use in Nepali language. For instance, the Nepalese people say *"Sagar Dadhyo"* when the west horizon appears glowish at the sun-set time and it is always remembered by local inhabitants. Similarly, *Math* or *Matha* signifies the sky or the head, the tallest part of the body. Generally, *Sagar* denotes the heaven or sky and *Matha* is the head or crest.

This was also the reason that Chairman Mao Tse-tung accepted that Chomolungma and Sagarmatha were the same peak and agreed to the border line according to the map presented by Nepal. He had also suggested to scrap the different names used in the two countries and outside such as Sagarmatha – Chomolungma – Mount Everest and rather to call the peak 'Friendship Peak' as a symbol of friendship between Nepal and

China..........But the naming of Sagarmatha as Friendship Peak could not be named because of lack of interest on the Nepalese side.

That time if Prime Minister Koirala had only nodded his head by way of concurrence, Nepal might not have been called these days as the country of Sagarmatha.

Chou En-Lai Settled the Issue

The Chinese Prime Minister Chou En-Lai paid a three-day visit to Nepal on the scheduled time to strengthen Nepal-China relations and to resolve the issue of Sagarmatha. In this connection after the Chinese prime minister said at a press conference at the Singha Durbar Gallery *Baithak* on 28 April 1960 that 'Sagarmatha belongs to Nepal', and the Sagarmatha issue was put off at once.

The Issue was Resolved at Prime Ministers Level

It should be noted that the issue of Sagarmatha was resolved at the level of the prime ministers. Who can say that this issue would be resolved to amicably if it had been taken up at the lower level?

Peak of Sagarmatha is Located in Nepal

Many people may wonder how Sagarmatha could be of Nepal if the borderline runs over the peak. On top of that there is the curiosity of which country should claim the rights to the peak or on which country the peak is located. The shortest and the easiest answer is that the peak or the highest portion lies on the Nepalese side and Sagarmatha belongs to Nepal..........

The most important matter about the peak of Sagarmatha is that there is about 2 meter by 2.3 meter of sloping terraced portion on the southern side of the demarcating line of water-parting ridge. And that piece of sloping terraced area with the highest portion lies on the Nepalese side.

But the Chinese side from the borderline is almost vertical, and anyone conquering Sagarmatha from the northern or Chinese face cannot set foot on the peak without stepping on that sloping terraced area of the Nepalese frontier and no one can remain standing on the water-parting ridge of the borderline. As that sloping terraced area of the world's highest portion is located on the Nepalese side of the borderline, so Sagarmatha is said to lay in Nepalese territory......... In short, it is because of the fact that the highest peak with the sloping terraced portion lied on the Nepalese side during demarcation and China gave up its claim to Sagarmatha.

Rebels : Beyond the Border

The Nepalese rebels who do not think safe and feel free within the territory of their own nation, flee beyond the border to India, no matter whoever may be the rebels. It may be a rebellious son of a cruel hearted father or the leaders of the political parties banned by the then government. If a father scolds and warns his mischievous son, the son intends to cross the open border suddenly to be safe from his father. When a Nepalese national commits crime or murder, rape or some illegal activities, he intends to cross the porous border to escape from the Nepali law and to get safe shelter in India, commonly referred to as *Mugalan* (land of the Mugal Emperors).

Rebels in the History

Not only the Kings, Princes, Regents and courtiers of high office, but the Queens of Nepal also had taken political asylum in India. Queen Rajya Laxmi and King Rajendra entered Varanasi after the infamous *Kot Parva*. The rebels managed to flee beyond the border though the border was not open at that time as it is today.

Democratic Movement

King Tribhuvan Bir Bikram Shah Dev had taken refuge beyond the border in New Delhi, India in 1950......... This may be one of the instances how even the King had to go beyond the border to bring democracy in the nation.

Anti-national Element of Partyless Panchayat System

In the political history of Nepal, late King Mahendra Bir Bikram Shah Dev banned all political parties, dissolved the parliament and established Partyless Panchayat System in 1961. After the ban on multi-party system, some of the political leaders and their supporters were put into custody while some others managed to flee beyond the border in course of time, because the border was open and there was no provision for restriction on the free movement of people......... In those days, the Nepalese political leaders namely, Bisheswore Prasad Koirala, Subarna Shumsher JB Rana, Ganesh Man Singh, Pushpa Lal Shrestha, Mana Mohan Adhikari, Mohan Bikram Singh, Nirmal Lama, Ram Raja Prasad Singh etc. launched their movement against the then Nepal government from the Indian soil. They were safe and sound beyond the border of Nepal.

Maoist Insurgency

For the last few years, India has been harbouring the Maoist rebels. Maoist leaders who have found shelter in the Indian territory were operating hostile movement in Nepal against the police force and royal Nepal army. Regarding the underground movement conducted by the Maoist rebels, former prime minister Girija Prasad Koirala has said that India has protected Maoists by giving them shelter in her land......... US State Department spokeswoman said "the Maoists need to lay down their arms immediately, stop their brutal and senseless attacks and engage in the peaceful pursuit of their aims within the democratic framework of Nepal's constitution." In the mean time, Shyam Saran, Indian Ambassador to Nepal said "there could be Maoists among the Nepalese crossing into India through the open international border. We have also reports of MCC and PWG cadres from India going to training camps in western mid-hills of Nepal."

Now the Maoist problem has been recognized as a movement, albeit the Maoist called it a "people's war." His Majesty's Government of Nepal had designated the Maoists as terrorists at first. But later on they were addressed as rebels. The government had put on price tag on the head of Maoist leaders up to 5 million rupees, if one could bring them live or dead. Now the government of Nepal has taken back the label of terrorist and rebels to the Maoists. On the other hand, the United States government on 30 April 2003 announced the names of 38 groups as "Foreign Terrorism

Organizations" and has named CPN (Maoists) among 38 outfits under "Other Terrorist Group".

The U.S. Department of state displayed the lists, determined by the Secretary of State from the "Patterns of Global Terrorism" on its website.

Actually, the Maoists had started people's movement on 13 February 1996 with a view to upgrading the economic condition of the general rural people of Nepal changing the political scenario by transferring power to the people, as they put it. Poor, uneducated and jobless young people became angry, frustrated and violent against the government administration. Besides, feelings of tyranny, injustice, ethnic differences and religious fundamentalism led the enthusiastic youngsters to resort to cult of terrorism and the Maoist movement was expanded.

During the Maoist insurgency common Nepalese people were of the view that the war was going on between two groups of Nepali people, but not with the aliens. Among them one is the government force and the other is the rebels which is known as people's force. And the same Nepalese people have been killed by both the forces.

Cease-fire between Maoist and Government Force

Realising this fact, both the sides agreed to make cease-fire and to hold talks for peace in the country. As a result, cease-fire was declared on 29 January 2003.

According to the Royal Nepal Army Spokesman, Colonel Deepak Gurung the seven years old insurgency which started on 13 February 1996 has claimed the lives of 7,973 Nepalese people, and over four thousand of them were killed after the imposition of a state of emergency on 26 November 2001. Those who lost their lives during insurgency were 6,011 Maoist rebels, 873 civilian policemen, 773 civilians, 219 army personnel and 97 armed policemen since its inception on 13 February 1966.

Fortunately, there is a cease-fire now and people have felt relief to conduct their affairs comfortably and businessmen move and transport merchandise from one place to another.

Fleeing of Corrupt Persons

There are some other examples of how not only the rebels but also people from other sections used to go beyond the border to India for the protection of their lives. Currently the corrupt persons have started to flee beyond the border to remain safe and sound away from the penal action of Commission of Investigation of Abuse of Authority (CIAA). The commission had raided the houses of twenty-two government officials of revenue departments, especially the customs and tax offices to investigate whether their property, cash or kind, had been earned legally or illegally.

Similarly, three former ministers, Khum Bahadur Khadka, Jaya Prakash Gupta and Chiranjibi Wagle had been taken into custody by the CIAA to find out the source of their huge amount of property including land and buildings, cash and gold and investment on commercial business.

In the mean time CIAA was searching Khadka very much. But he suddenly reached CIAA at 11 A.M. on Friday, the 4th of April 2003. He might have gone beyond the border for a long period of time. It is due to the fact that no identification card is necessary for exit and entry on the international border between Nepal and India. Because the border is open and any Nepali/Indian national can cross the porous border any time and so many times a day. At the same time, there is no record keeping system of those passengers of both nations, while they cross the international border.

Extradition of Culprits

If the law offenders of a country cross the border and enter into the other frontier, the security personnel could arrest him and extradite to the concerned government authority with the help of the record of border crossings, though there is a lack of effective articles in the Extradition Treaty between the two countries. .... But the meeting ended without any decision. Updating the treaty for extraditing the citizens of a third country to India was India's proposal. But Nepal had refused to agree to the Indian proposal to handover citizens of third countries to India.

Remarks

Because of lack of effective measures in the extradition treaty in general and weakness in border management system in particular, the rebels intend to move beyond the border to get safe havens on the other side of the frontier. The rebels range from the lower section of the society to leaders of the political parties and bureaucrats. It has been affected the security of the nation. Now there is a need realised by all to develop an appropriate system on border management, not to let the rebels go beyond the border, so that the prevailing laws and regulations could be enforced to them within the country's jurisdiction for the maintenance of national security as well as to check the evil designs and mischievous of the members of the Nepalese society.

'NEW FRONT' OF CHINA ON INDO-NEPAL BORDER

The Chinese clamour over Arunachal Pradesh has raised many eyebrows in India. Even as the meeting between Prime Minister Manmohan Singh and Chinese Premier Wen Jiabao in Thailand on Saturday was being looked at as an effort to cool down the tension between the neighbouring countries, the Dragon nation has opened another anti-India front. This time in Nepal. Silently but speedily China is spreading its wings in the erstwhile Hindu kingdom, mainly to unleash anti-India propaganda. Besides acquiring some major construction projects in Nepal, the Chinese are also making their presence felt by opening language centres in Nepali cities on the Indo-Nepal border. These centres are teaching Chinese language. But, what raises suspicions on Chinese intentions is the fact that these centres are open only for Nepali citizens.

The surge in Chinese activities in the neighbour country is a matter of concern for India which is already fighting terrorism being pushed into the country from Pakistan. It's a known fact that China often uses Nepal as a buffer state against India. After the Indo-China war of 1962, the Dragon country has made constant efforts to increase its influence in Nepal. Though it did not succeed much till Nepal was under the rule of monarchy, the fall of monarchy and growing Maoist grip over Nepal has given a fillip to Chinese plans.

A clear indicator of this is the construction of Sikta barrage in Agaiya village of Banke district (Nepal). Its construction was delayed for almost three decades owing to Indian protest. But, once Maoists held sway over the Nepali government, the construction was given a go-ahead in 2006. Moreover, the contract for the project was given to Chinese firm — Sinehydro. In fact, a team of 40 Chinese engineers is engaged in the construction of the Sikta barrage in Agaiya district of Nepal. The district touches the Indian district of Shravasti. The distance from Indian border to the barrage is barely 14 kilometres. The possibility of Chinese infiltration in important zones of war on Indian border areas due to the presence of Chinese engineers cannot be ruled out.

Also, after the completion of the barrage the flow of river Rapti towards India will be diverted towards Nepal which will create acute water shortage in Indian area. Efforts have also been started to divert the flow of rivers flowing towards Indian area from Parchu lake located in Chinese area adjoining the state which may lead to floods in the borders districts of India during monsoon. Not only this, if the and Sikta barrage ever breaks down due to technical reasons it will severely impact the security arrangements made on the India border. China, thus, seems to be working on these two projects under well-planned policy to tease India. Similarly, China has established the office of 'Maitri Sangh' in Nepal adjoining Indian border territory. Meanwhile, a 10-member team comprising five Chinese and five Tibetan national recently visited Nepalganj headquarters of Banke district (Nepal). The team toured the Indo-Nepal border and secretly clicked photographs of the Rupaidiha main gate located on Indo-Nepal border. The Indian intelligence agencies, however, learnt about this when the team had already left for Kathmandu. Assistant army Nayak Devendra of Shashtra Seema Bal (SSB), when contacted, told TOI that he will report the incident to his senior officers.

Nepal's Prime Minister Mr. Madhav Kumar Nepal and Chairman of the Nepalese Congress (NC) Party Girija Prasad Koirala have assured China that Nepali soil will not be allowed to be used against China under any circumstances. Talking with the Chinese delegation led by politburo member of the Chinese Communist Party, Mr. Zhang Gaoli, separately, September 1, 2009, the two veteran politicians of Nepal, according to the high placed sources, did try to convince China towards Nepal's firm stand on 'One China Policy'. However, Beijing is not that fool to believe such parroted/repetitive assurance of Nepali politician, say Kathmandu based analyst.

"The lame duck government has not even asked official clarifications from those lawmakers from the Madhesh parties who had assured the Tibetan community in exile in India that they will raise the issue of 'Free Tibet' in Nepal's Constituent Assembly (CA) during their last meet with Dalai Lama in Dharmasala of Himanchal Pradesh, India", laments a Kathmandu based analyst who preferred anonymity. 'The recent meet of the Nepal law makers has raised suspicion in the minds of the Beijing authorities as regards the Nepalese structured stance that she remains firm on "One China Policy' of Nepal. And Beijing understands the Nepali intentions well. According to PM's political advisor Mr. Raghujee Panta, PM's upcoming visit to China, Constitution drafting process and ongoing peace process were also discussed during the meet.

CHINA-SOUTH ASIA POLITICAL RELATIONS: A VIEW FROM NEPAL

"Peaceful co-existence" is the main principle in China-South Asia relations. The fundamentals of this principles are i) mutual equality, ii) non-interference in each other's internal affairs, iii) mutual respect to territorial integrity, iv) cooperation against hegemonism and power politics, and v) mutual accommodation and benefit (Wang Hongwei, 2005). In view of the colonial and feudal background, the main principle and fundamentals of China-South Asia ties are progressive. If one closely examines the natural and spiritual realities that persist between China and South Asia, the main principle and fundamentals of their ties can not truly be more than egalitarian.

China and South Asia are linked by land and water, mountains and rivers. Unlike East Asia and South East Asia and China,

Chinese and most of South Asian ties are contiguous, more natural and comprehensive. Mountains pass through and major rivers flow down to China and South Asia from the Tibet Autonomous Region (TAR) of China. Now, it is science and technology that is poised to harness snow and water for larger benefits of the people. In China and South Asia, it has yet remained a geo-political as well as ecological truism that link maintained by mountains and rivers are more stable than opportunistic alliances offered by nuclear power.

Another basic articulation of China-South Asia relations is Buddhism. Gautam Buddha, who was born and had acquired knowledge about the ultimate truth in South Asia, very much lives life-size every where in China. The civilization of China and South Asia thus holds common source of inspiration with a profound degree of continuity. As Buddhism does not stand as an anti-thesis for any other religion, it helps to create an internal capacity to absorb, acculturate and assimilate in both China and South Asia. In short, geo-politically charged neighborhood in an intense natural and spiritual sense is what stands out in China-South Asia relations.

China's politics till the recent past was concentrated on its east coast of the Taiwan Straits. Asia as a whole ranked relatively low in its security agenda since creation of the People's Republic of China. But the Cold War era did not leave China untouched. Tibet in particular conditioned China in formulation of its South Asia policy and to the stability in its frontier regions. The tenets of this policy were: Peace at the south-west border region of China. Efficient signing of border treaty with the neighboring countries was part of this policy to ensure peace along China's long border.

The Tibetan question. This question raised by the external forces had made China acutely sensitive of its national integration and domestic stability. Chinese policy recognized Tibetan separatism as having serious implications for the national integration and domestic stability. It also recognized that the forces supporting the Tibetan separatism were working by proxy, and many aspects of the separatist moves were utterly non-transparent. So trying its best to correctly understand the external as well as internal features of Tibetan question, and appreciating highly those neighboring countries and organizations who did not allow Tibetan separatists to engage in activities and also did not permit outside powers to support such activities on their soil, China's South Asia Policy tried proactively hard to work at the two inter-related fronts at the same time-discouraging the separatist elements and, praising and encouraging those countries and organizations who did not support and did not provide any ground to support the Tibetan separatism.

Independent relations with South Asian states. China was aware of the unequal interstate relations that do not allow development of cordial and trustily ties between them. Difference in size, power and interpretation of agreements had affected relations between states in South Asia. During the Cold War years, the dominating trend in the interstate relations was exploitation and gains at the cost of other, and a tendency to have "sphere of influence." Exchange and cooperation between China and a number of small South Asian states was not liked by India. But China continued to cultivate ties with small South Asian countries independently. It supported independence of these countries, and their independent decision making. After 1962 border war with India, the importance of independence of the countries in South Asia-particularly of those small and non-nuclear power countries-had increased for China. China realized that only unilaterally wishing for cooperation might not be wise and realistic.

Therefore in view of a Chinese analyst, "It is undeniable, ...after the 1962 border war, China's policy toward Nepal might have reflected, to some extent, a strategy in which China supported Nepal, along with other small countries in South Asia, to check India's influence" (Hua Han, 2005). Despite so, China provided unflinching support to late King Birendra's proposal to declare Nepal a "Zone of Peace" in mid 1970s. It was indicative of China's firmer conviction that the indigenous will and ability of neighboring small states in South Asia to independently conduct their foreign and defence affairs together with its independent foreign policy and self-defence strategy was more important and conducive for peace and stability of China's frontier regions than mere lonely Chinese efforts directed at the same. It was this sense of working together which had been the driving force for China to reciprocally commit to the independence of the small South Asian states. Whatever financial, material and military assistance China has provided to these countries were corollary of the said policy.

The United States of America (the US) has ever been at the centre stage whether it was the end of the bi-polar Cold War, 9/11 terrorist attacks and the subsequent US campaign against terrorism, and now the US campaign for democracy. It is the only power which could put troops in Iraq and Afghanistan at the same time and spend enough money to rebuild the economies. Indeed, despite the euphoria for multi-lateralism after the end of Cold War, the South Asian countries were "gravely relying on the assistance and loans provided by the World Bank and developed countries, which in turn resulted in the heavy burden of foreign debts and shortage of foreign exchange reserves and investment capital.

After 9/11, the new strategic development (beginning of the US offensive in Afghanistan) changed the security environment in Asia. US military presence in Uzbekistan and Afghanistan and the new military relationship of the US with Pakistan and India completed the US military involvement in the whole of the Asian continent. Until then South Asia was a gap between the US involvement in West Asia and East Asia. After the US completed its Asian military expansion by filling the gaps left by collapse of Soviet Union under its "war against terror" planning, it felt a need to address another gap which its own larger military involvement had created. The felt US need was primarily due to genuine domestic concerns. The felt need this time was democracy.

For China and the US "the week that changed the world" in February, 1972 when President Nixon visited China had a clear American objective, and that was "to transform the two-power world of the Cold War into a triangle then to manage the triangle in such a way that we would be closer to each of the contenders than they were to each other, thereby maximizing our options". With the disappearance of the Soviet Union, one of the two-power world, despite the initial instability and uncertainty, the US and China appear to move into a maturing stage, and carry out responsibilities particularly in Asia-Pacific region. The following statements of President Bush and Premier Wen confirm how they viewed their role in relation to each other.

Welcoming Chinese Premier Wen Jiabao at the White House on December 9, 2003, President George Bush of the United States of America described the US and China as "partners in diplomacy working to meet the dangers of 21st century."

He further added: "As our two nations work constructively across areas of common interest, we are candid about our disagreements. The growing strength and maturity of our relationship allows us to discuss our differences, whether over economic issues, Taiwan, Tibet, or human rights and religious freedom, in a spirit of mutual understanding and respect."

Replying to President Bush on the occasion, Chinese Premier Wen said, "Our cooperation in a wide range of areas such as counterterrorism, economy, trade and international and regional issues has effectively safeguarded our mutual interests and promoted peace, stability and prosperity in the Asia Pacific region and the world at large."

The key policy statements above from President Bush and Premier Wen, beyond any doubt, eloquently establishes the importance of Sino-US relationship for the Asia-Pacific region and the world at large over and above the bilateral ties existing between the two great countries. In the period ahead where agenda for democracy is pushed to the front, China-US ties may loose glitters; and China may face all the blames for being a "communist" state. And specifically in the context of South Asia, where the majority belongs to the poor and level of interstate cooperation is low, it is for the people and states of the South Asia to decide either for China-inspired peace with independence and self-governed development or for the US-inspired peace with global democracy and development. Whatever the choice the people and states of South Asia make, the decision of Thirteenth Dhaka SAARC summit to associate China and Japan with SAARC was indeed a very welcome unprecedented geopolitical development. The constructive role played by the small SAARC members in this decision making will certainly help fruitfully maximize comparative advantage of SAARC member's vis-à-vis the new partners (China and Japan).

South Asian states are poor. One major reason for such a condition is they do not have an effective good neighborly policy between themselves. At times certain state's behaviour suggests that it wants to live without neighbours. Mahatma Gandhi has provided an example of a good neighborly policy. In his words of wisdom, "One who serves his neighbours serves all the world."

Since 1978 when the modernization and reform process started, economic growth in China has averaged 9.5 percent per year which remains a truly astounding rate. Similarly, foreign trade has expanded at an annual rate of 15 percent over the same period. As for foreign investment China was able to attract $53.2 billion in 2002 as against $52.7 billion for the United States of America. Indeed, the economic transformation has been so rapid that even renowned investment banking firms like Golsdman Sachs predict that China could be the world's largest economy by 2050 with a GDP of $44.4 trillion ahead of the US GDP of $35 trillion and India's GDP of $27 trillion in the same period.

To correct some of the economic divide of a market based economy so that no part of the country remains left out in the great process of economic transformation, the Chinese government is allocating increasing resources including new investment funds from better off provinces in building new physical and social infrastructure and new industrial establishments in the western region. As a part of this strategy the Qinghai-Tibet railway is completed at a cost of $3.16 billion. Similarly, road network in Tibet is being expanded and improved with links to important cities in other provinces.

China's rapid economic growth has its neighbours change their perception on China. The shift from a "China threat" to "China opportunity" theory opens the alternative to explore the benefits that can be draw from the gigantic China's market-leading to deeper and inner natural and spiritual bonds with China. As the immediate neighbours, as many South Asian scholars and experts have wisely suggested, the SAARC members states should take full advantage of China's achievement, especially China's "western development program," which can facilitate a closer economic and trade interaction specially between Tibet, Xingjian, Sichuan and Yunnan and neighboring South Asian states. Opening of new transport and trade routes and just completed railway line over "the roof of the world" will provide China's western parts with efficient access to neighboring countries leading to a change in geo-political outlook.

The ultimate test of the South Asian ability will lie with its leaders' determination to practically conduct the principle of peaceful co-existence along with its fundamentals in relationship with China. Hopefully the Himalayan twins as if representing north face and south face of Kailash-China and South Asia-cherish more a vision of working together than a division of sphere of influence.

It was this spirit of working together that had inspired the press release that was issued after the international seminar on SAARC and China. China Study Centre, Nepal organized this seminar on 23 December, 2002 in Kathmandu, the venue of SAARC Secretariat. The press release stated: "Based on the papers presented and comments and observations made during the discussion, the participants of the seminar on SAARC and China …have come to the following consensus." There is a need for institutionalized dialogue mechanism between SAARC and China. The imperative for good neighbourhood and challenges and opportunities of the 21st century in regard to peace, cooperation and development dictate the needs for bold and speedy action to move forward in this direction. In this connection it is necessary to hold follow-up seminar focusing on the specific of the institutionalized dialogue mechanism between SAARC and China.

The SAARC member states may try to expand and intensify their social and economic interaction with China at sub-regional level. The Track II initiative prepares ground for promoting and complementing official level discussion. It is gratifying to note that Thirteenth SAARC summit at Dhaka in November last has gloriously taken initiative for establishing institutionalized dialogue mechanism between SAARC and China. The SAARC member leaders should be commended for their bold and glorious initiative.

It is hoped that they will also ensure speedy actions regarding the paraphernalia of China's institutionalized association with SAARC.

What is expected are upcoming SAARC official meetings at various levels will prepare grounds for the SAARC member states to expand and intensify their social and economic interaction with China at sub-regional level. Various sub-regional groupings within SAARC may find, for example, i) eastern Himalayan resource, ii) western Himalayan resources, iii) transportation links and networks, iv) nature tourism and v) spiritual tourism as important themes for sustainable cooperation to the various sub-regional groups within SAARC. It has been learned that attempts have been made to organize seminars on China and South Asian Relations in Colombo. Such activities are encouraging as they promote and compliment official level discussion on inter-regional collaborative dialogue between China and South Asian states.

It will be extremely good if the SAARC member states attempts to expand and intensify their social and economic interaction with China at sub-regional level. A sub-region (based on sub-geographical level-for example, eastern South Asia, western South Asia, and/or function-for example, culture, natural sources or infrastructure) is recognized as a practical mechanism to promote and strengthen SAARC's over all link with China. As more effective, immediate and direct geo-political link between China and South Asia will be through sub-regional grouping of South Asia; members of the South Asian sub-regional grouping will be more dependent on each other to realize the purpose. Whereas for China, this sort of cooperative arrangement will ensure required stability and peace in the frontier regions, for each South Asian sub-region value will be added to tourism, culture, and physical development which will enhance overall quality of life of its people.

3

India and Bangladesh: Calculus of Territorial Dispute Settlement

Given that instances of territorial dispute settlement in this sovereignty-conscious region have been few and far between, this exercise in statesmanship is both commendable and long overdue. A review of the principles and processes underlying the compromises reveals useful insights into territorial dispute settlement at New Delhi's end.

The India-Bangladesh boundary is no ordinary one. Hastily constructed in the dying days of British colonialism, it was the longest international boundary created during the age of decolonisation. The border was intended to separate a contiguous majority area of Muslims from that of non-Muslims — but for only about a quarter of its length does it separate a Muslim-majority in Bangladesh from a Hindu-majority in India. As many as 162 tiny enclaves (111 Indian and 52 Bangladeshi) dot a section of the frontier: in the extreme an Indian enclave sits within a Bangladeshi enclave, itself situated within a larger Indian enclave, all surrounded by Bangladeshi territory!

Shifting rivers, mapping errors and 'adversely possessed lands' — that is, lands unwittingly encroached upon and (illegally) occupied by both countries — added to the maze of identity, loyalty and insecurity along the Bengal borderland. Sixteen Indian and three Bangladeshi border guards were killed in 2001 following a show of force in a disputed area along the border. Demarcating a boundary has unsurprisingly been a protracted affair.

According to the recent agreement, the Indian enclaves in Bangladesh and the Bangladeshi enclaves in India are to be swapped, enabling unbroken territorial continuity — with minor exceptions — for both states. New Delhi's claim to compensation for the additional acreage ceded to Bangladesh is waived. The bewildered 51,000 residents in these enclaves will presumably be offered the choice of either relocating or, more likely, having their citizenship switched — although this is not accounted for in the *Protocol*. The 'adversely possessed lands' are to be mutually vacated, something that will be done in conjunction with the swapping of enclaves. Finally, the remaining disputed points are to be marked and delimited, enabling India thereafter to share its first *fully* demarcated land boundary with a neighbour.

The *Protocol* lays down weighty precedents for New Delhi's territorial dispute settlement practices. Especially notable is admitting an uncompensated swap of territory — during the course of exchanging the enclaves — in effect *ceding land to which it holds undisputed title*. Minor exchange of disputed territory by New Delhi is not groundbreaking. In 1951, India and Pakistan agreed to exchange two disputed territories on the India-East Pakistan (now Bangladesh) border. And in 1959 the two countries prepared modalities for future exchange of territories pending boundary demarcation. Letting-out undisputed territory on a 'perpetual lease' is not groundbreaking either. In 1974, New Delhi leased a narrow strip of territory (Tin Bigha corridor) to the then newly-inaugurated independent government of Bangladesh. The Indian Supreme Court interpreted the lease as a form of 'undisturbed possession' for Dacca's use which did not divest India of its sovereign rights.

But uncompensated cession of undisputed territory along its land border is altogether unprecedented. It also sets a useful precedent for that significant patch of disputed territory that will necessarily have to be ceded to China in the context of a Sino-Indian boundary arrangement in the foreseeable future. With New Delhi already having ceded a small, uninhabited island to Sri Lanka along their maritime boundary line in the mid-1970s, and with the Indian judiciary vesting treaty-making authority wholly to the executive, the swap of enclaves on the India-Bangladesh border should pass constitutional muster. Two fundamental principles and processes that underlie New Delhi's calculus of territorial dispute settlement are particularly noteworthy.

First, an imperative of good neighborliness has been a fundamental pre-requisite for settlement — New Delhi was willing to meet the Bangladeshi Prime Minister mid-way, even beyond, but only after the latter had met India's security concerns and walked the extra mile to extend the hand of friendship. Significant credit for the settlement belongs at the Bangladeshi end.

Second, and more important, is a practice of Indian boundary diplomacy which has seen New Delhi admit to the exigencies of *'zamini haqeeqat'* (ground realities) in disputed border areas — formally seeking to resolve territorial disputes according to the status quo, with least disturbance to local inhabitants. 'Ground realities' is formally acknowledged in the India-Bangladesh Joint Statement. Paired with the acceptance of a political parameters-based approach to dispute resolution, it has also unlocked potential for resolving the long-dormant Sino-Indian boundary dispute.

India and Bangladesh should use the goodwill generated through the settlement to resolve their long-pending maritime border dispute. That dispute consists of: (a) demarcation of the coastal boundary line around a tiny island at the point where a common boundary river meets the estuary on the Bay of Bengal, and (b) overlapping EEZ boundary and resource development claims emerging from the concave geography of the Bengal coastline.

For the former, international arbitration on the tried-and-tested lines of the 1968 settlement between India and Pakistan that divided a semi-submerged tract at the mouth of the Arabian Sea may provide a model for determining the coastal boundary. For the latter, New Delhi should desist from unilateral surveying of the overlapping maritime zones pending judgment of their respective claims at the Permanent Court of Arbitration (PCA) at The Hague. Better still, submitting to settlement principles in the analogous Myanmar-Bangladesh maritime baseline claims case, currently under fast-track International Tribunal for the Law of the Sea (ITLOS) proceedings would be an act of graciousness on New

Delhi's part. Best of all would be joint survey and development of the overlapping India-Bangladesh maritime zone without prejudice to the ITLOS or PCA verdicts. In doing so, New Delhi would also set a portentous precedent for claimants in the South China Sea.

BANGLADESH–INDIA BORDER

The border has created a narrow strip known as "Chicken's neck" that has made the communication and transportation between mainland India and Northeast India inconvenient

Bangladesh and India share a 4,096-kilometer (2,545-mile)-long international border, the fifth-longest land border in the world, including 262 km in Assam, 856 km in Tripura, 180 km in Mizoram, 443 km in Meghalaya, and 2,217 km in West Bengal. The Bangladeshi Divisions of Dhaka, Khulna, Rajshahi, Rangpur, Sylhet and Chittagong are situated along the border. A number of pillars mark the border between the two states. Small demarcated portions of the border are fenced on both sides.

History

The border of Bangladesh first came into being when the Bengal Presidency was created by the British. When India became independent from Great Britain in 1947, the country was divided among Muslim and non-Muslim majority areas. Likewise the provinces of Punjab, Bengal and the Sylhet district of Assam were also bifurcated and the border came into being. Muslims were the majority in the western part of India and the eastern part of Bengal province. These two areas formed the new Islamic republic of Pakistan. The eastern part, East Pakistan, became the People's Republic of Bangladesh in the Bangladesh Liberation War of 1971.

Geography

The border divides the Ganges delta region and the Sundarban mangrove forest. It is crisscrossed by a large number of rivers. The area is mostly flat with slight hilly terrain in Meghalaya, Assam, Tripura and Mizoram sections. The border area is densely populated. The land is extremely fertile and is cultivated right up to the border pillars. Sometimes the border line passes right through villages, even buildings. The area is patrolled by the Indian Border Security Force BSF of India and BGB, formerly known as Bangladesh Rifles or BDR of Bangladesh.

Issues

Moreover, illegal immigrants from Bangladesh cross the border to India. Because of a large number of illegal immigrants crossing from Bangladesh into India, a controversial shoot-on-sight policy has been enforced by the Indian border patrols. This policy was initiated with reports of violence between the illegal migrants and Indian soldiers. The border has also witnessed occasional skirmishes between the Indian Border Security Force and the Border Guards Bangladesh, most notably in 2001.

In July 2009, Channel 4 News reported that hundreds of Bangladeshis were killed by the BSF along the Indo-Bangladeshi Barrier. The BSF claims that the barrier's main purpose is to check illegal immigration and to prevent cross-border terrorism. In 2010, Human Rights Watch (HRW) issued an 81-page report which brought up uncountable abuses of the BSF. The report was compiled from the interviews taken from the victims of BSF torments, witnesses, members of the BSF and its Bangladeshi counterpart. The report stated that over 1000 Bangladeshi citizens were killed during the first decade of the 21st century. According to HRW, BSF did not only shoot illegal migrants or smugglers but even innocents who were seen near, sometimes even people working in fields (farmland) near the border..

BSF has often been accused by Bangladesh government of incursions into Bangladesh territory, and indiscriminate shooting of civilians along the India-Bangladesh borders. This was in retaliation to massive illegal immigration from Bangladesh to India, for which the Indo-Bangladeshi Barrier is underway/ In a news conference in August 2008, Indian BSF officials admitted that they killed 59 illegals (34 Bangladeshis, 21 Indians, rest unidentified) who were trying to cross the border during the prior six months. Bangladeshi media accused the BSF of abducting 5 Bangladeshi children, aged between 8 and 15, from the Haripur

Upazila in Thakurgaon District of Bangladesh, in 2010. The children were setting fishing nets near the border. In 2010, Human Rights Watch has accused the Border Security Force for the indiscriminate killings. BSF forces badly beaten, physically abused, Raped (later killed and hanged the dead body over the fence) Ms. Felani (a 15 years old Bangladeshi girl) on 7 January 2011.

Many conferences have been held between India and Bangladesh to discuss such issues as smuggling and trespassing, cattle lifting, trafficking of drugs and arms. Colonel Muhammad Shahid Sarwar of Bangladesh Rifles gave Border Security Force a list of miscreants which took place in India, and the BSF side also handed over a similar list to the BDR.

Exclaves

The border area is dotted with many Indian territory exclaves within Bangladesh, and many Bangladeshi territory (enclave) within India. They result from pre-colonial treaties between the Maharajah of Cooch Behar and the Nawab of Rangpur, and were maintained at the time of partition between India and what was then East Pakistan in 1947. Residents of the exclaves generally live in miserable conditions, lacking access to basic services such as healthcare or electricity. These are not provided by their own government, as they are isolated from it by a strip of foreign land; nor are they provided by the surrounding state. They cannot visit their own country without crossing the international border surrounding the territory (enclave).

In September 2011, the two countries verbally agreed on land swaps and resolve the issue, but till November 2013 nothing were done from both side. The exclaves' population, over 50,000 people, would have a say in the matter, and each person would ultimately be allowed to choose their nationality.

POLITICS AND ORIGIN OF THE INDIA-BANGLADESH BORDER

Every time Nazir Rahman Bhuiyan, a villager in Bangladesh, moves from one part of his house to another, he crosses an international border-the recently fenced India and Bangladesh border. A spokesman for the Indian Ministry of External Affairs cited the reasons for the fence as a combination of the same & that had made the United States and Israel to build fences with Mexico and the West Bank respectively to prevent illegal migration and terrorist infiltration.

The idea of protecting the Indo-Bangladesh border with a fence is not new. Regional politicians in Assam first proposed fencing the border in the 1960s in order to isolate the population of East Pakistan. During that period, the Government of Assam under Congress Chief Minister Bimala Prasad Chaliha launched a campaign to deport immigrants who had settled in Assam since January 1951. He ignored Prime Minister Jawharlal Nehru's request to go slow on the issue. He along with his party also advocated clearing up an area in sufficient depth along the border to control Pakistani infiltration which was taken up by the government in Delhi at that time but not implemented. Assamese politicians were not able to convince the Central government on illegal migration from East Pakistan but they managed to sanction 180 additional police watch posts and erect a barbed wire fence in selected places on the Assam-East Pakistan border.

In the late 1970s and early 1980s there was a violent protest and anti-Bengali program in Assam, which led to the establishment of the Assam Accord. The mainstream Indian political leaders discuss the issue and place it on the national agenda in 1985. In 1986, the Indian government approved the Indo-Bangladesh Border Road and Fence project to prevent illegal (also called irregular) migration from Bangladesh. However, the progress of that project was very slow.

The project was budgeted at Rs 3.7 billion in 1986. Progress on the fence construction on Bangladesh-Assam border was slow and irregular till 1998. Apart from fencing the border, the All Assam Student Union (AASU) and the Asom Gana Parishad (AGP) demanded the enactment of the Illegal Migrants (Determination by Tribunal) Act (IMDT Act), which came into force in 1983. A number of criticisms were made of the Act with a demand for its amendment and abolition throughout late 80s and 90s by AASU, AGP and section of Assamese print media. In response to that the

Supreme Court of India set aside the Act in a judgement in July 2005 and ordered the State Government of Assam to constitute a sufficient number of tribunals under the Foreigners Act to deal with illegal Bangladeshi migrants in Assam.

In December 2002, an estimation made by the Indian Ministry of Home Affairs (MHA) in 2004 claimed that Assam had a total of 26,490 foreigners staying illegally. Earlier, the Bharatiya Janata Party (BJP)-led National Democratic Alliance (NDA) Government had claimed that there were 1.20 million illegal migrants living in Assam and around 20 million Bangladeshis living in other parts of India including big cities like Kolkata, Delhi and Mumbai. The number of Bangladeshis varies with each media or official report. The issue of Bangladesh migrants residing in India (apart from North-east) became a concern of the Indian media when it became a political agenda of the Hindu nationalist mainstream political party Bharatiya Janata Party (BJP) in the 1980s and 1990s.

Management of Bangladesh India Border

A border is something that indicates a limit where one's responsibility ends and another's begin. The term "boundary" is used in similar sense inasmuch as it is one of the most significant manifestations of state territorial sovereignty. It delimits physical space and has proven to be quite a daunting task that can bedevil state relationship. But not so always if both sides understand each other better and are amenable to rational choices.

In the Eurocentric global model of modernity from which no culture in the world has remained untouched and which the Third World leaders have adopted, national borders left by their colonial rulers continue to provide them with challenges that so far many have been unable to resolve satisfactorily specially with their value system as tools. But this should not necessarily be the case. Borders could be sources of conflict as well as peace and prosperity depending on how the issues are tackled. This paper would look into the options that the two neighboring states Bangladesh and India can adopt in order to overcome the impediments that have alternately soured or given boost to their relationship from time to time taking necessary cue from the Eurocentric practices.

Prime Minister Sk. Hasina's planned visit to India from 11 January 2010 onward has raised tremendous positive expectations among the peoples of the two countries, media and policy makers for practical reasons. During her first term as Prime Minister of Bangladesh together with Indian Congress leaders like Mr. I. Gujral and regional leaders like Mr.Deve Gowda she was able to resolve some of the intractable issues like that of long term sharing of Ganges Water and the resolution of Chittagong Hill Tracts insurgency.

Similar concrete achievements, if not more, are now being expected by the peoples of the two countries as both the Prime Ministers of India and Bangladesh came to power in recent past with comfortable majority and do have positive track records of taking the bulls by the horn. The title of the today's roundtable discussion, namely "Bangladesh India Relations: Exploring New Horizons" does symbolize that upbeat expectation amongst all of us. Given the inter state post 1947 political culture in South Asia of keeping resolution of territorial issues pending, such expectations seem to be reflection of too much of the sunny side on the part of Bangladeshi psyche.

Meanwhile, the solemn declaration and its repeated affirmation of Sk. Hasina that Bangladesh's soil would not be allowed to be used by terrorists for attacking India followed by concrete action which lead to ULFA leaders surrender to Indian security apparatus have taken care of a serious security concern of Indian rulers and people on its eastern front. This has generated a huge surge of goodwill in the vocal Indian media whose Bangladesh critical columnists have not failed to note these unprecedented acts of friendship and tremendous risk to the person of Sk. Hasina and Bangladesh from the revenge seeking insurgent organizations of North east India.

But again to many Bangladeshis who got frustrated from little or no implementation of many settled agreements by India despite expression of concrete and repeated measures of goodwill shown by Bangladesh like handing over of Berubari enclave, lowering of tariff to Indian products entering Bangladesh under SAPTA passed without any reciprocal gestures, this unilateral daring act of strategic risk taking appears to be one more act of friendship gesture going to waste. Consequently, any mismatch in give and take from the two sides during her ensuing visit to India is going to have tremendous impact on the Bangladesh Prime Minister's political capital and goodwill among her people.

INDO-BANGLADESHI BARRIER

The project has run into several delays and there is no clear completion date for the project yet. The barrier when complete will be patrolled by the Border Security Force. The fence will also be electrified at some stretches.

The BSF claims that the barrier's main purpose is to prevent smuggling of narcotics.

Barbed Wire Fencing

India is constructing the Indo-Bangladeshi barrier, a 3,406 kilometres (2,116 mi) fence of barbed wire and concrete just under 3 metres high, to prevent smuggling of narcotics. Out of this, 2529 kilometres of fencing was completed at the cost of 28.81 billion (US$450 million) by November 2007.

The deadline for project completion was set to 2008–09 By October 2009, about 2649 kilometres of fencing along with about 3326 kilometres of border roads were completed. The deadline for project completion was revised to March 2010. By March 2011, 2735 kilometres of fencing was completed and the deadline was revised to March 2012.

Assam shares a 263 km of border with Bangladesh out of which 143.9 km is land and 119.1 km is riverine. As of November 2011, 221.56 km of fencing was completed.

Flood Lights

India has completed Flood lights installation for 277 kilometers in the West Bengal sector.

Sometimes between 2001-2006 Bangladesh Border security troops (BDR) clashed with the Indian Border Security Force when the fence were build beyond the no man's land.

INDIA AND BANGLADESH NEAR RESOLUTION ON BORDER DISPUTE

After years of negotiation, recent reports suggest that India is close to resolving its border dispute with Bangladesh, now that the current Indian government supports a resolution. Territorial changes in India need to be approved via constitutional amendment which explains why it would be most difficult for India to make territorial swaps with China or Pakistan without the entire Indian establishment being on board. Previous attempts at exchanging territory with Bangladesh all ran into trouble because of whichever party was in opposition in the Indian Parliament at the time.

The present agreement is known as the Land Boundary Agreement (LBA) and was negotiated by former Prime Minister Manmohan Singh with Bangladesh in 2011. The currently ruling Bharatiya Janata Party (BJP) and Prime Minister Narendra Modi opposed the agreement at the time and thus the agreement did not go through.

This is the same agreement that the BJP is now supporting. The reason given for this U-turn was given by Prime Minister Modi on Sunday in a speech given in Assam, which borders Bangladesh to the north. Modi declared that his government would in fact ratify the agreement in order to improve India's security and curb illegal immigration from Bangladesh. With all major Indian parties now in favor of a border agreement with Bangladesh, an amendment to the Indian constitution is expected to pass quickly and without much political difficulty.

Bangladesh's border with India is an interesting and unique case of a dispute – one that cannot be compared with India's border disputes with other countries. The nature of the Indo-Bangladeshi border makes a resolution involving a territorial swap all but necessary. Strewn along Bangladesh's northern border with India are hundreds of enclaves. There are 111 Indian enclaves in Bangladesh – Indian territory completely surrounded by Bangladesh, and 51 Bangladeshi enclaves in India. Some of these enclaves are second order enclaves. The result is an archipelago of enclaves along the Indo-Bangladeshi border.

The Indo-Bangladesh border is also home to the world's only third order enclave, the Indian Dahala Khagrabari. To see just how crazy this is, understand that this means that it is a piece of India within Bangladesh, within India, within Bangladesh.

India's strange boundary with Bangladesh came about because of pre-colonial politics during the Mughal Empire. While most of Bengal was a Mughal province, the state of Cooch Behar remained independent to its north. However, landowners from both Bengal and Cooch Behar owned properties and fiefs on both sides of the border, which resulted in the present situation. Sovereignty in this period in South Asia was not necessarily the result of straight territorial boundaries but a function of who paid taxes and was subordinate to whom. The current borders seem to be the "result of peace treaties in 1711 and 1713 between the kingdom of Cooch Behar and the Mughal Empire, ending a long series of wars in which the Mughals wrested several districts from Cooch Behar." A popular legend stating that the enclaves are the result of local rulers wagering villages in games of chess is anecdotal. Later on Cooch Behar became a princely state under British protection while Bengal was a province in British India. When Bengal was partitioned in 1947, a part of it became part of India and a part East Pakistan (later Bangladesh), while the princely state of Cooch Behar joined India. As a result, parts of it were surrounded by non-Indian territory and parts of East Pakistan were in India as a result of Cooch Behar joining India.

When Bangladesh became independent in 1971, India and Bangladesh attempted to resolve the problem of their enclaves. A 1974 agreement signed between then Indian Prime Minister Indira Gandhi and Bangladesh's leader Sheikh Mujibur Rahman was not ratified in India. The present treaty is broadly similar to the original one. India will acquire 51 enclaves and 2,777 acres of land and transfer 111 enclaves and 2,267 acres to Bangladesh. There is no doubt that this deal will be strongly beneficial for both India and Bangladesh by finally resolving a long standing cause of tension between both countries. It is also in the interests of the people of the enclaves, as it will finally give them access to the services of India and Bangladesh.

INDIA TAKES STEP TOWARD RESOLVING BORDER DISPUTE WITH BANGLADESH

India has inched closer to settling a long-simmering border dispute with Bangladesh, possibly signalling a softer line from nationalist Prime Minister Narendra Modi than when he was in opposition.

On Monday, a parliamentary committee urged the government to table a constitutional amendment that would pave the way for a land swap deal that Bangladesh and India have been negotiating for years. That followed a speech by Modi at the weekend that suggested a solution was in the offing.

In addition to Bangladesh, India has intractable territorial disputes with Pakistan and China. Modi called off peace talks with Pakistan in August but last week appointed a special envoy to China, a move that will allow border negotiations to resume.

A deal with Bangladesh would end decades of uncertainty for tens of thousands of citizens living in enclaves on the "wrong" side of their homeland's border.

Dozens of enclaves exist on either side of the border, a historical oddity left after British India's partition in 1947. The proposed solution would enable each side to acquire the enclaves within its borders, along with other disputed territories. On paper, the exchange appears to leave India with about 10,000 acres less territory and affects the more than 50,000 people living in the enclaves, as of a July 2011 headcount.

People living in the enclaves would have the right to move to live in their original country of nationality or to become nationals of their 'new' country after the exchange. Most are expected to stay put, according the Indian government.

Neither country would lose any territory they currently control, said Shashi Tharoor, head of the parliamentary committee and a minister in the last government.

Identity

"It is merely regularizing the existing reality in a way that permits both countries to extend normal public services to the residents of these areas," he told Reuters. Despite the BJP's past objections, Modi seemed to back such a deal on Sunday during a speech in Assam, one of the Indian states that would be affected.

"Whatever we do, there might be a perception of a short-term loss, but ultimately Assam will gain," said Modi, who discussed the border with his Bangladeshi counterpart last week. Modi said the deal could help curb illegal immigration from Bangladesh, a hot political issue in border areas. Bangladesh's foreign secretary declined to comment on the proposed deal.

Enclave dwellers in India welcomed the prospect of a deal. "I will finally have the chance to obtain an identity," said Jamal Hussain, a 20-year-old farm worker who lives in Masaldanya enclave nestled within West Bengal.

Not everyone was happy. "The land of Assam that is supposed to be handed over belongs to Assam," said Samujjal Bhattacharya, an advisor to the influential All Assam Students' Union. "[The BJP] are taking a U-turn today. How can that be?"

But as the Modi government looks to tackle bigger regional problems, resolving the border dispute with Bangladesh would be a solid start, some say. "They have to sort out some of the issues that are low-hanging fruit," said Anand Kumar, of the New Delhi-based think-tank the Institute for Defence Studies and Analyses.

INDO-BANGLADESH ENCLAVES

The Indo-Bangladesh enclaves, also known as the chitmahals , sometimes called pasha enclaves, are the enclaves along the Bangladesh–India border, in Bangladesh and the Indian states of West Bengal, Tripura, Assam and Meghalaya.

There are 106 Indian enclaves and 92 Bangladeshi enclaves. Inside the main part of Bangladesh, 102 of these are first-order Indian enclaves, while inside the main part of India, 71 of these are Bangladeshi first-order enclaves. Further inside these enclaves are an additional 24 second order- or counter-enclaves (21 Bangladeshi, 3 Indian) and one Indian counter-counter-enclave, called *Dahala Khagrabari #51*. They have an estimated combined population between 50,000 and 100,000.

In September 2011, Prime Ministers Manmohan Singh of India and Sheikh Hasina of Bangladesh signed an accord on border demarcation and exchange of adversely held enclaves; however, the Indian parliament has yet to ratify it. Under this intended agreement, the enclave residents could continue to reside at their present location or move to the country of their choice.

History

According to a popular legend, the enclaves were used as stakes in card or chess games centuries ago between two regional kings, the Raja of Koch Bihar and the Maharaja of Rangpur. As far as history records, the little territories were apparently the result of a confused outcome of a 1713 treaty between the Kingdom of Koch Bihar and the Mughal Empire. Possibly, the Kingdom and the Mughals ended a war without determining a single boundary for what territories had been gained or lost.

After the partition of India in 1947, Rangpur was joined to East Pakistan, and Koch Bihar was merged in 1949 with India. The desire to "de-enclave" most of the enclaves was manifested in a 1958 Nehru-Noon agreement for an exchange between India and Pakistan without considering loss or gain of territory, but the matter then worked into a Supreme Court case in India and Supreme Court ruled that constitutional amendment is required to transfer the land. So the ninth amendment was introduced to facilitate the implementation of the agreement. The amendment could not be passed due to objection to transfer of southern Berubari enclave. Due to detoriated relation with Pakistan, the issue remained unsolved. With that agreement unratified, the negotiations had to restart after East Pakistan became independent as Bangladesh in 1971.

The Land Boundary Agreement was signed on 16 May 1974 between Indira Gandhi and Mujibur Rehman which provided for exchange" of enclaves and the "surrender" of adverse possessions. Under the agreement, India retained Berubari Union No. 12 enclave while Bangladesh retained Dahagram and Angorpota enclaves with India providing access to it by giving 178 metre × 85 metres corridor, called the Teen Bigha Corridor. Bangladesh quickly ratified the agreement in 1974 but India failed to do so. The issue of undemarcated land boundary of approximately 6.1 km in three sectors — Daikhata-56 in West Bengal, Muhuri River-Belonia in Tripura and Lathitila-Dumabari in Assam — also remained unsolved. The Teen Bigha Corridor was leased to Bangladesh in 1992 amid local opposition.

The list of enclaves was prepared in 1997 by both nations. Two Joint Boundary Working Groups was formed to work out the details of enclaves in 2001. The joint census was carried out it May 2007. In September 2011, India signed the Additional Protocol for the 1974 Land Boundary Agreement with Bangladesh. The both nations announced an intention to swap 162 enclaves, giving residents a choice of nationality. Under the agreement, India will receive 51 out of the 71 Bangladeshi enclaves (from 51 to 54 of the 74 chitts) that are inside India proper (7,110.2 acres), while Bangladesh will get from 95 to 101 of the 103 Indian enclaves (111 out of 119 chitts) that are inside Bangladesh proper (17,160.63 acres). India will also acquire 2777.038 acres adverse possession areas and transfer 2267.682 acres adverse possession areas to Bangladesh. According to July 2010 joint census, there were 14,215 people residing in Bangladeshi enclaves in India and 37,269 people residing in Indian enclaves in Bangladesh. Apparently Bangladesh would retain the 4617 acres of its Dahagram-Angarpota exclave. The Constitution (119th Amendment) Bill, 2013 was introduced to the Rajya Sabha, the Upper House of Parliament of India, on 18 December 2013. The parliament panel, Standing Committee on External Affairs, approved the bill in November 2014.

NOTABLE ENCLAVES

Bangladesh

Dahagram–Angarpota: The largest Bangladeshi composite enclave (combining the first- and third-largest Bangladeshi chhits by area), administered as part of Patgram upazila in Lalmonirhat zila, lies within the Indian province of West Bengal. It is separated from the contiguous area of Bangladesh at its closest point by less than 200 meters. The enclave has an area of 25.95 km (10 sq mi) with a resident population of 20,000 people. The enclave lacks all facilities. The lone health complex remains virtually useless for lack of power supply, as India refused to allow Bangladesh to run power lines to the enclave.

The Tin Bigha Corridor, the 178 x 85 meter strip of Indian territory separating the Dahagram–Angarpota composite enclave from other Bangladeshi territory, was leased to Bangladesh for 999 years for access to the enclave. It is available for use by the residents of Dahagram–Angarpota during specified hours of the day. India

Dasiar Chhara, the fourth largest Indian chhit by area, is the largest stand-alone Indian enclave (i.e., not a composite of adjoining chhits). It lies 3 km (2 mi) from the main part of India and has an area of 6.65 km^2 (3 sq mi).

According to the Census Report issued by Bharat Bangladesh Enclave Exchange Co-ordination Committee (31 July 2010), the total population of 9510 includes: male 4941, female 4569; Hindu 640, Muslim 8870; cultivator 2426, non-cultivator 840; literate 4148; disabled 6; with Indian EPIC 193, with BD EPIC 1173; under 5 years 378; 6 to 18 years 1072.

Dahala Khagrabari is the world's only third-order enclave, being Indian territory inside a Bangladeshi territory which is itself inside an exclave of India in Bangladesh.

EVERYTHING YOU NEED TO KNOW: LAND SWAP IN OFFING WITH BANGLADESH TO END DISPUTES

What is the genesis of the Land Boundary dispute? India and Bangladesh have a common land boundary of approximately 4,096.7 km. The India-East Pakistan land boundary was determined as per the Radcliffe Award of 1947. Disputes arose out of some provisions in the award.

What is the Land Boundary Agreement (LBA) of 1974? It was an agreement signed on May 16, 1974, soon after the independence of Bangladesh, to find a solution to the complex nature of border demarcation. While Bangladesh ratified the agreement, India didn't as it involved seceding territory and indicating these precise areas on the ground. The 1974 agreement provided that India would retain half of Berubari Union No. 12 and in exchange Bangladesh would retain the Dahagram and Angarpota enclaves. The Agreement further provided that India would lease in perpetuity to Bangladesh a small area near Dahagram and Angarpota (the "Tin Bigha" corridor) for the purpose of connecting Dahagram and Angarpota with Bangladesh.

Finally the agreement was implemented in entirety, though India did not ratify, with the exception of three issues pertaining to un-demarcated land boundary of approximately 6.1 km in three sectors — Daikhata-56 (West Bengal), Muhuri River-Belonia (Tripura) and Lathitila-Dumabari (Assam); exchange of enclaves; and adverse possessions.

What is the issue of enclaves? The flawed nature of the Partition left 111 Indian enclaves in Bangladesh (17,160.63 acres) and 51 Bangladesh enclaves in India (7,110.02 acres). Their inhabitants do not enjoy full legal rights as citizens of either country or proper facilities such as electricity, schools and health services. Even law and order agencies do not have proper access to these areas.

A joint headcount estimates the population in the enclaves to be around 51,549 (37,334 of them in Indian enclaves within Bangladesh).

What does the LBA say on enclaves? It states that people in these areas have the right to stay where they are as nationals of the State to which the areas were transferred. But a joint India-Bangladesh delegation that visited these enclaves in May 2007 found that people residing in Indian enclaves in Bangladesh and Bangladeshi enclaves in India did not want to leave their land and would rather be in the country where they had lived all their lives. Movement of people, if any, is therefore expected to be minimum.

What about land 'in adverse possession'? 'An adverse possession' is territory that is contiguous to India's border and within Indian control, but which is legally part of Bangladesh. Residents of these adverse possessions are Indian citizens. The same applies to Bangladeshi adverse possessions. In respect of adverse possessions, India is to receive 2,777.038 acres of land and to transfer 2267.682 acres to Bangladesh.

However, the reality is that the area to be transferred is already in the possession of Bangladesh and its handing over to Bangladesh is merely a procedural acceptance of the de facto situation on the ground.

What happened when the LBA was signed in 2011? The protocol was signed by the two countries on September 6, 2011, after written concurrence of the concerned state governments was obtained. *People* living in the border areas were not to be dislocated. The protocol only addresses the unresolved issues of the 1974 LBA. It does not depart from it on any point other than the *maintenance* of status quo on adverse possessions and only adds details on some other aspects of the 1974 LBA.

What about the concerns of Assam? Regarding adverse possessions of Pallathal and Nayagaon in Assam, the interests of tea and betel-leaf planters have been protected while finalising the border between India and Bangladesh in this sector. With regard to demarcation of the Lathitilla and Dumabari sector, the line drawn by Radcliff and actual position on the ground has been followed.

What about the people living in these areas? Over time, it became extremely difficult to implement the terms of 1974 LBA as it meant uprooting people living in adverse possessions from the land in which they had lived all their lives and to which they had developed sentimental and religious attachments. Both India and Bangladesh, therefore, agreed to maintain the status quo in addressing the issue of adverse possessions instead of exchanging them as was earlier required for in the LBA 1974.

ENCLAVES BETWEEN INDIA AND BANGLADESH

The Land that maps Forgot

THOSE of us who keep an eye out for anomalies in the world's maps have long held a fond regard for what might be called Greater Bengal. A crazed array of boundaries cuts Bangladesh out of the cloth of easternmost India, before slicing up the surrounding Himalayan area and India's north-east into most of a dozen jagged mini-states. But the *crème de la crème,* for a student of bizarre geography, is to be found floating along the northern edge of Bangladesh's border with India.

EVER since Bangladesh achieved its independence in 1971, struggles over territory and terrorism, rather than the exchange of goods and goodwill, have dominated its relations with its mega-neighbour. Forty years on, both countries appear to be nearing an agreement to solve the insoluble—by swapping territory.

The planned exchange of parcels of each other's territory is concentrated around some 200 enclaves.

These are like islands of Indian and Bangladeshi territory surrounded completely by the other country's land, clustered on either side of Bangladesh's border with the district of Cooch Behar, in the Indian state of West Bengal. Surreally, these include about two dozen counter-enclaves (enclaves within enclaves), as well as the world's only counter-counter enclave—a patch of Bangladesh that is surrounded by Indian territory...itself surrounded by Bangladeshi territory.

Folklore has it that this quiltwork of enclaves is the result of a series of chess games between the Maharaja of Cooch Behar and the Faujdar of Rangpur. The noblemen wagered on their games, using villages as currency. Even in the more sober account, represented by Brendan R. Whyte, an academic, the enclaves are the "result of peace treaties in 1711 and 1713 between the kingdom of Cooch Behar and the Mughal empire, ending a long series of wars in which the Mughals wrested several districts from Cooch Behar."

That was before the days of East India Company rule, before the British Raj and long before the independence of South Asia's modern republics. These places have been left as they were found by both India and Bangladesh: in a nearly stateless state of abandonment. They are today pockets of abject poverty with little or nothing in the way of public services.

In a 2004 paper titled "An historical and documentary study of the Cooch Behar enclaves of India and Bangladesh", Mr Whyte, in reference to the intractability of the boundary issues at partition, asks whether India is still "waiting for the Eskimo".

When in 1947 Mr Feroz Khan Noon suggested that Sir Cyril Radcliffe should not visit Lahore for he was sure to be misunderstood either by the Muslims or the Sikhs, The Statesman *wrote: "On this line of argument, he [Sir Cyril] would do better to remain in London, or better still, take up residence in Alaska. Perhaps however there would be no objection to his surveying the boundaries of the Punjab from the air if piloted by an Esqimo".*

Apparently the newspaper thought that anyone's sorting this border dispute anytime soon was highly improbable. Sir Cyril's success seemed as implausible—in those waning days of the British empire—as the notion of an Inuit flying an aeroplane. Most of a century later and a flying "Esqimo" seems like no big deal, while progress on the zany borders of Cooch Behar has made no progress at all.

There is now talk that a land swap might be sealed when India's prime minister Manmohan Singh visits Bangladesh later this year. If it goes ahead, India stands to lose just over 4,000 hectares of its territory, or about 40 square kilometres. It has 111 enclaves of land within Bangladesh—nearly 70 square kilometres. Bangladesh has 51 enclaves of its own, comprising 28 square kilometres surrounded by India. The transfer proposed would simplify the messy boundary immeasurably—and entail something like a 10,000-acre net loss for India.

For India's governing Congress party, making a gift of land to Bangladesh—in all an area equivalent to the size of 2,000 test-cricket stadiums—will not come easy. During a time of ideological waffle, it is an issue which India's opposition Bharatiya Janata Party (BJP) can use to flaunt its nationalistic (oftentimes pro-Hindu, ie anti-Muslim) credentials and to attack Congress at a weak spot—its perceived softness towards illegal immigrants from Bangladesh, most of them Muslims. By many estimates, more than 15m illegal migrants have entered India from Bangladesh since 1971. The BJP has been trotting out the round figure of 20m for years.

Meanwhile, construction of a border fence, 2.5m high, on India's 4,100km border with Bangladesh, the world's fifth-longest (due to all its zigging and zagging), continues unabated. It is a bloody border, too. Indian soldiers enforce a shoot-to-kill order against Bangladeshi migrants caught making their mundane way from one side of the line to the other.

But what's in it for India? Its broader desire to clarify its fuzzy borders with all its neighbours provides one attraction. The dispute with Pakistan over Kashmir has eluded resolution. China's claim of the Indian state of Arunachal Pradesh remains an open sore. Drawing one steady borderline in the east looks comparatively easy.

India must also hope that its generous co-operation in the territorial dispute might help Bangladesh's prime minister, Sheikh Hasina Wajed, secure popular Bangladeshi support for a rapprochement with India. Her Awami League (AL) government has proven itself a willing partner: working to deny Bangladeshi territory to the insurgent groups who challenge Indian sovereignty in its north-eastern states; and cracking down Bangladesh's homegrown Islamic-extremist fringe. But as many of Sheikh Hasina's fellow citizens see things, India has yet to reciprocate following their government's consent last year to allow India to use Bangladesh's ports and roads. The main opposition party, the Bangladesh National Party (BNP), whose leader likes to say that no foreign vehicles should be allowed to use Bangladesh's territory, scents blood.

Indian diplomats know this. A diplomatic cable from the American embassy, leaked to the world by WikiLeaks, summarises discussions held in 2009 between India's then High Commissioner to Bangladesh and the American ambassador. India, the Americans thought, would like to establish a bilateral agreement with Bangladesh on counterterrorism, but was impeded by its understanding "that Bangladesh might insist on a regional task force to provide Hasina political cover from allegations she was too close to India".

Such international intriguing tends to ignore the people who actually in the enclaves—150,000 by some estimates—who are left waiting. Their chief grievance is a complete lack of public services: with no education, infrastructure for water, electricity etc, they may as well not be citizens of any country. NGOs are barred from working in the enclaves. The question of their citizenship is a major obstacle in resolving the problem: referendums are out of the question, as India does not want to create a precedent which could inspire Kashmiris or north-easterners fighting for independent statehood.

The people who actually live in enclaves (and counter-enclaves) in a certain sense "don't see" the borders. They speak the same language, eat the same food and live life without regard to the politicians in Dhaka, Kolkata and Delhi. Many of them cross the border regularly (the bribe is US$6 a trip from the Bangladeshi side).

A few years ago, away from Cooch Behar, on the eastern border with India, I met a man who lived smack on the border between Tripura state and Bangladesh. His living room was in Bangladesh, his toilet in India.

He had been a local politician in India, and was now working as a farmer in Bangladesh. As is typical in such places, he sent his daughters to school in Bangladesh, and his sons to India, where schools, he thought, were much better. To his mind, the fence dividing the two countries was of little value. But, he conceded, "at least my cows don't run away anymore."

THE INDO-BANGLADESH BORDER FENCING PROJECT

The Government of India sanctioned the erection of fencing in two phases. The Indo-Bangladesh Border Works under Phase-I had been initiated in 1989. Fencing in 854.35 kilometres was erected and 2606.35 kilometres of road was completed as. Under Phase II, the government had approved additional fencing of 2429.5 kilometres and 797 kilometres road at an estimated cost of Rs 287.617 million.

This project was budgeted at Rs. 10.5 billion in 1998. It involved the construction of 900 km of border fence, 2800 km of border roads and 24 km of bridges along the India-Bangladesh border in the states of West Bengal, Assam, Meghalaya, Tripura and Mizoram. The Assamese government and media were not satisfied with the fence on the Assamese side. As a local newspaper had put it, 'crossing the fence border remained as easy as slicing butter with a knife '.

In 2001, the Director General of the Border Road Organization calculated that 1 km of border fence cost Rs. 2.2 million and 1 km of border road Rs 4.5 million.

A high BSF official admitted that 80 percent of the 4000 km border was unfenced, while the Indian External Affairs Minister claimed in a statement to Parliament that the border would completely be fenced in 2006-07. In 2001, BSF and BDR exchanged gunfire leading to the killing of BSF personnel which obviously had a negative impact on India-Bangladesh relations.

Former Prime Minister of Bangladesh Sheikh Hasina resolved the dispute jointly with Indian Prime Minister Vajpayee. Work on erecting barbed wire fences along the Indo-Bangladesh border was again resumed by the NDA government headed by Vajpayee in 2002. The Indian government tripled its budget for border security in 2003.

The work had been in actual progress from early 2004, when tenders were called and closed. Various public sector institutions of India undertook activities to fence different parts of the border, such as Indian Railways Construction Corporation (NBCC), Borders Road Organization (BRO), the Central Public Works Department (CPWD), and the state Public Works Departments in Assam, Tripura, Meghalaya and West Bengal. In May 2004, the Central government of India changed and BJP-led National Democratic Alliance handed over power to the United Progressive Alliance (UPA) led by the Indian National Congress.

After the newly formed government assumed power and formed their coalition government in 2004, the construction of fence was put on hold for review in June. According to Karlekar (2005), one of the main reasons was the strong opposition of the Bangladesh government that argued that the fence violated the India-Bangladesh Agreement in 1974 which prohibited the construction of any defence structure within 150 yard of the border and the fence was a defensive structure. National level talks were held between the Home Secretaries of Bangladesh and India in Dhaka in September 2004 to cover security issues, implementation of the 1974 Land Boundary Agreement, cooperation in combating the problems of drugs and narcotics, border patrolling be security forces, cross border movements, visa regime and extradition treaty and agreements on mutual legal assistance in criminal matters. Construction resumed after a meeting on 14 October 2004 in Delhi where the Cabinet Committee on Security decided to continue fencing the border. The UPA government allocated funds for border fencing, road and maintenance as well as for boats and aircraft for the BSF. India's seriousness about the fence was demonstrated by the fact that they spent Rs 2404.7 million for fencing the Bangladesh border during 2004-5. This was stated in the Indian Lok Sabha by the State Minister for Home Affairs Mr S. Raghupathy.

According to the Annual Report 2005-2006 of Indian Ministry of Home Affairs, fencing was necessary in order to prevent illegal infiltration and other anti-national activities from across the border. By the year 2004-2005, 1502 kilometers had been fenced. Similarly, work was completed on 2670 kilometers out of 3663 kilometers of roads to be constructed. To date, a total of 2535.80 kilometres fencing has been completed in Phase I and II out of 4096.7 km long Indo-Bangladesh border. For border roads 3250.60 kilometres has been completed in Phase I and II (Government of India, 2007-08).

In 2007, India decided to replace the entire 861 km. of fence constructed under Phase-I in West Bengal, Assam and Meghalaya, as most of this fence have been damaged by adverse climatic conditions and repeated submergence. The replacement work has already commenced in the States of Assam and West Bengal. 193.70 km. of fencing has been replaced so far (Ministry of Home Affairs, Annual Report 2007-08, p: 30)

Illegal Migration and the Census of India 2001

According to the Census 2001 report released in 2005, the number of Bangladeshi migrants during the decade 1991-2001 was about 280,000, which was a decrease of 53% from almost 600,000 migrants between 1981 and 1991. In the 2001 Census, about 5.1 million persons were reported as migrant by last residence from across the international border from India's neighbour countries mainly Pakistan, Afghanistan, Sri Lanka, Nepal, Bhutan and Bangladesh. About 97% of these migrants by last residence were from eight neighbouring countries including Afghanistan. Of these migrants, 3 million were from Bangladesh, 0.9 million from Pakistan, 0.5 million from Nepal and 0.1 million from Sri Lanka. About 65.2% of these migrants from neighbouring countries had migrated to India at least 20 years ago perhaps many of them during the time of partition and later during the Bangladesh liberation war in 1971.

The total number of migrants by last residence from neighbouring countries by duration of residence is 3.08 million from Bangladesh -all residents living in India for more than 20 years. The '20 years or above' category indicates migration at the time of the 1949 partition or the formation of Bangladesh in 1971. Yet the report also revealed the number of migrants who came from Bangladesh during the decade 1991-2001.

In case of Bangladesh as the last place of residence, the total number of migrants with duration from 0 to 9 years is 279,878 in 2001and 591,572 in 1991. Another notable figure in the report was the flow of migrants from another neighbouring country Nepal-175,195 in 1991 and 261,451 in the 2001 census which is close to the total number of Bangladeshi migrants.

The decadal variation during 1991 –2001 has been negative - a reduction of 52.7% for Bangladesh and an increase for Nepal by 49.2%. It can be assumed that most of the migrants coming from Nepal were Hindu. According to the census 2001 in Nepal, 80.6% of the population is Hindu, 10.7% is Buddhist, 4.2% of the population is Muslim and 3.6% of the population follows the indigenous Kirant Mundum religion.

Christianity is practiced by less than 0.5% of the population. It is very significant that the Shiv Sena-BJP government never complained about the migrants from Nepal, though statistics indicate the number of migrants was larger. They kept quiet on illegal Nepalese migrants as far as the literature and media are concerned. It can be interpreted that they did not take Hindu illegal migrants from Nepal as an economic or security threat to

India. Another interesting feature of their campaign on detection and deportation of illegal Bangladeshi migrants is that, BJP appeared to be sympathetic towards Hindu migrants from Bangladesh. So this was not about jobs or security;it is really an anti-Muslim campaign.

INDIA-BANGLADESH RELATIONS: TOWARDS INCREASED PARTNERSHIP

The last decade has seen a new development in India's foreign policy. Both the Congress-led United Progressive Alliance (UPA) and the BJP-led National Democratic Alliance (NDA) governments have sought to improve political relations and deepen economic partnerships with neighbouring countries.

India's quest for self reliance, initiated soon after Independence, steadily reduced the salience of economic engagement with its neighbours. This approach cost India economically and diplomatically; trade barriers within South Asia have limited growth potential. Certain key unresolved issues between the two countries resulted in the under-exploitation of the potential for mutual growth. While India played a critical role in 1971 in the birth of Bangladesh, this did not however result in close bilateral ties. India was even present in Bangladesh's threat perception, with public opinion in Bangladesh accusing India of embracing a heavy-handed approach.

But the opening up of India's economy and the renewed political emphasis on building a peaceful periphery represented a unique opportunity for India to realise its ambition of resecuring strategic ties in its immediate neighbourhood. Additionally, geo-strategic equations with China, whose rise has cast a lengthening shadow over the subcontinent, presented an added urgency in New Delhi to transform its regional policy.

Bangladesh formed an important component in this strategy. India and Bangladesh, two sub-continental neighbours, have always shared strong cultural, linguistic and geographical ties. Historically the destiny of the Bangladeshi people has never been far removed from that of the other communities that make up the Indian sub-continent. Bangladesh has fought alongside India twice in the cause of the right of peoples to self determination, and the two countries have shared a porous border for over 40 years. Today, as the recent improvement in relations suggests, there is a growing realisation that increased cooperation will bring substantial socio-economic benefits that can no longer be overlooked.

Bangladesh Prime Minister Sheikh Hasina's landmark visit to India in 2010 was followed by Prime Minister Manmohan Singh calling on Dhaka in September 2011. These visits unveiled a sweeping agenda for the transformation of bilateral relations by committing the two leaders to resolve all major outstanding issues left behind since the partition.

The ambition in 2010 was to reaffirm their shared history and build a new basis for a cooperative relationship, with both sides making a substantive effort to overcome issues. A comprehensive framework of cooperation for development aimed at promoting trans-border cooperation in the management of shared water resources, hydro-power potential and eco-systems and in the areas of connectivity and trade and economic cooperation was signed between the two countries.

However, some of the progress that was made in the run-up to the second visit was undermined when the Teesta Waters Agreement did not fructify at the last minute. Given the emotion attached to the water issue in Bangladesh, there was some disappointment during Indian Prime Minister Dr. Manmohan Singh's visit to Dhaka. Neverthless, it is to be noted that the Joint Communiqué of 2010 and the Joint Statement of 2011 were major steps in charting the future course of relations between India and Bangladesh. It is now up to both the countries to restore confidence and rebuild upon what has already been achieved and advance the bilateral relationship.

4

Sino-Indian Border Dispute

Sovereignty over two large and various smaller separated pieces of territory have been contested between China and India. The westernmost, Aksai Chin, is claimed by India as part of the state of Jammu and Kashmir and region of Ladakh but is controlled and administered as part of the Chinese autonomous region of Xinjiang. It is a virtually uninhabited high altitude wasteland crossed by the Xinjiang-Tibet Highway. The other large disputed territory, the easternmost, lies south of the McMahon Line. It was formerly referred to as the North East Frontier Agency, and is now called Arunachal Pradesh. The McMahon Line was part of the 1914 Simla Convention between British India and Tibet, an agreement rejected by China.

The 1962 Sino-Indian War was fought in both of these areas. An agreement to resolve the dispute was concluded in 1996, including "confidence-building measures" and a mutually agreed Line of Actual Control. In 2006, the Chinese ambassador to India claimed that all of Arunachal Pradesh is Chinese territory amidst a military buildup. At the time, both countries claimed incursions as much as a kilometre at the northern tip of Sikkim. In 2009, India announced it would deploy additional military forces along the border.

THE SINO/INDIAN DISPUTE

Ever since its establishment in 1949, the attitude of the Communist Chinese Government towards India has been bound up with the Tibetan issue. India had, on gaining independence in 1947, inherited the British "special position" in Tibet, along with the Mission in Lhasa and trade agencies in larger towns. It had retained the services of British officials stationed in Tibet. When, in 1949, Tibetan leaders made their bid to contact foreign Governments, they first contacted these officials, and it was only a short step for the suspicious minded Chinese to regard this as evidence of Indian collusion with the British.

The Communist Chinese also had ideological reasons for believing that such collusion existed. At the time of their coming to power, Moscow was propagating the line of a world divided into two camps, with the Indian Government depicted as a tool of British imperialism and firmly situated in the opposing camp. The Communist Chinese leaders, who previously had had little contact with the outside world, faithfully repeated these accusations against Nehru and his Government.

Following the Chinese occupation of Tibet in late 1950, Peking's suspicions of the Indians were further aroused when Nehru, in notes to the Chinese Government, expressed the "surprise and regret" of his Government at the Chinese action. He described as "deplorable" the Chinese use of force in Tibet.

Standard diplomatic practice stipulates that a state does not criticise the behaviour of another state acting within its own territorial boundaries unless there are special reasons for so doing. The Indians justified their criticism of the Chinese on the ground of their special interest in Tibet, from which the Chinese inferred that the Indians were implying some restriction on Chinese sovereignty. A sharp reply was received from the Chinese accusing the Indians of unwarranted interference and claiming that the policy of the Indian Government was "affected by foreign influences hostile to China in Tibet".

Nevertheless, whatever suspicions the Chinese may have felt about the Indians in 1949-50 must to some extent have been allayed by subsequent developments. India opposed the 1950 Tibetan appeal to the United Nations; it was one of the few non-communist countries not to condemn China's intervention in the Korean War; it sought to have China seated an the United Nations. The culmination of these moves to improve relations with China was the signing, in April 1954, of an agreement by which India recognised without qualification China's sovereignty over Tibet and conceded many of India's former rights there. A few months later the Chinese Premier, Chou En-lai, paid a successful visit to India, and in October of the same year Nehru visited Peking.

The very considerable improvement in Sino/Indian relations from 1950 to 1954 was on the Indian side almost entirely the result of efforts by Nehru, who saw friendship between China and India as the starting point of a new order in world affairs. It must have been obvious to the Chinese that considerable opposition to Nehru's pro-China policies, at least as far as Tibet was concerned, existed both within and outside the Indian Government. It should also have been clear that problems were going to arise over wide discrepancies in the claimed Sino/Indian border, as shown in maps published by both sides.

However, as long as Nehru's China policy appeared to produce results, his opposition in India remained silent. It was important for both Nehru and the Chinese that this policy continued to appear to give results, and hence the efforts made by both sides to keep intact the edifice of good relations.

The Chinese, under the 1954 agreement, allowed India to maintain certain trade and pilgrimage rights in Tibet. They sought to play down the significance of border differences, stating that they had simply inherited their claimed Sino/Indian frontier from the pre-1949 Nationalist Government and that it would be "revised" in due course. Nehru, for his part, avoided public mention of the reality and extent of border differences, and it seemed that both sides were moving towards a compromise settlement of the question.

What were these differences, and what evidence was there that both sides were in fact prepared to compromise?

The Sino/Indian border can be divided into three sectors:

(i) an eastern sector where 99,000 square kilometres of territory described by the Indians as the Northeast Frontier Agency, or N.E.F.A is in dispute:

(ii) a middle sector where some 2.000 square kilometres of territory on either side of the main Himalayan passes is disputed: and

(iii) a western sector where the Indian province of Ladakh borders on Tibet and Sinkiang and where both the Indian/Tibet and Indian/Sinkiang borders are disputed, in particular the ownership of some 30,000 square kilometres of high plateau country known as the Aksai Chin.

To an outside observer looking at the frontier as it stands, an apparent basis for a compromise settlement would be for China to drop its claim to the N.E.F.A. in exchange for India dropping its claim to the Aksai Chin, with both sides making concessions over the middle sector and the Ladakh/Tibetan border. Such a settlement accords with the realities of both geography and administrative control two important criteria in the settlement of border disputes. The N.E.F.A. lies to the south of the Himalayan watershed and is controlled by India. The Aksai Chin, for the most part, lies to the north of the main range, and the Chinese claim to have controlled the area since 1950. In 1956-7, they built a strategic road across the Aksai Chin, linking Sinkiang with Tibet. That the Indians learnt about the road only from a map published by the Chinese in 1958 is substantial evidence that India was not in control of the area.

The historical basis of the border is more confused. The Indian claim to the N.E.F.A. rests almost entirely on acceptance of the McMahon Line, a line agreed to by the Tibetans and British in 1914 as the border in this area. In the Aksai Chin area no agreement has ever been reached on the alignment of the border. Nevertheless, if both sides were to take a generous view of the historical data, a basis for a N.E.F.A./Aksai Chin exchange could be found.

During the post-1954 honeymoon period of Sino/Indian relations, both sides did in fact seem prepared to take a generous view of the situation and to move towards a compromise settlement. In 1956, Chou En-lai admitted privately to Nehru that, although lie thought the McMahon line "was not fair", nevertheless China would accept the line as the border with India after they had "consulted with the Tibetan authorities". Chinese recognition of the McMahon Line was also implied when its eastern extension was accepted as a basis for border negotiations with Burma, and by Chinese de facto acceptance of the line as the dividing line between Chinese and Indian forces in the area.

Nehru, for his part, appeared willing to play down the Indian claims to the Aksai Chin. He tried to delay disclosure if the news that the Chinese had built a road in the area. After the news had been revealed, he sought to play down the economic significance of the area, describing it as a "barren tundra". He even went so far as to cast doubt on the validity of the Indian claim to the area. In statements to the Indian Parliament during early 1959, Nehru pointed out that "during British rule, this area was neither inhabited: nor were there any outposts", adding that "this place, Aksai Chin area, is distinguish completely from other areas. It is a matter for argument which part belongs to us and which part belongs to somebody else. It is not clear".

Nehru's efforts to take the heat out of the Aksai Chin question were not entirely successful. (One of his critics even suggested building an atomic reactor in the area to promote its economic development.) News of the Chinese road in the area appeared to trigger off long-suppressed Indian sensitivity over the border issue, and, in August 1958, the Indian Government made a formal claim to the disputed territory in all three sectors.

In a letter to Nehru of January 1959, Chou En-lai claimed that the Aksai Chin was Chinese territory and added that the McMahon Line was a "product of British aggression", illegal, and had "never been recognised by the Chinese Central Government". He proposed that the existing status quo he maintained, however, pending a negotiated settlement of the dispute, and added that China would take a "realistic attitude" over the McMahon Line.*

The Tibetan uprising of March 1959 upset the delicate balance of Sino/Indian relations. Reports of Chinese military action to suppress the uprising, together with the sight of thousands of Tibetan refugees crossing into Indian territory, quickly aroused feelings of alarm and anger in India, particularly among those who believed their country had an historic interest in Tibet. Nehru's Right-Wing critics charged that India should never have allowed the Chinese into Tibet in the first place. Nehru, influenced possibly both by Indian public opinion and his own feelings on the question, came out in open condemnation of Chinese behaviour in Tibet.

The Chinese reacted even more strongly than they had in 1950. Nehru, in addition to condemning the Chinese, had spoken of his sympathy with "the aspirations of the Tibetans for autonomy". He had given asylum to the Dalai Lama, who was also allowed facilities to make his 1959 appeal for U. N. action over Tibet. And finally, the Chinese had reason to believe that the Tibetan guerrillas were receiving arms from across the Indian border.

In May 1959 the Chinese published a long article urging, almost begging, Nehru not to be swayed by his reactionary Right-Wing critics and to return to the path of Sino/Indian friendship. With a frankness and detail probably unmatched by any other Chinese statement on foreign policy, the article set out the Chinese case over Tibet, and accused the Indians of unjustified interference. Indian trade with Tibet was greatly restricted. Clashes involving casualties occurred at several points along the disputed border as the Chinese Army extended its control over border areas in an effort to restrict the move- court of Tibetans across the frontier.

These border clashes, following in the wake of the Tibetan uprising, appeared to put an end to Nehru's willingness to compromise over the border dispute.

Having earlier in 1959 cast doubt on the Indian claim to the Aksai Chin, in September he stated before the Indian Parliament that the Chinese claims were "absurd" and would mean "handing over the Himalayas to them as a gift". A Chinese call in November 1959 for negotiations and a twenty-kilometre military withdrawal from the McMahon Line in the east and the "line of actual control" in the west to prevent a recurrence of border clashes was met with an Indian demand for a prior Chinese withdrawal from the Aksai Chin. A Chinese reply pointing out that this should also be paralleled by an Indian withdrawal from the NE.F.A. was ignored. In the end the Chinese appeared to settle for a freezing of the existing status quo - without negotiations or a twenty-kilometre withdrawal.

However, if the Chinese were happy to keep things as they were (keeping also their road across the Aksai Chin), Nehru and his Government were not. Throughout 1960-61 Indian opinion progressively hardened, and demands for the Government to do something about Tibet and the disputed border increased. The army was given full control over the frontier districts and it proceeded to build up its strength in these areas.

During the summer (northern) of 1962, Indian military patrols repeatedly crossed the Chinese-claimed line of actual control in the western sector of the frontier. Posts were established well behind the Chinese forward positions in territory claimed and occupied by the Chinese. Frequent and insistent Chinese protests were met with the bald statement that the Indians were merely operating in Indian territory. By August 14, Nehru was able to announce that India had three times as many posts in the western sector as the Chinese. He asked for a free hand to continue the build-up of Indian strength in the area.

The Chinese had repeatedly warned that a continuation of such activity would end in hostilities. On July 9, they had warned the Indians "to rein in on the brink of the precipice". On August 4, they called for immediate negotiations on the border. The Indians replied that negotiations could not be held until the Chinese had ceased their occupation of "every square inch of sacred Indian territory", and that the Chinese must first "vacate their aggression" in the Aksai Chin. The Chinese replied on September 13 proposing talks to begin on October 15 "without preconditions", that is, without a Chinese withdrawal from the Aksai Chin. The Indians refused the offer.

While Indian military pressure was building up along the Chinese-claimed border in the western sector, a curious situation was developing along the McMahon Line in the eastern sector. The Indians claim that at its western end the McMahon Line was not accurately drawn: that it was meant to have followed the crest of a line of hills known as the Thag La ridge. The Chinese claim, and have produced the original McMahon Line from the Tibetan archives to prove their point, that the line as originally drawn lies approximately twelve miles south of this ridge along the southern side of a small river valley. (Western maps show the McMahon Line in conformity with the Chinese claim.) The area between the Indian and Chinese versions of the McMahon Line is described by the Indians as the Dho La strip.

This was not the only unilateral revision of the McMahon Line carried out by the Indians. In his letter to Chou En-lai of September 29, 1959, Nehru admitted that in the Migyitun area (to the east of the Dho La strip) the border shown on Indian maps "differs slightly from the boundary shown in the Treaty map". He claimed that when the McMahon line was drawn, "the exact topographical features in this area were not known". The Indians have also now come to admit that "blind adherence" to the original McMahon Line would leave the Dho La strip on the Chinese side at the border.

It is not clear who first occupied the Dho La strip. The Chinese claim that the area had always been under their control and that Indian troops moved in during 1962. The Indians claim they had long occupied the area and that the Chinese began a to establish posts in the area after September 8, 1962. What is clear is that on October 12, 1962, Nehru announced in the Indian Parliament that he had given the order to drive the Chinese out of the Dho La strip.

Eight days later, on October 20, the Chinese attacked in force across the Thagla La ridge and into the disputed strip, while advancing their troops into the Chinese-claimed territory in the western sector where the Indians had earlier established posts. Four days later, the Chinese called for a ceasefire to be followed by a withdrawal of both sides from the line that separated them at that moment (the so-called October 24 line of actual control).

Failing to get a satisfactory response from the Indians, they advanced troops south of the Dho La strip into the N.E.F.A., defeating Indian military forces in the area.

Two weeks later, they withdrew to the positions occupied on October 24. The main point of contention between the Chinese and Indians ever since has been whether the Chinese should maintain their October 24 positions or withdraw further to the positions they occupied before fighting broke out.

The Chinese attack of October 1962 has led to an almost complete breakdown in relations between China and India. The level of each country's diplomatic representation in the other has been greatly reduced. Many thousands of Chinese nationals have been expelled from India. The few Indian nationals living in China have, in one way or another, been forced to leave. Border incidents have continued. Both sides have launched extreme propaganda campaigns against each other, the Chinese denouncing Nehru as a representative of the "big bourgeoisie" and a tool for U. S. aggressive designs against Tibet, while the Indians denounce the Chinese for having aggressive, imperialist designs against Indian territory. Both sides have gone to great lengths to discredit each other inter- nationally. Both sides have increased their military preparedness along the Himalayan frontier, particularly India, which has doubled its military budget to a level it cannot afford.

The question thus arises: Who is primarily to blame for the hostility in Sino/Indian relations? From the account already given, the primary cause of the hostility was the post-1959 dispute over the Sino/Indian border leading to the Chinese attack of October 20. But why the sudden emergence of such a dispute between two countries previously enjoying good relations?

Reverting to the terminology of our previous discussion on hostility between states, both sides see the breakdown in relations as being caused by the active hostility of the other side. This hostility, they claim, is both ideologically and national- interest based. The Chinese are accused of having acted in a hostile manner out of a desire to acquire territory and out of strong ideological dislike for the Indian Government. The Chinese claim the Indians have designs against Chinese territory and that their Government is under the influence of anti-Chinese and pro-U. S. reactionary elements.

Both sides realise that they have somehow or other to explain why the other side suddenly, in 1959, decided that its interests were no longer served by the maintenance of normal relations. The Indian explanation is that Chinese pre-1959 policy was designed to lull India into a false sense of security and so facilitate Chinese ambitions. The Chinese explanation was that reactionary elements began to gain the upper hand in the Indian Government in 1959, and point to the post-1959 increase in U. S. aid to India as evidence.

In fact there is good reason to believe that the hostility shown by each side towards the other was reactive rather than active: that each side was reacting to the believed hostility of the other. To take the Chinese side of things first.

In terms of the account already given, it seems likely that the Chinese attack of October 20, 1962, was primarily a reaction to Indian military pressure along the disputed frontier during preceding months.

It could be argued, however. that the behaviour of the Chinese before October 20, and in particular their propaganda attacks against the Indians from 1960 onwards, cannot be explained simply as a reaction to previous events: that overall Chinese behaviour must therefore include some aggressive component.

The Chinese had in fact made their first hostile move against the Indians back in 1959 when they restricted Indian trading and other rights in Tibet. The Chinese had also, according to the Indians, extended somewhat the area they claimed in the western sector. And they had, according to the Indians, been responsible for the 1959 border clashes already mentioned. The Indian charge is based on alleged differences between the frontier claimed by the Chinese to 1956 and that shown on a map of the claimed Sino/Indian frontier handed to the Indians by the Chinese in 1960. The Chinese deny any difference between the two lines.

Unless these apparently hostile acts of the Chinese can be explained in reactive terms., in terms of their reacting to previous Indian actions, then it would seem that the Chinese had taken the initiative in hostility towards India and were largely responsible for the eventual breakdown in relations.

The hardening of the Chinese attitude towards India in 1959 was clearly related to Tibetan developments in that year. In judging the behaviour of the Chinese, we need, in effect, to ask whether their sensitivity over Tibet was sufficient to explain this hardening of attitude.

To accept that the Communist Chinese are, in fact extremely sensitive toward Tibet does not necessarily imply a simple acceptance of Chinese propaganda. What we know of Chinese thinking and behaviour, strongly suggests that this sensitivity does exist. If all non-communist Chinese believe that China has the right to consider Tibet as an integral part of her territory, we should accept that Communist Chinese are equally convinced. If many non-communist Chinese believe (as they do) that Britain had designs against Tibet, we should accept that Communist Chinese, educated to believe in the evils of US Western imperialism, will be at least equally fearful. We do not need accept that these views are correct; we may even consider they are absurd. But if we are going to get anywhere in trying to understand China's behaviour, we should start from the assumption that these views may be sincerely hold in Peking.

Nor may it be so absurd for the Communist Chinese to think along these lines. The Chinese legal claim to Tibet, it has been argued, appears difficult to refute. As for fears of foreign designs, if the British had earlier convinced themselves that the activities of one Russian agent in Lhasa could lead the politically unstable Tibetans to ally themselves with Tsarist Russia, the Chinese could be excused for thinking that the presence of a British Mission in Lhasa dealing directly with the independent-minded Tibetans and arranging on occasion for the supply of arms from India was evidence of British ambitions eventually to detach Tibet from China, and that India may have inherited these ambitions. Similarly, it would not be entirely surprising if the Chinese viewed the supply of foreign arms to Tibetan guerrillas from northern India in 1959 as confirmation that such ambitions existed. Finally, the Chinese were hound to be impressed by the demands of the Indian Right Wing for action against the Chinese in Tibet.

For example: some weight could be attached to the fact that the then Chief of the Indian Army Staff wrote a not unenthusiastic foreword for a book published in 1961 entitled The Chinese Aggression. The author of the hook, a Dr. Satyanarayan Sinha, predicted that the "clash of the Indochinese weapons for the possession of the Himalayas will lead to making Tibet an independent country again", and suggested ways in which this could be done.

These, then, are the reasons for believing the Chinese may he sensitive about Tibet. Chinese behaviour provides further confirmation. British officials captured in Tibet in 1950 were subjected to long imprisonment and continual interrogation - treatment far more severe than that meted out to British nationals who fell into communist hands elsewhere in China. And there was Nehru's sad admission to the Indian Parliament in 1959 after talks with Chou En-Iai, of the Chinese having "some sort of kink in their minds... of foreign countries, United Kingdom or America, somehow making incursions into Tibet".

In sum, therefore, it does not seem unreasonable to conclude that the Communist Chinese sincerely believed they had a right to Tibet and that their position in the area was threatened from the direction of India. In which case they would have interpreted Indian behaviour in 1959 as an indication of hostility to which they felt compelled, or entitled, to react.

However, if Chinese behaviour in 1959 can be explained in reactive terms, can the same be said about the Chinese attack of October 1962? Even if the Indian claim to the Dho La strip was doubtful, does not the violence and intensity of the 1962 attack suggest that China was doing more than retaliate for any wrongs she may have believed the Indians to base committed?

By 1962, the Chinese were confronted not only by Indian agitation over Tibet, but also by two further aspects of Indian behaviour which would even more easily have been misunderstood. They were: (i) the Indian military build-up along the Sino/Indian border in 1961-2 and (ii) rigid Indian insistence that, as a precondition to border negotiations, the Chinese must first evacuate the whole of the Aksai Chin.

At the time, the Indians justified their position on negotiations and their military build up in terms of the correctness of their border claims. Indeed, the official Indian position was that the line claimed by India as a border had already been defined historically, and that the only purpose of negotiations was to demarcate on the ground the exact alignment of this border. From this it followed that they were justified (a) in regarding rival Chinese claims, and the occupation of the Aksai Chin, as evidence of Chinese hostility, and (b) in insisting that occupied territory had to be vacated before there could be negotiations. In the meantime the Indians had no alternative but to use military means to counter the Chinese "aggression".

If India was in fact the injured party in the territorial dispute, the Indian attitude over the disputed border would have been explicable at least to an impartial observer, and possibly even to the less impartial Chinese. There would be less justification for the Chinese reacting in the way they did. But was this the case? To answer this question we need to take a closer look at the historical background to the Sino /Indian frontier, and shall begin with the eastern sector, or N.E.F.A.

Until the 1920's, the region now known as the N.E.F.A. was largely unexplored. It was, and still is, inhabited by tribes of Tibeto-Burmese origin, some of which enjoyed trade and tributary relations with Tibet. Certain areas in the north of the region, the Tawang district for example, were inhabited by Tibetans and were under administrative control from Tibet.

The McMahon Line was negotiated with the Tibetans in 1914 at the time of the Simla Conference. It was drawn as far to the north as possible, since the British at the time sought to forestall a feared Chinese expansion into the foothills bordering the Assam plains. The McMahon Line as part of a bargain whereby the British would press the Chinese to concede territory elsewhere to Tibet.

Even so, the Tibetans were not entirely happy about losing territory south of the McMahon Line, the Tawang district in particular. Their acceptance of the line was conditional on possible future adjustments in their favour. No such adjustments, were ever made. The British also failed to extract the promised concessions from the Chinese, since the latter refused to accept the Convention produced at the Simla Conference. Thus, even as a Tibetan/British frontier, the McMahon Line does not have full validity, particularly as the Tibetans subsequently, in 1936, made a formal request to the British for revision of the line in their favour a request which the British ignored. As late as 1946, the Tibetans were still collecting taxes in the Tawang area. And, in 1947, the Tibetans approached the newly established Indian Government, seeking the "return" of "Tibetan territories" from Assam to Ladakh.

The Indian reply to this approach may be of interest in the light of complaints to be voiced later by the Indians over the manner in which the Chinese spoke of their border claims being inherited from previous Chinese Governments "The Government of India should be glad to have an assurance that it is the intention of the Tibetan Government to continue relations an the existing basis until new Agreements are any reached... This is the procedure adopted by all other countries with which India has inherited Treaty relations from His Majesty's Government".

The validity of the McMahon Line as a Chinese/Indian frontier is considerably more doubtful. True, in rejecting the draft Simla Contention, the Chinese did not specifically object to the McMahon Line as drawn on the map of Tibet attached to the Convention. But, as the Chinese point out, the then Chinese Government had no way of knowing what this line was supposed to represent, since the terms of the McMahon Line agreement were for some reason kept secret by the British and Tibetans until 1929. It could, in theory, have been a border between Tibet and a Chinese-owned N.E.F.A. Moreover, Chiang Kaishek's Government was later to make it clear to the British (and the Indians after 1947) that it did not accept the McMahon Line. The Chinese have also pointed out that, since neither the British nor the Chinese regarded Tibet as a sovereign entity, the Tibetans were obliged to obtain Chinese approval for any frontier negotiated with a foreign power. * Failure to obtain this approval, both at the Simla Conference and later, meant that the McMahon Line never at any stage enjoyed international legality. And finally, as the Chinese never tire of pointing out, many Western and Indian maps, including one reproduced in a book by Nehru himself, Discovery of India, have, even in recent years., shown the Sino/Indian border as running along the edge of the Assam plain in conformity with the traditional Chinese claim.

The 1906 Convention between Britain and China had required China to accept responsibility for Tibet's foreign relations. "The 1907 Anglo/Russian Convention required Britain 'not to enter into negotiations with Tibet except through the intermediary of the Chinese Government". Negotiations with the Tibetans over the McMahon Line were thus a breach of both conventions - a possible reason why the terms of the McMahon Line agreement were kept secret.

For the Communist Chinese to appear to be willing to drop their N.E.F.A. claim is no small concession in view of the very considerable doubts as to the validity of the McMahon Line. Indeed, the Nationalist Government in Taiwan feels so strongly shout the justice of the Chinese clams that its official newspapers have accused Peking of being willing to abandon "sacred" Chinese territory. They have predicted that the present Communist Chinese leaders will be condemned by future generations of Chinese for their betrayal of China's interests.

Nevertheless, the Indian position was that the Chinese should not only drop their claim to the N.E.F.A. but to the Aksai Chin also. How strong is the Indian claim in the western sector of the disputed frontier?

The province of Ladakh, which lies on the Indian side of the disputed western sector, was originally a semi-independent state with a complex tributary relationship with Tibet. It was far from being clearly defined Indian territory. These links with Tibet were severed as a result of the 1841 invasion of Tibet from Kashmir, and Ladakh was incorporated into India. In the agreement which followed the invasion, the Ladakh/Tibet border was defined simply as following "the old established frontier", and it was only subsequently that British cartographers decided where this frontier should lie. A small area lying between the Chinese-claimed and Indian-claimed frontiers is in dispute.

By far the larger area in dispute, the Aksai Chin, lies for the most part north of the Ladakh/Tibet frontier, and its ownership depends on a definition of the Ladakh/Sinkiang border. At the end of the nineteenth century, the British decided an effort should be made to define this border, and in 1899 a note was delivered to the Chinese suggesting a possible alignment. This alignment is shown on the map above, and it will be seen that it leaves with China much of the territory at present in dispute. The Chinese never replied to the note. Shortly afterwards, the British attitude changed. Alarmed by growing Chinese weakness in Central Asia, and fearing Russian expansion into the area (fears similar to those being entertained in connection with Tibet), the British felt they should establish the border as far north as possible to forestall any southward advance by the Russians. British maps began to show the border as lying far to the north along the Kun Lun mountains. Chinese agreement was never sought for this claimed border (despite the fact that the British recognised Chinese sovereignty in Sinkiang) ; presumably it was only being put forward as an emergency measure in case the Russians attempted to seize Sinkiang. By the 1920's the Russian threat had disappeared, and it was deemed safe to drop this particular claim.

In subsequent years, British and Indian maps showed a variety of claim lines some coinciding with the present Chinese claim line, some the claim line along the Kun Lun mountains, and some an in-between claim line which ran south of the Kun Lun mountains but which included the Aksai Chin as Indian territory. Maps showing this last claim line were in general use at the time of the 1947 transfer of power, and appear to constitute the basis of the present Indian claim to the Aksai Chin. However, the only border to have ever been officially proposed to the Chinese by the British in this area was that of 1899, and, as already mentioned, this border left most of the Aksai Chin with China.

Whatever the merits of rival Chinese and Indian claims to the Aksai Chin area, it does seem clear that the Indians can hardly speak of the frontier they claim in this area as being already defined by history and therefore subject only to demarcation. In this connection a rather curious aspect of the Indian position should be mentioned - an aspect which has been overlooked by most students of the Sino/Indian dispute. Numerous Indian authorities, including Nehru himself, have claimed historical validity for their version of the Indian! Sinkiang frontier on the ground that the line proposed by the British in 1899 "ran along the Kun Lun range to a point east of 80° longitude, where it met the eastern boundary of Ladakh". In fact, the 1899 line ran well to the south of the Kun Lun mountains, and the text of the proposal speaks only of the tine meeting "the spur running south from the Kun Lun range, which [the spur] has hitherto been shown on our maps as the eastern boundary of Ladakh. This is a little east of 80° east longitude".* A misquotation of these dimensions is rather serious, particularly when it is used to justify an official claim to some 30,000 square kilometres of territory, and when, on the basis of this claim, negotiations are refused in favour of a military solution of a complex border dispute.

The only observer who appears to have noted this misquotation is Alastair Lamb. In his book, *The China-India Border*, he gives the full text of the British note of 1899 and lists some of the Indian authorities who have misquoted the 1899 proposal. Distribution of his book within India has been banned.

It would seem, therefore, that an impartial observer who takes into account not only the historical background of the border dispute, but also the equally relevant criteria of geography and administrative control, would agree that the Chinese are not being unreasonable when they call for border negotiations on the basis of the present status quo. If, as seems to be the case, the Chinese are prepared to do a N.E.F.A./Aksai Chin exchange leaving India in control of far the largest and most valuable of the territories in dispute, he may even feel that the Chinese are being quite generous. And if our impartial observer were to reach such a conclusion, it seems highly likely that the Chinese would be convinced of the reasonableness of their position and the unreasonableness of the Indian demand for a unilateral Chinese withdrawal from the Aksai Chin.

If the Chinese were in fact convinced that they were in the right over the border dispute, they would in all probability have interpreted the Indian military build-up along the disputed border in 1961-2 as evidence of active hostility. Striking confirmation that this was the case is contained in the "Tibetan Documents" - official Chinese documents which were captured by Tibetan rebels in 1961 and which subsequently found their way to the U.S., where they have been translated and published. These documents were intended as background briefing to senior Chinese military commanders stationed along the Sino/ Indian border. As such, their contents cannot be dismissed simply as propaganda. The documents warned of U.S./Indian collusion to build up pressure along the Tibetan frontier as a prelude to a joint attack against Tibet. Military commanders were instructed to observe strictly the twenty-kilometre troop withdrawal from the line of actual control and to avoid clashes with advancing Indian patrols since this would provide the "imperialists" with the pretext they needed to justify their planned attack.*

1960 MEETINGS TO RESOLVE THE BOUNDARY QUESTION

In 1960, based on an agreement between Nehru and Zhou Enlai, officials from India and China held discussions in order to settle the boundary dispute. China and India disagreed on the major watershed that defined the boundary in the western sector. The Chinese statements with respect to their border claims often misrepresented the cited sources.

AKSAI CHIN

From the area's lowest point (on the Karakash River at about 14,000 feet (4,300 m) to the glaciated peaks up to 22,500 feet (6,900 m) above sea level, this is a desolate, largely uninhabited area. It covers an area of about 37,244 square kilometres (14,380 sq mi). The desolation of Aksai Chin meant that it had no significant human importance other than ancient trade routes crossing it, providing brief passage during summer for caravans of yaks from Xinjiang and Tibet.

One of the earliest treaties regarding the boundaries in the western sector was issued in 1842. The Sikh Confederacy of the Punjab region in India had annexed Ladakh into the state of Jammu in 1834. In 1841, they invaded Tibet with an army. Chinese forces defeated the Sikh army and in turn entered Ladakh and besieged Leh. After being checked by the Sikh forces, the Chinese and the Sikhs signed a treaty in September 1842, which stipulated no transgressions or interference in the other country's frontiers. The British defeat of the Sikhs in 1846 resulted in transfer of sovereignty over Ladakh to the British, and British commissioners attempted to meet with Chinese officials to discuss the border they now shared. However, both sides were apparently sufficiently satisfied that a traditional border was recognised and defined by natural elements, and the border was not demarcated. The boundaries at the two extremities, Pangong Lake and Karakoram Pass, were reasonably well-defined, but the Aksai Chin area in between lay largely undefined.

THE JOHNSON LINE

W. H. Johnson, a civil servant with the Survey of India proposed the "Johnson Line" in 1865, which put Aksai Chin in Jammu and Kashmir. This was the time of the Dungan revolt, when China did not control Xinjiang, so this line was never presented to the Chinese. Johnson presented this line to the Maharaja of Jammu and Kashmir, who then claimed the 18,000 square kilometres contained within his territory and by some accounts he claimed territory further north as far as the Sanju Pass in the Kun Lun Mountains.

Johnson's work was severely criticised for gross inaccuracies, with description of his boundary as "patently absurd", and he was reprimanded by the British Government and resigned from the Survey. The Maharajah of Jammu and Kashmir apparently sent a few soldiers to man the abandoned fort at Shahidulla (modern-day Xaidulla) at one point, by the time most sources placed Shahidulla and the upper Karakash River firmly within the territory of Xinjiang.

According to Francis Younghusband, who explored the region in the late 1880s, there was only an abandoned fort and not one inhabited house at Shahidulla when he was there – it was just a convenient staging post and a convenient headquarters for the nomadic Kirghiz. The abandoned fort had apparently been built a few years earlier by the Dogras. In 1878 the Chinese had reconquered Xinjiang, and by 1890 they already had Shahidulla before the issue was decided. By 1892, China had erected boundary markers at Karakoram Pass.

In 1897 a British military officer, Sir John Ardagh, proposed a boundary line along the crest of the Kun Lun Mountains north of the Yarkand River. At the time Britain was concerned at the danger of Russian expansion as China weakened, and Ardagh argued that his line was more defensible. The Ardagh line was effectively a modification of the Johnson line, and became known as the "Johnson-Ardagh Line".

THE MACARTNEY-MACDONALD LINE

In 1893, Hung Ta-chen, a senior Chinese official at Kashgar, handed a map of the boundary proposed by China to George Macartney, the British consul-general at Kashgar. This boundary placed the Lingzi Tang plains, which are south of the Laktsang range, in India, and Aksai Chin proper, which is north of the Laktsang range, in China. Macartney agreed with the proposal and forwarded it to the British Indian government. This border, along the Karakoram Mountains, was proposed and supported by British officials for a number of reasons.

The Karakoram Mountains formed a natural boundary, which would set the British borders up to the Indus River watershed while leaving the Tarim River watershed in Chinese control, and Chinese control of this tract would present a further obstacle to Russian advance in Central Asia. The British presented this line, known as the Macartney-MacDonald Line, to the Chinese in 1899 in a note by Sir Claude MacDonald. The Qing government did not respond to the note, and the British took that as Chinese acquiescence. Although no official boundary had ever been negotiated, China believed that this had been the accepted boundary.

1899 to 1947

Both the Johnson-Ardagh and the Macartney-MacDonald lines were used on British maps of India. Until at least 1908, the British took the Macdonald line to be the boundary, but in 1911, the Xinhai Revolution resulted in the collapse of central power in China, and by the end of World War I, the British officially used the Johnson Line. However they took no steps to establish outposts or assert actual control on the ground. In 1927, the line was adjusted again as the government of British India abandoned the Johnson line in favour of a line along the Karakoram range further south. However, the maps were not updated and still showed the Johnson Line.

From 1917 to 1933, the "Postal Atlas of China", published by the Government of China in Peking had shown the boundary in Aksai Chin as per the Johnson line, which runs along the Kunlun mountains. The "Peking University Atlas", published in 1925, also put the Aksai Chin in India.

When British officials learned of Soviet officials surveying the Aksai Chin for Sheng Shicai, warlord of Xinjiang in 1940–1941, they again advocated the Johnson Line. At this point the British had still made no attempts to establish outposts or control over the Aksai Chin, nor was the issue ever discussed with the governments of China or Tibet, and the boundary remained undemarcated at India's independence.

Since 1947

Upon independence in 1947, the government of India used the Johnson Line as the basis for its official boundary in the west, encompassing Aksai Chin. However, India did not claim the northern areas near Shahidulla and Khotan, for including which in Indian territory, among other things, Johnson had been criticised. From the Karakoram Pass (which is not under dispute), the Indian claim line extends northeast of the Karakoram Mountains north of the salt flats of the Aksai Chin, to set a boundary at the Kunlun Mountains, and incorporating part of the Karakash River and Yarkand River watersheds. From there, it runs east along the Kunlun Mountains, before turning southwest through the Aksai Chin salt flats, through the Karakoram Mountains, and then to Pangong Lake.

On 1 July 1954 Prime Minister Nehru wrote a memo directing that the maps of India be revised to show definite boundaries on all frontiers. Up to this point, the boundary in the Aksai Chin sector, based on the Johnson Line, had been described as "undemarcated."

During the 1950s, the People's Republic of China built a 1,200 kilometres (750 mi) road connecting Xinjiang and western Tibet, of which 179 kilometres (111 mi) ran south of the Johnson Line through the Aksai Chin region claimed by India. Aksai Chin was easily accessible from China, but was more difficult for the Indians on the other side of the Karakorams to reach. The Indians did not learn of the existence of the road until 1957, which was confirmed when the road was shown in Chinese maps published in 1958.

The Indian position, as stated by prime minister Jawaharlal Nehru, was that the Aksai Chin was "part of the Ladakh region of India for centuries" and that this northern border was a "firm and definite one which was not open to discussion with anybody".

The Chinese minister, Zhou Enlai argued that the western border had never been delimited, that the Macartney-MacDonald Line, which left the Aksai Chin within Chinese borders was the only line ever proposed to a Chinese government, and that the Aksai Chin was already under Chinese jurisdiction, and that negotiations should take into account the status quo.

In April 2013 India claimed, referencing their own perception of the Line of Actual Control (LAC) location, that Chinese troops had established a camp in the Daulat Beg Oldi sector, 10 km on their side of the Line of Actual Control. This figure was later revised to a 19 km claim. According to Indian media, the incursion included Chinese military helicopters entering Indian airspace to drop supplies to the troops. However, Chinese officials denied any trespassing having taken place. Soldiers from both countries briefly set up camps on the ill-defined frontier facing each other, but the tension was defused when both sides pulled back soldiers in early May. In September 2014, India and China had a standoff at the LAC, when Indian workers began constructing a canal in the border village of Demchok, and Chinese civilians protested with the army's support. It ended after about three weeks, when both sides agreed to withdraw troops.

Trans Karakoram Tract

The Johnson Line is not used west of the Karakoram Pass, where China adjoins Pakistan-administered Gilgit–Baltistan. On

13 October 1962, China and Pakistan began negotiations over the boundary west of the Karakoram Pass. In 1963, the two countries settled their boundaries largely on the basis of the Macartney-MacDonald Line, which left the Trans Karakoram Tract in China, although the agreement provided for renegotiation in the event of a settlement of the Kashmir dispute. India does not recognise that Pakistan and China have a common border, and claims the tract as part of the domains of the pre-1947 state of Kashmir and Jammu. However, India's claim line in that area does not extend as far north of the Karakoram Mountains as the Johnson Line

THE MCMAHON LINE

British India and China gained a common border in 1826, with British annexation of Assam in the Treaty of Yandabo at the conclusion of the First Anglo-Burmese War (1824–1826). Subsequent annexations in further Anglo-Burmese Wars expanded China's borders with British India eastwards, to include the border with what is now Myanmar.

In 1913–14, representatives of Britain, China, and Tibet attended a conference in Simla, India and drew up an agreement concerning Tibet's status and borders. The McMahon Line, a proposed boundary between Tibet and India for the eastern sector, was drawn by British negotiator Henry McMahon on a map attached to the agreement. All three representatives initiated the agreement, but Beijing soon objected to the proposed Sino-Tibet boundary and repudiated the agreement, refusing to sign the final, more detailed map. After approving a note which stated that China could not enjoy rights under the agreement unless she ratified it, the British and Tibetan negotiators signed the Simla Convention and more detailed map as a bilateral accord. Neville Maxwell states that McMahon had been instructed not to sign bilaterally with Tibetans if China refused, but he did so without the Chinese representative present and then kept the declaration secret.

V.K. Singh argues that the basis of these boundaries, accepted by British India and Tibet, were that the historical boundaries of India were the Himalayas and the areas south of the Himalayas were traditionally Indian and associated with India. The high watershed of the Himalayas was proposed as the border between India and its northern neighbours. India's government held the view that the Himalayas were the ancient boundaries of the Indian subcontinent and thus should be the modern boundaries of British India and later the Republic of India.

Chinese boundary markers, including one set up by the newly created Chinese Republic, stood near Walong until January 1914, when T. O'Callaghan, an assistant administrator of North East Frontier Agency (NEFA)'s eastern sector, relocated them north to locations closer to the McMahon Line (albeit still South of the Line). He then went to Rima, met with Tibetan officials, and saw no Chinese influence in the area.

By signing the Simla Agreement with Tibet, the British had violated the Anglo-Russian Convention of 1907, in which both parties were not to negotiate with Tibet, "except through the intermediary of the Chinese Government", as well as the Anglo-Chinese Convention of 1906, which bound the British government "not to annex Tibetan territory." Because of doubts concerning the legal status of the accord, the British did not put the McMahon Line on their maps until 1937, nor did they publish the Simla Convention in the treaty record until 1938. Rejecting Tibet's 1913 declaration of independence, China argued that the Simla Convention and McMahon Line were illegal and that Tibetan government was merely a local government without treaty-making powers. In 1947, Tibet requested that India recognise Tibetan authority in the trading town of Tawang, south of the McMahon Line. Tibet did not object to any other portion of the McMahon line. In reply, the Indians asked Tibet to continue the relationship on the basis of the previous British Government.

Tibetan officials continued to administer Tawang and refused to concede territory during negotiations in 1938. The governor of Assam asserted that Tawang was "undoubtedly British" but noted that it was "controlled by Tibet, and none of its inhabitants have any idea that they are not Tibetan." During World War II, with India's east threatened by Japanese troops and with the threat of Chinese expansionism, British troops secured Tawang for extra defence.

China's claim on areas south of the McMahon Line, encompassed in the NEFA, were based on the traditional boundaries. India believes that the boundaries China proposed in Ladakh and Arunachal Pradesh have no written basis and no documentation of acceptance by anyone apart from China. Indians argue that China claims the territory on the basis that it was under Chinese imperial control in the past, while Chinese argue that India claims the territory on the basis that it was under British imperial control in the past.

The last Qing emperor's 1912 edict of abdication authorised its succeeding republican government to form a union of "five peoples, namely, Manchus, Han Chinese, Mongols, Muslims, and Tibetans *together with their territory in its integrity*" However, V.K. Singh cites the presence of the Mauryan Empire and Chola Dynasty in regions India does not place a claim to but which were heavily influenced by Indian culture.

India's claim line in the eastern sector follows the McMahon Line. The line drawn by McMahon on the detailed 24–25 March 1914 Simla Treaty maps clearly starts at 27°45'40"N, a trijunction between Bhutan, China, and India, and from there, extends eastwards.

Most of the fighting in the eastern sector before the start of the war would take place immediately north of this line. However, India claimed that the *intent* of the treaty was to follow the main watershed ridge divide of the Himalayas based on memos from McMahon and the fact that over 90% of the McMahon Line does in fact follow the main watershed ridge divide of the Himalayas. They claimed that territory south of the high ridges here near Bhutan (as elsewhere along most of the McMahon Line) should be Indian territory and north of the high ridges should be Chinese territory. In the Indian claim, the two armies would be separated from each other by the highest mountains in the world.

During and after the 1950s, when India began patrolling this area and mapping in greater detail, they confirmed what the 1914 Simla agreement map depicted: six river crossings that interrupted the main Himalayan watershed ridge. At the westernmost location near Bhutan north of Tawang, they modified their maps to extend their claim line northwards to include features such as Thag La ridge, Longju, and Khinzemane as Indian territory. Thus, the Indian version of the McMahon Line moves the Bhutan-China-India trijunction north to 27°51′30"N. India would claim that the treaty map ran along features such as Thag La ridge, though the actual treaty map itself is topographically vague (as the treaty was not accompanied with demarcation) in places, shows a straight line (not a watershed ridge) near Bhutan and near Thag La, and the treaty includes no verbal description of geographic features nor description of the highest ridges.

Sikkim

India's annexation of Sikkim in 1975 was rejected by China at the time. The Sino-Indian Memorandum of 2003 was hailed as a *de facto* Chinese acceptance of the annexation. China published a map showing Sikkim as a part of India and the Foreign Ministry deleted it from the list of China's "countries and regions". However, the Sikkim-China border's northernmost point, "The Finger", continues to be the subject of dispute and military activity.

INDIA, CHINA TO MEET ON BORDER DISPUTE

Indian and Chinese officials are meeting in New Delhi this week for talks on a border dispute that has for decades strained relations between the neighbors — the first such negotiations since Indian Prime Minister Narendra Modi took office last year.

The two Asian countries are separated by a nearly 2,200-mile border whose exact location is a subject of bitter dispute. China claims India's northeastern state of Arunachal Pradesh, which it calls southern Tibet. India claims a Chinese-controlled region it calls Aksai Chin as part of its northernmost state of Jammu and Kashmir.

India periodically accuses Chinese troops of "transgressions" across the two countries' ill-defined boundary, known as the Line of Actual Control. Officials on both sides say such incidents are likely to continue – and perhaps escalate as India further develops its border lands – until the boundary is properly marked and settled.

The dispute cast a shadow over Chinese President Xi Jinping's visit to India last year – and on Mr. Modi's efforts to improve relations with China.

As Mr. Xi held his first official talks with Mr. Modi in September last year, their countries' armies were locked in a tense face-off in the Himalayan region of Ladakh. Roughly 1,000 troops were called in on both sides, making it the biggest border confrontation between the two nations in decades.

Such episodes have interfered with the two countries' efforts to deepen commercial relations as India seeks foreign investment to modernize its infrastructure. Mr. Modi is scheduled to visit China in May as part of those efforts.

Talks this week between China's representative on the boundary question, Yang Jiechi, and India's national security advisor, Ajit Doval, are aimed at giving momentum to the border talks.

Indian analysts say China may be more willing to negotiate given Mr. Modi's steps to strengthen India's ties with the United States. Mr. Modi visited the White House last year and U.S. President Barack Obama traveled to India to review a symbolically important military parade in January, signaling a willingness on India's part to move closer to Washington.

But, Indian officials said, it won't be easy. "It is an incredibly difficult problem if you look at the amount of real estate at stake and the length of the border," said a senior official at the foreign ministry, who declined to be named. The Indian government's approach, the official said, is "let's not let it drift."

A BRIEF REVIEW OF THE CHINA-INDIA BORDER DISPUTE

The entire China-India boundary has never been formally delimited by any mutually-accepted treaty. There has existed a boundary line of actual control between the two countries. It took shape on the basis of the extent of each other's administrative jurisdiction over a long course of time. The entire boundary has been traditionally divided into three sectors—the eastern sector, the middle sector, and the western sector with all in dispute. The western sector involves the dispute over the Aksai Chin area India claims as part of Latah andChina claims as part of Xinjiang. The middle sector involves a dispute over various points between the Tibet-Kashmir- Punjab border junction and the Nepal-Tibet-Uttar Pradesh border junction. The eastern sector involves a dispute over the area between the pre-1914 Outer Line and the McMahon Line.

In the eastern sector, the British–Indian government had observed the foothills of the Himalayas as the "Outer Line" of its administrative jurisdiction by 1914. Although the Chinese-Tibetan authorities had claimed the tribal areas beyond the British Outer Line within the Tibetan jurisdiction, their administrative jurisdiction actually covered only Tawang tract, the Walong area along the Lohit valley, and some other scattered enclaves in the tribal areas.

Today the line of actual control observed by both sides conforms to the McMahon Line. The disputed area between the pre-1914 Outer Line and the McMahon Line covers a total area of 90,000 square kilometers. According to China, this area is composed of Tibet's three districts of Monyul, Loyul and lower Zayul. According to India, this area is its Arunachal Pradesh, formerly the North-East Frontier Agency of Assam State.

In the western sector, the line of actual control runs roughly along the Karakoram range, conforming to the Chinese claim. The Indian government claims that the boundary runs along the Kunlun range from theKarakoram Pass. The disputed Area is the Aksai Chin region between the two ranges, covering a total area of about 33,000 square kilometers. This area falls mainly in China's Xinjiang and part of it belongs to the Ari District of Tibet. India claims that it is part of its Ladakh area of the State of Jammu and Kashmir. This area, sparsely inhabited, serves as the traffic artery linking Xinjiang and Tibet.

Therefore, in terms of the general China-India border dispute, the McMahon Line in the eastern sector and Aksai Chin in the western sector have been central to the negotiations on the settlement of the border dispute.

The Mystery of the McMahan Line

After Russia successfully divided Mongolia into Outer and Inner Mogolia with the Outer Mongolia as a buffer zone between China and Russia, the British- Indian authorities dreamed the same dream and tried to divideTibet into Outer Tibet and Inner Tibet and made the Outer Tibet as a buffer zone between British India andChina.

To achieve such a objective, the Simla conference was held in 1914,with British Henry McMahon, Chinese Chen Ivan, and Tibetan Lonchen shatra as representatives.

There were actually two parallel conferences at Simla, the tripartite conference focusing on the division ofTibet, and the other was the secret one, keeping Chen Ivan out of their negotiations on the Indian-Tibetan boundary. In early 1914, Henry McMahon and Lonchen Shatra secretly negotiated on the division of Tibet and the boundary between Assam and Tibet as a package deal. An agreement was reached through a secret exchange of notes in Delhi on March 24 and 25, 1914. This boundary line, later known as the McMahon line, was shown on a map in two sheets.

The tripartite conference focused on McMahon's proposal referring to China's suzerainty over Tibet and the outer-inner division of Tibet. On the map attached to the draft convention of the conference, two lines were drawn, one red and the other blue. The red line showed Tibet as a geographical and political unit, and the blue line divided Inner from Outer Tibet. In its southern extension, the red line curves around along the crest of theHimalayas, roughly conforming to the McMahon Line except in the Tawang tract where the McMahon Line reached short of the Tawang tract , implying that the Tawang tract remained part of Tibetan territory. On this map, the Tawang tract was not put within the British-Indian territory.

Without the consent of the Chinese government, Chen Ivan, under McMahon's threat and pressure, initiated the draft convention on April 27, 1914, but with the clear understanding that "to initial and to sign are two different actions," and that his initials would not bind his government, whose views he would immediately seek. The next day, the Chinese government instructed Chen Ivan that "The Chinese representative was forced to initial the draft convention. The Chinese government cannot accept it. You should declare it invalid." Since Chen Ivan refused to sign the draft convention, it was then amended and initialed by McMahon and Lonchen Shatra on July 3, 1914. On the map attached to the draft convention, the McMahon Line was marked just across the town of Tawang, indicating that the area to the north of Tawang would fall within the Tibetan territory.

The British-Indian government did not accept the Simla convention. Viceroy Hardinge forwarded McMahon's report on the Simla conference to London on July 23, 1914, stating that the Indian government recognized that a consideration of the northeastern frontier did not form part of the functions of the conference, and the views and proposal put forward might be regarded as personal to Henry McMahon, not carrying the endorsement of the Government of India. Chen was also instructed to declare that the Chinese government "would not recognize any treaty or similar document that might now or hereafter be signed between Great Britain andTibet." The Tibetan authorities understood that without securing the Sino-Tibetan boundary, they could not accept the Indo-Tibetan boundary.

The Dalai Lama even recognized the logic relationship between the status of Tibet and the legality of the McMahon Line. In his 1959 address to the Indian Council of World Affairs, he contended that if Tibet had no sovereignty when the Simla convention laid down the McMahon Line, that line was invalid. He challenged Nehru that if you deny the sovereign status to Tibet, you deny the validity of the McMahon Line."

Three maps are related to the Simla conference. One is attached to the March 24 notes; one to the April 27 convention, and the third to the July 3 convention. As far as the Tawang Tract is concerned, the three maps show the McMahon line quite differently. On the first map, the McMahon Line was shown running alng south of the Thagla range far north of Tawang; on the second map, it is not shown in the Tawang tract; and on the third one, it is superimposed on the word " Tawang".

In 1936, Basil Gould, Political Officer in Sikkim, was dispatched to Lhasa and discussed the Tawang issue with the Tibetan government. The Tibetan attitude was Tawang had been Tibetan up to 1914 and they regarded the adjustment of the Tibet-Indian boundary as part and parcel of the general adjustment and determination of boundaries contemplated in the 1914 convention. If they could, with British help, secure a definite Sino-Tibetan boundary, they would observe the Indo-Tibetan border as defined in 1914.

In 1944, just before the British quit from India, basil Gould informed the Tibetan authorities that the Bitish-Indian government was willing to modify the McMahon Line soas to exclude Tawang from the territory it claimed. He also proposed that the Se La range should be a new boundary line. However, The Tibetan authorities did not accepted it and continued to collect revenues in the Tawang tract and remained administrative control over the Tawang tract.

It was in February1951 that the Indian government took over the Tawang tract by force before the PLA entered and liberated Tibet. The Tibetan authorities organized protest demonstrations in Tawang and Lhasaagainst India's occupation of the Tawang tract, but no avail.

As far as the objective of the Simla conference was concerned, it certainly aborted. The McMahon Line was not even accepted by the British-Indian government. After the Simla conference, from 1914 to 1935, on the official maps published by the Survey of India, the McMahon Line was not shown, but instead the Outer Line along the foothills of the Himalayas was shown. The Tibetan authorities continued to exercise administrative jurisdiction in the tribal areas as they did before. The Simla conference went down in history as an unaccomplished cause.

As to the Simla conference, the first official record appeared in Volume XIV of the 1929 edition of Aichison'sTreaties. It did not refer to the McMahon Line, but to the discussion on the Sino-Tibetan frontier. It was stated that a tripartite convention was drawn up and initialed in 1914, but the Chinese government refused to permit its representative to proceed to full signature.

In 1935, Olaf Caroe, deputy secretary of the Foreign and Political Department of the British-Indian Government discovered the secret documents of the Simla conference in dealing with a case involving the illegal entry into Tibet through the Tawang tract. He realized that the northeastern frontier might be a matter of dispute with the Chinese in the future. He proposed to revise the official record of the Simla conference in the Aichison's Treaties and show the McMahon Line on the official maps. The British government approved his proposal.

This original 1929 edition was soon withdrawn from circulation and replaced by a spurious edition, actually printed in 1938, but with an imprint of 1929. However, at least three copies of the original 1929 edition survived, one in Peking Library, one in Harvard University library, and one in the India Office. In the revised edition, it was stated that the Simla conference negotiated an agreement on the status of Tibet and the boundary of Tibet with both China and India. Such a revision was nothing but scandalous diplomatic forgery. Then the McMahon Line began to appear o the Indian official maps. However, it was still marked as "Undemarcated Boundary."

The Puzzle of Aksai Chin

In the western sector of the China-India border, the dispute has centered on the Aksai Chin area. The British left Aksai Chin area as "undefined" at the time of their transfer of power in 1947.nehru himself once stated that " it is a matter of argument as to what art of it (Aksai Chin) belongs to us and what part of it belongs to somebody else.... The point is, there has never been any delimitation there in that area and it has been a challenged area."

Before the British left India, the British-Indian government had shown no boundary at all in that area on its official maps. In Volume XII of Aichison'd Treaties published in 1931, it was stated that"The northern as well as the eastern boundary of the Kashmir state is still undefined." The Survey of India maps published in the 190s and 1930s did not indicate any boundary alignment or show any color difference inthis are, and wide spaces between

Kashmir and Xinjiang and between Kashmir and Tbet were shown blank. Louis Dane, Indian Foreign Secretry, stated clearly in a letter to the Indian office that Aksai Chin was I Chinese Xinjiag. The neighborhood of the Lanak Pass at the head of the Changchenmo valley was supposed to be the most northerly boundary point on the Kashmir-Tibet border.

In 1945, guided by Olaf Caroe, then foreign secretary of India, on new Survey of India maps the Aksai Chin area bgan to be shown by a color-wash with the words"Boundary Undefined" marked on it. In 1947, the Indian Army in its "top secret" m submitted to the British Cabinet Mission accepted the Karakoram range as the northern boundary of India in the western sector.

However, after the signing of the trade agreement concerning Tibet in 1954, following Nehru's instructions, new Survey of India maps began to show an international boundary in the western sector running along the crest of the Kunlun range, which for the first time placed the whole Aksai Chin area within the Indian territory. According to Sir H.A.F. Rumbold, an official in the Indian Office, the Simon Commission wished to include a map of India in Volume I of their report in 1929. Rumbold found nothing in the India office to justify the line on the Kunlun range shown on some maps. The Commission accordingly adopted a line roughly along the crest of the Karakoram range, excluding the Aksai Chin area. Nehru, even on August 28, 1959, stated in the Lok Sabha that "This was the boundary of the old Kashmir statewith Tibet and Chinese Turkestan. Nobody had marked it."

On the other hand, Chinese maps have shown the Karakoram range as its boundary in the western sector at least since the 1920s. There was no evidence that the British-Indian authorities ever disputed this with the Chinese government before they left India in 1947.

The widely accepted modern concept of boundary marking involes three steps: delimitation, delineation and demarcation. Delimitation involves defining the boundary in written terms through treaties and agreements. Delineation involves sketching the boundary in maps through joint boundary surveys. Demarcation involves marking the boundary line on the ground through pillars, chains and other markers. Reviewing the historic facts for the entire China-India border, such a China-India boundary has never existed, though each side has made its own territorial claims. Historical facts have also showed that, in the old days, wide desolate tracts in the remote high mountains between the two countries were physically inaccessible. Therefore, the China-India border dispute has been the dispute on the "zone" rather than the " line" in the eastern and western sectors. Mutual understanding and recognition of such historical evolution of the China-India border should become the starting point for the future border deliberations.

FACTS BEHIND CHINA-INDIA BORDER DISPUTE

If a general of the Chinese imperial government representing the Manchu dynasty had, by force of arms, pillage and plunder, succeeded in subjugating the North American continent and on that basis had artificially created a border line between the United States and Canada called, let us say, The Manchu Line, would a sovereign U.S. government abide by thus border line?

Let us suppose further that the boundary line demarcated by this general included, for the Canadian side, parts of Buffalo, Detroit, Seattle and Duluth.

Let us suppose again that the treaty between Canada and the U.S. dictated by this general had never been accepted by any government of the United States, and that in truth the people of the U.S. regarded this treaty and its boundary line as illegal, null and void, and as the imposition of a foreign power at a time when the U.S. was weak, divided and under the domination of a foreign imperialist power.

All we have to do with this analogy is to just change the name — Canada to India, United States to China and China to Great Britain — and the picture becomes immeasurably clearer than it is represented in the U.S. press.

THE MCMAHON LINE

It is the position of the Chinese People's Republic that the so-called McMahon Line — named after the British General McMahon

— is illegal, null and void, and the result of a predatory, imperialist imposition of the British government in the year 1914.

No Chinese government ever accepted the McMahon Line. Neither did the Imperial Government of China in 1914, nor the Chiang Kai-Shek government ever agree to it. The very fact that even the Chiang Kai-Shek clique, which is nothing but a tool of U.S. imperialism, has not dared to dispute the Chinese People's Republic's position of the China-India border dispute, it in itself the most eloquent testimony to the correctness of the Chinese position.

Nevertheless, the Chinese People's Republic has made every effort to achieve a reasonable and just settlement of the territory in dispute. It has consistently shunned the use of arms.

CHINA AND INDIA WANT A BREAKTHROUGH ON THEIR BORDER DISPUTE

Indian Foreign Minister Sushma Swaraj was in Beijing this week to participate in a trilateral meeting with her Russian and Chinese counterparts. While there, she also held separate meetings with both President Xi Jinping and Foreign Minister Wang Yi. Swaraj told reporters that, in addition to the trilateral meeting, one of the main purposes for the visit was laying the groundwork for Prime Minister Narendra Modi's trip to China in May 2015. Apparently, part of that groundwork will be a concerted effort to see concrete progress in discussions over China and India's disputed border.

The Telegraph, citing an Indian government official, said that New Delhi in particular hopes to hammer out the Framework for a Resolution of the Boundary Question. "That's the next big diplomatic target for the government," one official told *The Telegraph of India.* "The breakthrough has to be ready to be announced when the PM visits in May." India's national security adviser, Ajit Doval, is expected to travel to Beijing soon to continue the negotiations.

India and China dispute two large swaths of territory: Arunachal Pradesh to the east of Bhutan and Aksai Chin on the western edge of the India-China border. Arunachal Pradesh is administered by India as a state while Aksai Chin is administered by China as part of Xinjiang. In the 1990s, China and India effectively agreed to hold to the status quo, with both countries agreeing to abide by the Line of Actual Control until their governments could agree on a true border. However, the LAC remains ill-defined and incursions by both sides are frequent.

Since 2003, China and India have held a total of 17 rounds of border talks, with little to show for it. But new leadership in both Beijing and New Delhi has raised hopes that the two sides can reach the Holy Grail of their bilateral relationship: a demarcated border.

Since Modi came to power last year, China and India have taken to emphasizing the newness of their relationship. "I have been told that the Lunar Year of Sheep is known as the year of creativity and innovation… I feel that your India visit was about creativity and innovations," Swaraj told Xi during their meeting this week. Xi also affirmed that "China-India relations entered a new development stage" with his fall 2014 trip to India. He added, "I have full confidence on the future of China and India relations and I believe that good progress will be achieved in the growth of bilateral relations this year."

The question, then, is whether this new "creativity and innovation" can actually lead to a diplomatic breakthrough on the border issue. China and India both were hoping to have such a breakthrough to showcase during Xi's September visit to India. That didn't pan out – instead, the presence of Chinese troops in a disputed region highlighted how the border issue continues to strain China-India ties. That led to Modi raising India's "serious concern over repeated incidents along the border" in talks with Xi.

Last year, in the wake of Xi's visit, both he and Modi said their governments were committed to an "early" settlement of the border question. This time around, Indian diplomats have taking the daring step of putting a time-frame on the negotiations, raising expectations for a major announcement in May. That will be a difficult goal to reach – neither Modi nor Xi appears to be particularly flexible when it comes to territorial issues. But a border agreement will be a major coup for both Modi and Xi if they can pull it off.

India-China Border Dispute

On assuming power, the People's Republic of China (PRC) renounced all prior foreign agreements as unequal treaties imposed upon it during the "century of humiliation" and demanded renegotiation of all borders. The Sino-India border remains the only major territorial dispute, other than South China Sea disputes, that China has not resolved. China's growing assertiveness in its territorial claims, especially on Arunachal Pradesh, and its relentless development of infrastructure in Tibet will shape the prospects of Sino-India relations.

The territory stretching from the jungles of northern Myanmar, westward to the Karakoram Range, and northward to the edge of the Tibetan plateau can be seen as a single geopolitical system referred to as the Himalayan-Tibetan massif.

The ruggedness of this terrain makes movement of men and materiel extremely difficult, thus preventing Indian and Chinese civilizations from intermingling or projecting military power in these remote areas effectively. Not until 1962 did the Chinese and Indian armies fight each other over these desolate heights, thus altering the geopolitics of the region significantly.

The McMahon Line boundary dispute is at the heart of relations between China and India. China has land and sea boundary issues with 14 neighbors, mostly for historical reasons. The Chinese have two major claims on what India deems its own territory. One claim, in the western sector, is on Aksai Chin in the northeastern section of Ladakh District in Jammu and Kashmir.

The other claim is in the eastern sector over a region included in the British-designated North-East Frontier Agency, the disputed part of which India renamed Arunachal Pradesh and made a state. In the fight over these areas in 1962, the well-trained and well-armed troops of the Chinese People's Liberation Army overpowered the ill-equipped Indian troops, who had not been properly acclimatized to fighting at high altitudes.

In the early 20th Century Britain sought to advance its line of control and establish buffer zones around its colony in South Asia. In 1913-1914 representatives of China, Tibet and Britain negotiated a treaty in India: the Simla Convention. Sir Henry McMahon, the foreign secretary of British India at the time, drew up the 550 mile (890 km) McMahon Line as the border between British India and Tibet during the Simla Conference.

The so-called McMahon Line, drawn primarily on the highest watershed principle, demarcated what had previously been unclaimed or undefined borders between Britain and Tibet. The McMahon line moved British control substantially northwards.

The Tibetan and British representatives at the conference agreed to the line, which ceded Tawang and other Tibetan areas to the imperial British Empire. However the Chinese representative refused to accept the line. Peking claimed territory in this far north down to the border of the plain of Assam.

The land is mostly mountainous with Himalayan ranges along the northern borders criss-crossed with mountain ranges running north-south. These divide the state into five river valleys: the Kameng, the Subansiri, the Siang, the Lohit and the Tirap. High mountains and dense forests have prevented intercommunication between tribes living in different river valleys. The geographical isolation thus imposed has led different tribes to elove their own dialects and grow with their distinct identities. Nature has endowed the Arunachal people with a deep sense of beauty which finds delightful expression in their songs, dances and crafts.

A slow forward move towards the McMahon Line was begun on the ground, to establish a new de facto boundary. The McMahon Line was then forgotten until about 1935 when the British government decided to publish the documents in the 1937 edition of Aitchison's Collection of Treaties.

The NEFA (North East Frontier Agency) was created in 1954. On 7 November 1959, Chou En-lai proposed that both sides should withdraw their troops twenty kilometers from the McMahon line. The issue was quiet during the decade of cordial Sino-Indian relations, but erupted again during the Sino-Indian War of 1962.

During the 1962 war, the PRC captured most of the NEFA. However, China soon declared victory and voluntarily withdrew back to the McMahon Line.

China is in occupation of approximately 38,000 sq. kms of Indian territory in Jammu and Kashmir. In addition, under the so-called China-Pakistan "Boundary Agreement" of 1963, Pakistan ceded 5,180 sq. kms. of Indian territory in Pakistan Occupied Kashmir to China. China claims approximately 90,000 sq. kms. of Indian territory in Arunachal Pradesh and about 2000 sq. kms. in the Middle Sector of the India-China boundary. Beijing has stated that it does not recognise Arunachal Pradesh.

The border between China and India has never been officially delimited. China's position on the eastern part of the border between the two countries is consistent. Not a single Chinese government recognizes the "illegal" McMahon Line. For China, the McMahon Line, stands as a symbol of imperialist aggression on the country. The so-called "Arunachal Pradesh" dispute is China's most intractable border issue. Because the gap between the positions of China and India is wide, it is difficult for both nations to reach consensus. The area of this disputed region is three times that of Taiwan, six times that of Beijing and ten times that of the Malvenas islands, disputed by Britain and Argentina. It is flat and rich in water and forest resources.

Arunachal Pradesh is the only issue which has a potential for conflict between India and China. If ever India and China go to war one day, it will be on this issue. India considers recurring Sino-Indian border clashes a potential threat to its security. Since the war, each side continued to improve its military and logistics capabilities in the disputed regions. China has continued its occupation of the Aksai Chin area, through which it built a strategic highway linking Xizang and Xinjiang autonomous regions. China had a vital military interest in maintaining control over this region, whereas India's primary interest lay in Arunachal Pradesh, its state in the northeast bordering Xizang Autonomous Region.

Barring an armed clash at Nathu La in eastern Sikkim in 1967, the border between India and China (Tibet) - and specifically the ill-defined Line of Actual Control (LAC) in Ladakh/Aksai Chin and Arunachal Pradesh - had remained free of any major incidents through the 1970s and the early 1980s. While relations between the two countries remained cool,, official statements from Beijing and New Delhi professed a desire to solve the border tangle peacefully through mutual consultations. Beginning in December 1981, officials from both countries held yearly talks on the border issue.

With the improvement of logistics on the Indian side, the Indian Army sought to reinforce and strengthen forward areas in Arunachal Pradesh in the early 1980s. Patrols resumed in 1981 and by the summer of 1984 India had established an observation post on the bank of the Sumdorong Chu [referred to as Sangduoluo He in the Chinese media].

In July 1986 there were reports in the Indian media of Chinese incursions into the Sumdorong Chu [S-C] rivervalley in Arunachal Pradesh. By September-October, an brigade of the Indian Army 5 Mountain Division was airlifted to Zimithang, a helipad very close to the S-C valley. Referred to as Operation Falcon, this involved the occupation of ridges overlooking the S-C valley, including Langrola and the Hathung La ridge across the Namka Chu rivulet.

This was followed by reports of large-scale troop movements on both sides of the border in early 1987, and grave concerns about a possible military clash over the border. In February 1987, India established the so-called Arunachal Pradesh in its ["illegally occupied"] Chinese-claimed territories south of the McMahon Line. The Chinese side made solemn statements on many occasions that China never recognizes the "illegal" McMahon Line and the "so-called" Arunachal Pradesh. After these events, and India's conversion of Arunachal Pradesh from union territory to state, tensions between China and India escalated. Both sides moved to reinforce their capabilities in the area, but neither ruled out further negotiations of their dispute.

China, which had always maintained a large military presence in Tibet, was said to have moved in 20,000 troops from the"53rd Army Corps in Chengdu and the 13th Army in Lanzhou by early 1987, along with heavy artillery and helicopters. By early April, it had moved 8 divisions to eastern Tibet as a prelude to possible belligerent action. Reinforcements on the Indian side began with Operation Falcon in late 1986, and continued through early 1987 under Exercise Chequerboard. This massive air-land exercise involved 10 Divisions of the Indian Army and several squadrons of the IAF. The Indian Army moved 3 divisions to positions around Wangdung, where they were supplied solely by air. These reinforcements were over and above the 50,000 troops already present across Arunachal Pradesh.

Although India enjoyed air superiority in 1987, rough parity on the ground existed between the two military forces, which had a combined total of nearly 400,000 troops near the border. The Indian Army deployed eleven divisions in the region, backed up by paramilitary forces, whereas the PLA had fifteen divisions available for operations on the border. Most observers believe that the mountainous terrain, high-altitude climate, and concomitant logistic difficulties made it unlikely that a protracted or larges-cale conflict would erupt on the Sino-Indian border.

That the Sino-Indian border has not suffered any major disruptions since 1986, as compared to the incessant firing incidents and infiltration on the Indo-Pak borders, made the Sino-Indian border an example of good neighbourly relations.

In December 1988, Indian Prime Minister Rajiv Gandhi visited China. The Prime Ministers of the two countries agreed to settle the boundary questions through the guiding principle of "Mutual Understanding and Accommodation and Mutual Adjustment". Agreement also reached that while seeking for the mutually acceptable solution to the boundary questions, the two countries should develop their relations in other fields and make efforts to create the atmosphere and conditions conducive to the settlement of the boundary questions. The two sides agreed to establish a Joint Working Group (JWG) on the boundary questions at the Vice-Foreign Ministerial level.

An Agreement on the Maintenance of Peace and Tranquility along the Line of Actual Control in the India-China Border Areas was signed on 7 September 1993. After more than thirty years of border tension and stalemate, high-level bilateral talks were held in New Delhi starting in February 1994 to foster "confidence-building measures" between the defense forces of India and China, and a new period of better relations began. In November 1995, the two sides dismantled the guard posts in close proximity to each other along the borderline in Wangdong area, making the situation in the border areas more stable. During President Jiang Zemin's visit to India at the end of November 1996, the Governments of China and India signed the Agreement on Confidence Building Measures in the Military Field along the Line of Actual Control in the China-India Border Areas, which is an important step for the building of mutual trust between the two countries. These Agreements provide an institutional framework for the maintenance of peace and tranquility in the border areas.

Though lot had been done during the Sino-Indian official border talks, with number of border related CSBMs put in place, the border issue remains mired in various bilateral and domestic compulsions and contradictions on both sides. Border 'encounters' between India and China are not rare and arise from the very real disagreements that exist between the two sides in demarcating the LCA on the ground. Such incidents have usually been handled, not in full media glare, but by the two sides discreetly withdrawing to their earlier positions.

The two sides withdrew sentries along the eastern section that were considered to be too close to each other. During early 1990s, India unilaterally withdrew about 35,000 troops from its eastern sector. On the other hand, the PLA maintains a force between 180,000 and 300,000 soldiers and has directly ruled Tibet from 1950 to 1976, and indirectly thereafter. Tibet today is connected to other military regions through four-lane highways and strategic roads. And Beijing's capability to airlift troops from its other neighbouring military regions has advanced very far from its comparative inability to use air force in 1962.

During the Indian Prime Minister's visit to China in June 2003 India and China signed a Memorandum on Expanding Border Trade, which adds Nathula as another pass on the India-China border for conducting border trade. The Indian side has agreed to designate Changgu of Sikkim state as the venue for border trade market, while the Chinese side has agreed to designate

Renqinggang of the Tibet Autonomous Region as the venue for border trade market.

During Chinese Premier Wen Jiabao's visit to India in April 2005, the two sides signed an agreement on political settlement of the boundary issue, setting guidelines and principles. In the agreement, China and India affirmed their readiness to seek a fair, reasonable and mutually acceptable solution to the boundary issue through equal and friendly negotiations.

India after 1962 adopted a policy to not develop the border areas. The idea was that if India developed the border areas, the Chinese can easily use these facilities in the event of a war. This policy had changed by 2008.

To redress the situation arising out of poor road connectivity which has hampered the operational capability of the Border Guarding Forces deployed along the India-China border, the Government has decided to undertake phase-wise construction of 27 road links totaling 608 Km in the border areas along the India-China border in the States of Jammu & Kashmir, Himachal Pradesh, Uttarakhand, Sikkim and Arunachal Pradesh at an estimated cost of Rs.912.00 crores. The work of construction of 2 roads in Arunachal Pradesh has started. The construction of these roads was expected to start during 2008-09.

The two sides have differences in perception of the Line of Actual Control (LAC) in the India-China border areas. Both sides carry out patrolling activity in the India-China border areas. Transgressions of the LAC are taken up through diplomatic channels and at Border Personnel Meetings/Flag Meetings. India and China seek a fair, reasonable and mutually acceptable settlement of the boundary question through peaceful consultations.

Chinese President Hu Jintao met with Indian Prime Minister Manmohan Singh in Sanya City, south China's Hainan Province, April 13, 2011. Hu said China is willing to further push forward negotiations on border issues on the basis of peace and friendliness, equal consultation, mutual respect and understanding. The two sides should consider setting up a consultation and coordination mechanism on border issues so as to achieve consensus as soon as possible and to better maintain peace and stability at the border regions before the issues are solved.

China wants India to put behind the 1962 war as an "unfortunate" thing of the past and that the two countries should strengthen their military ties including formalising a border management pact under which their troops will not fire at each other. The Chinese assessment was conveyed to the Indian defence ministry team which visited Beijing on 14-15 January 2013 for the third round of the annual defense dialogue between the two countries.

Border tensions between China and India flared after New Delhi claimed a contingent of 30 to 50 PLA soldiers crossed about 12 miles beyond the Line of Actual Control between the two countries on 15 April 2012 and stayed there for three weeks. According to New Delhi, PLA soldiers frequently conduct border incursions (more than 600 times over the last three years) but do not usually cross more than a few miles over the Line of Actual Control nor stay there longer than several hours.

Beijing denied Chinese troops had crossed into Indian territory. A Chinese Ministry of Foreign Affairs spokesperson said, "China has always acted in strict compliance with relevant agreements and protocols between the two countries on maintaining peace and tranquility in the Line of Actual Control area along the border... Chinese patrol troops have never crossed the line." Chinese Premier Li Keqiang attempted to downplay the incident and the risk of conflict. During a state visit to India, he insisted that "a few clouds in the sky cannot shut out the brilliant rays of our friendship." Premier Li did not directly address the alleged Chinese incursion, though he said "both sides believe we need to improve various border-related mechanisms that we have put into place and make them more efficient, and we need to appropriately manage and resolve our differences."

President Xi Jinping met Indian Prime Minister Manmohan Singh at the BRICS Summit in Durban, South Africa, 29 March 2013. Xi urged both sides to use special representatives to strive for a fair, rational framework that can lead to a solution to the border issue as soon as possible. India will abide by political guidelines set by both sides and seek a solution to the border issue with a commitment to safeguarding peace, Singh said. Since 2003, more than a dozen rounds of talks had been launched to resolve the border disputes. But ties have still been occasionally strained by the issue and overshadowed by closer India-US relations amid Washington's accelerating Asia "pivot" policy.

Beijing and New Delhi resolved the April border impasse in May after a series of talks and agreed to pursue a formal agreement to build trust and confidence between the border troops. The two sides signed the agreement during the Indian prime minister's trip to China in October 2013. China and India concluded a border defense cooperation pact 24 October 2013, making it a highlight of Indian Prime Minister Manmohan Singh's visit to the Asian neighbor. The Indian Express newspaper said the pact also puts no restrictions on India developing border infrastructure or enhancing military capabilities along the border. It quoted India's Ambassador to China S. Jai Shanker as saying: "This principle allows both countries to take appropriate measures according to their own security needs."

Nevertheless, the potential for periodic low-level confrontations between border patrols to escalate likely will persist. Indian media have reported several additional albeit briefer incursions by Chinese troops since the April standoff. Furthermore, both China and India continue to boost their militaries' capabilities on the border, adding to mutual suspicion. This has left both sides sensitive to each other's border activities and disposed toward worst-case perceptions of the other sides' intentions and activities. Ely Ratner and Alexander Sullivan of the Center for a New American Security, warn: "more intense strategic competition between India and China would reverberate throughout the continent, exacerbating tensions in Central Asia, the Indian Ocean, and Southeast Asia. Disruptions to the Asian engine of economic growth caused by these tensions could debilitate the global economy."

Chinese troops entered disputed territory along the Sino-Indian border, Indian media sources reported, claiming it's not the first time China has made an incursion into the Indian border region. "Chinese troops are reported to have entered 25 to 30km deep into Indian territory in Burtse area in Ladakh where they had pitched their tents last year that had led to a tense three-week standoff," The Times of India reported on 18 August 2014. Citing official sources, the media outlet notes that troops from the People's Liberation Army were spotted on Monday near the 'New Patrol base' post in Ladakh's Burtse area. According to these sources, the PLA has crossed a de-facto border known as the Line of Actual Control (LAC) and moved deeper into Indian-held territory. The PLA reportedly carried flags reading "this is Chinese territory, go back" in their hands.

India Prime Minister Narendra Modi urged visiting Chinese President Xi Jinping to resolve a boundary dispute after holding talks in New Delhi 18 September 2014 that lasted much longer than the stipulated 90 minutes. Modi said he had raised serious concerns over the issue with Chinese President Xi Jinping. He said the boundary dispute must be resolved soon. The Indian leader said they were clear that peace on the border has to be the foundation of the trust and relationship between the two nations. Modi called for an early clarification of the "line of actual control" which presently separates the two countries. He said if this happened "we can realize the potential of our relations." Xi's visit to India took place as troops from both countries were engaged in a border standoff in the Ladakh region - one of their worst in recent years. The Chinese leader played down the tensions, attributing such incidents to their undemarcated border.

India's foreign minister said 26 September 2014 that India and China had resolved a tense, two-week military border standoff in the northern Himalayan region. Sushma Swaraj said after meeting with Chinese counterpart Wang Yi in New York that Chinese troops would begin withdrawing Friday 26 September 2014 and would be finished by Tuesday. She described the resolution as a "big accomplishment." Hundreds of Chinese troops moved into a territory claimed by India, sparking the standoff on the remote mountainous frontier of Ladakh. India said the Chinese troops wanted to extend a road they were building on their side of the border into territory claimed by India. China agreed not to extend the road into the disputed territory. In return, India agreed to demolish a recently built observation hut.

CHINA AND INDIA'S BORDER DISPUTE RISES TO DANGEROUS NEW HEIGHTS

On September 19 the Chinese president, Xi Jinping, concluded a three-day trip to India. As he set off to meet Narendra Modi, Xi wrote in The Hindu that China and India "need to become co-operation partners." This does not explain why his soldiers entered Indian territory without authorisation on the first day of his visit.

As Xi landed in Gujarat, Indian media was abuzz with reports of a Chinese intrusion into Indian territory in Ladakh, with 130 Indian troops facing down 230 Chinese troops. Both sides publicly downplayed the face-off – but it was apparently serious enough for Modi to raise it twice with Xi.

Whatever he said did nothing to relieve the tension, which is still high: around 1,000 soldiers from each side have now been stationed in Ladakh and the dispute is playing out through a seemingly endless series of rushed tit-for-tat construction of military huts and roads. Clearly, the latest increase in tension is not just an everyday mishap; thanks to constant mistakes, misperception and mistrust, it risks escalating into a more intense conflict.

CROSSING THE LINE

Chinese-Indian border incursions are nothing new: according to the Indian government, 334 "encroachments" have already happened in 2014 (with 411, 426 and 213 incidents in 2013, 2012 and 2011, respectively). Disputed since China annexed all of Tibet in 1950, the border still eludes clarification. India claims about 15,000 square miles of Chinese-controlled territory in Aksai Chin, while China claims Indian Arunachal Pradesh (about 34,000 square miles) as "Southern Tibet".

The failure to clearly demarcate the China-India border has led to overlapping perceptions of where the so-called Line of

Actual Control (LAC) lies, guaranteeing that rival border patrols will run into each other and force the issue.

It's possible that troops stationed high up in the Himalayas are just horribly out of touch with international politics. Alternatively, the People's Liberation Army could be airing its own foreign policy views in opposition to the civilian leadership.

Then again, this could also be a co-ordinated strategy on the part of the Chinese: talking peace and dangling economic incentives while implementing hard-nosed security policies, just as Beijing is doing in the East and South China Seas.

But whatever is behind the latest dial-up in tensions, it has taken emotions to a height unseen in years.

Making a scene

Territorial issues haunt Indian-Chinese relations even at the best of times – and so it went during Xi's visit. India had mixed success keeping Tibetan protests out of the Chinese president's path: to safeguard the atmosphere before his arrival in Ahmedabad, 52 Tibetan students were pre-emptively detained, and north-east Indian staff in Xi's hotel were banned from their workplace.

But still, Tibetan girls descended onto Hyderabad House, site of the Delhi meeting, shouting anti-Chinese slogans. Other activists scaled scaffolding outside Xi's hotel and unfurled pro-Tibetan banners.

Some Indians speculated that the authorities deliberately allowed the protesters to reach Hyderabad House in retaliation for the border incursion. If true, beating up the protesters and bundling them away within minutes is a strange and feckless way to send a message to China.

In any case, ahead of Xi's arrival, it had been predicted that he would pressure New Delhi to help curtail the Dalai Lama's activities and shut down the Tibetan "government-in-exile". New Delhi reportedly rejected these demands – but in a signal that the incursions had introduced a *froideur* into proceedings, it also refused to resurrect its expression of support for "One China Principle" in the customary joint declaration.

All this might sound like it calls for a reasonable sort of detente – but the problem is, New Delhi and Beijing need far more from each other than that.

Forced co-operation

The economic case for co-operation is obvious. China and India are currently trading only at the volume of US$66.4 billion, although India suffers a trade deficit of around US$35 billion. The 16 deals signed during Xi's visit will bequeath a Chinese investment of US$20 billion in Indian power equipment, automobiles, infrastructure development and airlines.

For India, securing foreign investment is a crucial priority. China has plenty of capital to invest, and if Modi is serious about co-operating in global institutions with the other BRICS, he will have to defrost New Delhi's relations with Beijing.

But for China, embroiled in various sharp territorial disputes with neighbours on its eastern Pacific front, improving relations with India is a point of paramount security importance.

With Modi headed to the US with an imperative to repair relations with Washington, this just weeks after he implicitly decried Chinese "expansionism" in Tokyo, hopes that the world's two largest countries will manage to improve their relationship may be premature at best.

Dalai Lama Visit Ignites Sino-Indian Border Dispute

In early November, the Dalai Lama is going to visit the majestic Tawang Monastery, perched atop a ridge in the Indian province of Arunachal Pradesh. Surrounded by thick clouds and perennial mist, the monastery sometimes seems almost to be suspended from heaven.

It is also at the very centre of thousands of square kilometres of terrain claimed by both China and India, although India currently possesses it. It now risks becoming a proxy battleground on which both India and China seek to proclaim their sovereignty. The religious leader's visit can be seen as a card played by both India and the Tibetan exile community to keep pressure on China.

Home to one of the most sacred Buddhist monasteries, Tawang is the birthplace of the sixth Dalai Lama, Tsayang Gyatso, in the 17th century. The current Dalai Lama passed through this region when he fled into exile in 1959. Chhime Chhoekyapa, the exiled Tibetan spiritual leader's aide, told the media that the Dalai Lama is "going there for teaching. This has nothing to do with politics, there is nothing political about it." In Chinese eyes, however, and perhaps Indian eyes as well, everything the Dalai Lama does has something to do with politics. And this is a region that Beijing calls "Southern Tibet."

When asked about the Dalai Lama's upcoming visit, Beijing officials have fumed. "China expresses strong concern about this information," said Jiang Yu, the spokeswoman for China's Foreign Ministry. "The visit further reveals the Dalai clique's anti-China and separatist essence. China's stance on the so-called Arunachal Pradesh is consistent. We firmly oppose Dalai visiting the so-called Arunachal Pradesh." Tension has slowly been ratcheting up between the two Asian giants, with media commentators fanning the flames. "Is China itching to wage war on India?" asked Professor Brahma Chellaney in the September issue of the Far Eastern Economic Review. Reports have appeared in Chinese state media alleging that India was moving troops and fighter aircraft to the northeast, specifically into Sikkim and Arunachal Pradesh.

India, however, is acutely aware of its shortcomings in the territory it controls. The Chinese, with their extensive roads and railways, can actually come up to the Line of Actual Control, take a stroll and walk back. Two years ago, Chinese soldiers demolished a Buddhist statue that Indians had erected at Bumla, the main border pass above Tawang, according to a member of the Indian Parliament, Nabam Rebia. It takes several days for India's troops to get to the border. But slowly India is finding its voice as it struggles to speed up its own preparedness.

China claims around 90,000 square kilometres of territory, roughly the size of Arunachal Pradesh, regarding the area as "disputed." China lays claim to Tawang on behalf of the Tibetans. But in the exile community in Dharamsala, where the Dalai Lama and thousands of Tibetan refugees live, the community is not impressed. They do not claim Tawang as Tibetan, let alone Chinese territory. The Dalai Lama's travel plans were announced a week after his recent visit to Taiwan to visit victims of tropical storm Morakot. China denounced the Taiwan trip, although its complaints were remarkably muted. The visit to Arunachal Pradesh has now drawn further attention to China's treatment of Tibetan activists and the Dalai Lama's calls for cultural and religious freedom and autonomy.

Tawang became part of modern India when Tibetan leaders signed a treaty with British officials in 1914 that established the McMahon Line between Tibet and British-run India. Tawang fell south of the line. The treaty, the Simla Convention, is not recognized by China. "We recognize it because we agreed to it," said Samdhong Rinpoche, prime minister of the Tibetan government-in-exile. "If China agreed to it now, it would be a recognition of the power of the Tibetan government at that time."

Tawang's native population is almost entirely Buddhist. Its origin is obscure. It was a part of the kingdom of Tibet in medieval times although local tribal rulers have governed it from time to time. The British declared the area off-limits in 1873. India's independence from Britain severed it from Tibet. In 1962 Chinese troops conquered Tawang during the invasion of Tibet and for six months it was controlled by the Chinese. After their retreat, Tawang again came under Indian control.

India denied the Dalai Lama permission to visit Tawang the last time he requested to do so. This time it is playing the Dalai Lama card to the full. Officials in India's Ministry of External Affairs insist that "things are changing" and that India is getting more assertive. On Sept. 16, India's foreign minister, S.M. Krishna, rejected China's opposition to the visit.

In an interview on IBN7, the sister channel of India's CNN-IBN, Krishna said China's objections had no merit. While the government has not explicitly said the visit will be permitted, Krishna said: "Arunachal Pradesh is a part of India and the Dalai Lama is free to go anywhere in India. The only question is that he is not expected to comment on political developments." Analysts say the Tibetan leader's visit will reassert Arunachal's status as an

Indian territory. "The timing of his trip [to Arunachal Pradesh] is significant. It comes while the debate over his visit to Taiwan is still hot," said Bhaskar Roy, a New Delhi-based China analyst. "Tibetans are as good at playing these games as the Chinese. They know such a visit will keep up the pressure on China."

In Dharamsala, Samdhong Rinpoche, Tibet's prime minister in exile, called Beijing's objections to the visit "absurd," adding that "Arunachal Pradesh and the Tawang region are an integral part of India. If the Dalai Lama, who has stayed in India for the last 50 years, is visiting any part of the country why does this bother China?

If the Dalai Lama goes to Chinese territories it can raise objections but in this case has no business to interfere." The Arunachal Pradesh government is urging New Delhi to ignore the Chinese opposition. "Chinese claims over Arunachal Pradesh are simply baseless and not correct. Arunachal Pradesh is an integral part of India and would continue to be so," said Chief Minister Dorjee Khandu. "They [the Chinese] are opposed to everything that His Holiness does," said a spokesman for the Dalai Lama's private office in Dharamsala.

Tawang's strategic importance cannot be ruled out. The place provides the shortest route from Tibet into India. The Dalai Lama himself took this route to escape into India in 1959. Indian defence officials have already raised alarms declaring China and not Pakistan to be India's biggest threat. They believe that control over Sikkim and Arunachal Pradesh would enable Chinese forces to overrun the entire northeast border region. Chinese troops repeatedly have attempted to gain control of Sikkim's evocatively named Finger Area, a tiny but key strategic location where Beijing does not dispute the frontier.

In June this year, General J J Singh, governor of Arunachal Pradesh and former chief of army staff, announced the deployment of two army divisions of around 25,000 to 30,000 soldiers each along the Arunachal Pradesh border with China. The strength of India's Sukhoi fighter jet fleet in the Northeast is being increased. It remains to be seen if the Dalai Lama's visit will be the trigger that causes them to be used.

5

India's Border Dispute with Pakistan

2014–15 INDIA–PAKISTAN BORDER SKIRMISHES

The 2014–15 India–Pakistan border skirmishes are a series of ongoing armed skirmishes and firing exchange between the Border Security Force and Pakistan Army along the Line of Control (LoC) in the disputed Kashmir area and Punjab. Started from mid-July 2014, military officials and media reports of both countries gave different accounts of the incident, each accusing the other of initiating the hostilities. The incident sparked outrage both in Pakistan and India and harsh reactions by the Indian army and Pakistan armed forces and governments.

Later in October, the situation became aggressive following which then Indian Defence Minister Arun Jaitley urged Pakistan to stop "unprovoked" firing and warned that the response by India would be "unaffordable". His Pakistani counterpart, Khawaja Asif replied to the warning with subtle mention of "nuclear power" that the country would be able to respond "befittingly" to the Indian aggression.

On 12 October 2014, Pakistan's Foreign and National Security Adviser, Sartaj Aziz, sent a letter to UN and appealed to resolve the crises. However, the United Nations rejected Pakistan's proposal to intervene in the crisis and reiterated that the dispute be resolved through bilateral discussions.

INCIDENTS

2014

In May

- On May 19, reports emerged that an Indian Soldier named Sepoy Bhikale Uttam Balu of the 2 Maratha Light Infantry (MLI) was killed in an encounter with terrorists near the Line of Control in Nathua Tibba area of Akhnoor

In July

- In mid July one BSF soldier was killed and three others injured after Pakistani Rangers fired upon Pittal border outpost along international border in Arnia forward area of R S Pura in Jammu district.
- On July 20 and 23, two civilian from Azad Kashmir were killed in Mirajke during a skirmish between Indian BSF and Pakistani forces.
- On July 22, An Indian soldier was reportedly killed in firing by Pakistani troops at Indian positions on the Line of Control. Later it was revealed he was killed by infiltrating militants and not by firing by Pakistani troops

In August

- Another incident occurred early August when an Indian soldier, allegedly trying to cross the border from Bajwat sector in Sialkot, was arrested by Pakistani Rangers. He was freed two days later on August 8.
- In late August, two civilians were allegedly killed by the Indian BSF in Sialkot region.

In October

- Early October, a 17-year old girl was killed in alleged cross-border firing by Pakistani troops in Poonch district while four other civilians were injured. Pakistani military official accused India of violating the ceasefire and opening fire in Pakistani village near Sialkot, after which Pakistani military retaliated.
- On October 6, Indian Border Security Forces (BSF)

personnel fired along the working boundary in Sialkot, killing four and injuring five. The Indian media reported death of 5 civilians injuring 34 others in a ceasefire violation from Pakistan in Arnia belt of Jammu district. It is said to be the highest Indian civilian causality in a decade across the Line of Control in the India-Pakistan conflict. The Indian and Pakistani forces did not exchange sweets along with the Wagah border taking a break from the traditional festival' meet on the occasion of Eid al-Adha.

- The following day, one woman was killed in Charwa sector by Pakistani troops. and eight people were killed and three injured as Indian security forces allegedly fired and shelled a village the Chaprar Sector. Later that day, two women were killed and 11 injured as Pakistani troops targeted 50 security outposts along the LoC.
- On October 9, two Pakistani civilians were killed on by Indian forces. Meanwhile two Indian women were killed by Pakistani forces in an unrelated incident.
- On October 11, Indian forces allegedly violated the ceasfire after a brief lull. No loss of life was reported. later Pakistan army allegedly violated ceasefire in Arnia targeting BSF outpost

In November

- On November 8, a civilian Gulshan Bano and a soldier were killed by Pakistani troops in Kamalkot area of Uri sector.
- After a day of handed over a 13 years old student, to Indian authorities at Chakoti-Uri crossing point by Pakistani Officials.
- On November 20, a Pakistani soldier was killed by Indian troops in the Pandu sector near Muzaffarabad, Azad Kashmir.

In December

- On December 30, Pakistani officials handed over 16 year old girl to her family who had mistakenly crossed the Line of Control (LoC).

- On December 31, One BSF soldier, Constable Sri Ram Gowria was killed in Pak firing in Jammu & Kashmir's Samba sector.
- On December 31, Two Pakistan rangers, Naik Riaz Shakir and Lance Naik Muhammad Safdar were killed in Indian BSF firing at Shakargarh Sector of Narowal district. According to Pakistani sources, the soldiers were heading to participate in the flag-meeting when they were fired upon by BSF troops at Zero Point. The Pakistani officials also claimed that the BSF fired at those who went to rescue the injured soldiers too. The BSF officials claimed that the firing was in retaliation to the previous day's Pakistani firing and that four Pakistani soldiers were killed instead. On 1 January 2015, two funeral prayers were offered for the two Pakistani soldiers killed.

2015

In January

- On January 2, a 13-year old girl, Sumaira was killed by Indian army firing in Pakistani residential areas of Zafarwal, while a 5 year old child, Mursaleen was injured in the Shakargarh sector of the Sialkot.
- On January 2, a woman and two army soldiers ware killed by Pakistani army firing. 11 people were also injured. The Hindu reported that 2 Pakistani Rangers were killed after 9:30 PM IST during the exchange of Fire.
- On January 5, Four civilans were killed by Indian firing and shelling on Pakistani residential areas, including 18 years old Azeem from Bore Chak and a woman from Sukhmal village in Zafarwal sector and two other civilians. Pakistani soldiers also responded by firing on BSF posts. ISPR reported that the Pakistani retaliatory firing on BSF posts caused heavy losses to them.
- On January 5, A BSF soldier was killed by Pakistani firing on BSF posts at Hiranagar in Samba sector of Jammu & Kashmir. The Pakistani media reported that at least 5 Indian soldiers were killed by Pakistani retaliation.

In February

- On 14 February, a sixty-year old villager was killed by Indian firing in Rawalakot sector along Line of Control, while he was cutting wood 150 meters inside the Pakistani territory.

REACTIONS

India

The Indian Prime Minister Narendra Modi said, "I want to assure the people that we will not let down our country" and 'everything will be fine soon'." While then Defence Minister of India, Arun Jaitley said that, "If Pakistan persists with this adventurism, our forces will make the cost of this adventurism unaffordable". The Indian Home Minister, Rajnath Singh said that the Pakistan must stop ceasefire violations across the border, "times have changed in India".

According to Indian claims, 18 militants were also killed and 19 alleged militant camps destroyed in October.

Pakistan

The Pakistani military officials and the government accused India of violating the ceasefire and opening fire in Pakistani territory, after which Pakistani military retaliated. Both condemned the LoC violation by Indian forces. The Pakistani Defence Minister, Khawaja Asif responded to the Indian counterpart on 'unafforable adventurism', "We don't want to convert border tension between two nuclear neighbours into confrontation".

In a rally in Multan, Pakistani politician Imran Khan stated that "Modi had been given a mandate by the Indian people, but if he chooses to use it for war, then he will regret it." Unofficial statement issues by the ISPR, Chairman joint chiefs General Rashad Mahmood reportedly marked that Narendra Modi is threat to peace and if he wants war then he will see just what the unified Pakistani military will do to India. On 12 October 2014, Pakistan's National Security Adviser (NSA), Sartaj Aziz, sent letter to UN and appealed to resolve the crises. However, the United Nations rejected Pakistan's proposal to intervene in the crisis and reiterated that the dispute be resolved through bilateral discussions.

India fired close to 30,000 mortar rounds between 2010 and 2014. The DG Rangers Punjab, Pakistan said Indian violation of ceasefire was up to the intensity of fighting a small-scale war.

On 31 December, National Security Adviser Sartaj Aziz directed a letter through the Embassy of Pakistan, New Delhi, to External Minister Sushma Swaraj protesting the "breach of trust" over the killing of two Rangers personnel. In response to letter, External Minister Sushma Swaraj reportedly dismissed Pakistan allegations.

World

On 9 October 2014, United Nations general secretary Ban Ki-moon's spokesperson issued a statement that he wants the both countries "to engage constructively to find a long-term solution for peace and stability in Kashmir". On October 14 United Nation military observer group in Pakistan and India visited Charwah, Chaprar and Pukhlian sectors and on the Working Boundary near Sialkot to gather firsthand account of damage caused to human lives and property due to recent ceasefire violation between Pakistan and India.

KASHMIR DISPUTE

1947: August 14/15. British India is partitioned into India and Pakistan as part of the independence process. Majority Muslim areas in the West (now all of Pakistan) and East (the place now called Bangladesh) form Pakistan. The British also allow the nominal rulers of several hundred "princely states," who were tax collectors for the British and served at British pleasure, to decide whether they wanted to join India or Pakistan. Pakistan demands Kashmir accede to it.

The Hindu ruler of Kashmir does not make a choice. Kashmir has three major ethnic areas: Ladakh in the northwest, which is majority Buddhist; the Kashmir Valley (controlled by India) and the part now controlled by Pakistan, which is majority Muslim, and Jammu (in the south), which is majority Hindu. The overall majority is Muslim.

1948: "Tribesmen" from Pakistan invade Kashmir with the support of the Pakistani government. The ruler of Kashmir asks India for help. India demands that Kashmir should accede to India first. The ruler agrees. India sends forces to Kashmir and the invasion is blocked. Kashmir is divided into a Pakistani controlled part and an Indian controlled part. This de facto partition continues to this date with the dividing line being known aş the Line of Control.

1948: India takes the Kashmir issue to the U.N. Security Council, which passes a resolution calling on Pakistan to do all it can "secure the withdrawal" of Pakistani citizens and "tribesmen" and asking that a plebiscite be held to determine the wishes of the people of Kashmir. Neither the force withdrawal nor the plebiscite has taken place.

1962: India and China fight a border war. China occupies a part of Ladakh.

1965: India and Pakistan fight a border war along the India-West Pakistan border and the Line of Control in Kashmir. U.N. brokered cease fire and withdrawal to pre-war lines affirmed by the leaders of the two countries at a 1966 summit meeting in Tashkent, USSR (now Toshkent, Uzbekistan).

1970-1971: An election in (East and West) Pakistan results in an overall majority for an East Pakistani party, which is ethnically mainly Bengali. The Pakistani military refuses to allow the Parliament to convene. East Pakistanis demand autonomy, then independence in the face of brutal repression by the Pakistani military. Guerilla warfare ensues. About ten million refugees stream into India from East Pakistan.

India also provides sanctuary to Bangladeshi guerillas. Pakistan attacks airfields in India and Indian-controlled Kashmir. India strikes back in West Pakistan and also intervenes in the East on the side of the Bangladeshis. The U.S., in a "tilt" towards Pakistan, sends a nuclear-armed aircraft carrier, the Enterprise, and its battlegroup, to the region, in an implicit nuclear threat to India (which influences nuclear politics of India in favor of nuclear testing). Pakistan loses the war on both fronts and Bangladesh becomes independent.

1972: India and Pakistan sign a peace accord, known as the Simla (or Shimla) agreement, according to which both sides agree "to settle their differences by peaceful means through bilateral negotiations or by any other peaceful means mutually agreed upon between them." Both countries agree that they will not unilaterally try to alter the Line of Control in Kashmir.

1974: India tests a nuclear device. Pakistan accelerates its nuclear weapons program.

1980s: U.S. supports Islamic resistance to Soviet occupation of Afghanistan and also the dictatorship of Zia-ul-Haq in Pakistan, which promotes Islamic fundamentalism in Pakistan.

Late 1980s: There is a state-level election in the Indian-controlled portion of Kashmir. There is evidence of fraud. Militancy rises in Kashmir. In 1989, the Soviets quit Afghanistan. Islamic militants from outside South Asia now become engaged in Kashmir, with the support of the Pakistani government. The violence in Kashmir becomes more dominated by foreign fighters and by religious fundamentalism. In the late 1980s and early 1990s, Hindu fundamentalism begins to become more powerful as a political force in India.

1990s: Violence intensifies in Kashmir. Islamic militants carry out ethnic cleansing in the Kashmir Valley, terrorizing non-Muslims, mainly Kashmiri pundits, causing large numbers of people to flee, mainly to Jammu. Pakistan supports the cross border infiltration. The Indian military responds with repression to the terrorism, foreign infiltration, and the domestic insurgency, which are now all mixed up. There are serious human rights abuses on all sides.

1998: A coalition led by the Hindu-fundamentalist party, the BJP, comes to power in India. India and Pakistan carry out nuclear weapons tests and declare themselves nuclear weapon states. Pakistan announces that it may, under certain circumstances, use nuclear weapons first to neutralize India's conventional superiority, making reference to NATO's Cold War doctrine of potential first use in case of a European war with the Soviets. India says it will not use nuclear weapons first.

1999: Indian Prime Minister, Atal Behari Vajpayee, travels to Lahore, Pakistan for a peace meeting with Prime Minister Nawaz Sharif. There is great hope for peace.

Three months later Pakistan-based militants invade the Kargil area in Indian-controlled Kashmir, with the support of the military. A military confrontation, with the possibility of nuclear war, ensues. Nawaz Sharif travels to Washington and President Clinton convinces him to withdraw Pakistani forces from Kargil. Confrontation ends. Nawaz Sharif is overthrown in a military coup led by General Musharraf, one of the architects of the Kargil war. (Musharraf proclaims himself President of Pakistan in the year 2000.)

September 11, 2001: Well-known tragic events in the United States. Terrorist attacks kill about 3,000 people.

October 1, 2001: A terrorist attack on the Kashmir state legislature in Srinagar. 38 people are killed.

October 7, 2001: U.S. launches a war in Afghanistan, under the rubric of the War on Terrorism. President Musharraf becomes a U.S. ally and allows Pakistan to become a base of operations for the United States. Al Qaeda, Taliban, and their supporters in Pakistan feel severe pressure.

December 13, 2001: A terrorist attack on India's Parliament. Fourteen people (including five attackers, as well as security guards and two civilians) are killed.

Aftermath of December 13: India mobilizes and moves hundreds of thousands of soldiers to the border with Pakistan, including the Line of Control in Kashmir. The danger of conventional and nuclear war rises.

May 14, 2002 to date (early Sept 2002): A terrorist attack on families of Indian servicemen. More than 30 people killed. India threatens to retaliate. Pakistan makes implicit threats of nuclear weapons use in case of Indian attack. Peak of the conventional and nuclear confrontation reached in May-June 2002. Greatest threat of nuclear war since the Cuban missile crisis of 1962. U.S. troops and war strategy in the region imperiled. U.S. shuttle diplomacy defuses the immediate crisis as Pakistan promises to end cross border infiltration. India does not retaliate. Tensions remain high and the threat of war and nuclear weapons use persists.

KASHMIR: INDIA AND PAKISTAN'S BITTER DISPUTE

Violent protests erupted this summer in India's Kashmir region, resulting in the worst bloodshed in a decade. Many of the demonstrators want independence from India, while New Delhi has always said the unrest is fueled by Pakistani-sponsored extremists. Here is a brief look at the dispute.

What is Kashmir?

Kashmir is a Himalayan region that borders India, Pakistan and China. Known for its majestic landscape, Kashmir has figured prominently in the history and legends of the Indian subcontinent. It was known as "paradise on Earth" and before the insurgency, Indians flocked to Kashmir for vacations and blockbuster Bollywood movies were filmed there.

On the Pakistani side, Kashmir includes the areas known as Azad (Free) Kashmir and Gilgit-Baltistan. The territory under dispute lies in India's Kashmir Valley, separated from Pakistan by the 450-mile Line of Control. That area is part of the northern Indian state of Jammu and Kashmir.

Indian Kashmir is mostly Muslim; Jammu is Hindu. The city of Srinagar is the summer capital of the state while the city of Jammu, further south and much warmer, serves as the winter capital. How did the trouble start? Kashmir's suffering is rooted in the painful birth of the two South Asian nations.

India's Muslim leaders demanded a Muslim homeland as a condition for independence in 1947. The British relinquished their hold on the subcontinent, giving way to a predominantly Hindu India and a Muslim Pakistan. Kashmir was free to accede to either nation. Maharaja Hari Singh, the ruler of the kingdom, initially chose to remain independent but eventually opted to join India, thereby handing key powers to the central government in New Delhi. In exchange, India guaranteed him military protection and vowed to hold a popular vote on the issue.

How dangerous is the situation? The South Asian rivals have fought two of three wars over the territorial issue — in 1947 and in 1965. A third conflict between India and Pakistan erupted in 1999 after Pakistani-backed forces infiltrated Indian-controlled Kashmir in the Kargil area.

Both India and Pakistan have fired across the demarcating Line of Control. Such incidents have become common but India has so far refrained from incursions into Pakistani territory. In 1998, both nations successfully tested nuclear weapons, raising the stakes in the Kashmir conflict and in turn, overall regional and global security.

What do India and Pakistan say about Kashmir? Islamabad has always maintained that majority-Muslim Kashmir should have been a part of Pakistan. A United Nations' resolution adopted after the first war called for a referendum allowing the people of Kashmir to choose which country they wanted to join, but that vote for self-determination has never been held. Pakistan wants that referendum to take place.

India claims that Pakistan lends support to separatist groups fighting against government control and argues that a 1972 agreement — signed after the Bangladesh war — mandates a resolution to the Kashmir dispute through bilateral talks. Neither country wants Kashmir to become an independent nation.

What is the separatist movement? Over the years, India sent thousands of security forces to Kashmir, making it one of the most highly militarized areas of the world. In 1989, militants began an armed uprising against New Delhi's control, taking up guns for the cause of independence. India accused its arch-rival Pakistan of fueling terrorism by sponsoring the armed insurgency.

Among the larger separatist groups are the Jammu and Kashmir Liberation Front (JKLF), but it gave up guns for politics in 1994 and its power is believed to have declined. Key separatist groups now fall under the umbrella of the All Parties Hurriyat Conference, which has engaged in talks with the Indian government. The last time the two sides met was in 2006. India claims that organizations designated as terrorist groups by the U.S. State Department are involved in Kashmir's violence. They include Lashkar-e-Tayyiba, which was blamed for the 2008 terrorist attacks in Mumbai, and Jaish-e-Mohammed, blamed for an attack on parliament in New Delhi. What happened to the insurgency? Tens of thousands of people have been killed in Kashmir since the insurgency took hold.

Parts of once-idyllic Srinagar now look apocalyptic — buildings are riddled with bullet marks and roads and infrastructure have not been improved in years. Children have grown up not knowing the meaning of peace. The "paradise on Earth," many say, has turned to hell. When talks between the Indian government and the All Parties Hurriyat Conference began in 2004, the bloodshed declined. But the problem was hardly resolved.

In a poll taken earlier this year by the London think tank Chatham House, most Kashmiris listed unemployment as the most significant problem plaguing their lives. Joblessness along with a sense of alienation from India has added to popular discontent. How do Kashmiris feel about India? The Chatham House poll last spring found that between 74 percent to 95 percent of residents of the mainly Muslim Kashmir Valley, where the conflict is centered, would vote for independence. In mostly Hindu Jammu, that support dropped to 1 percent.

What triggered the latest uptick in violence? Discontent with India has never gone away and manifests itself repeatedly in street demonstrations. Human rights groups say that India's Armed Forces Special Powers Act — which gives security forces wide-ranging powers to shoot, arrest and search in battling a separatist insurgency — further alienates Kashmiris.

In June, the death of a teenager hit by a teargas shell, triggered a series of violent protests. Since then, angry mobs have taken to the streets chanting: "Freedom."

INDIA AND PAKISTAN BORDER DISPUTE

The Government of India administers almost 60% of the state of Jammu and Kashmir and is unequivocal on its stand - "Kashmir is an integral part of India". The official map of the state, as approved by the Indian Government, shows the entire state of Jammu and Kashmir, including Gilgit-Baltistan, Azad Kashmir, and Aksai Chin, as part of Indian Territory. According to the Indian government the Instrument of Accession was a legal act executed without any deceit or coercion.

Pakistan authorities refer to the 1933 Pakistan Declaration and claim Kashmir to be one of the Indian units that were to secede from India and join Pakistan. Pakistan claims that the accession to India was unconstitutional since it violated the terms of the 'Standstill Agreement' between Pakistan and the Princely State of Jammu and Kashmir. Pakistan was formed on the basis of the Two Nation Theory. Since most of the people inhabiting the Kashmir valley are Muslims,

A HISTORY OF DISSENT

In 1947, before they withdrew colonial authority, the British Government divided the Indian subcontinent into two states, based largely on religious demographics. The primarily Muslim nation, Dominion of Pakistan, was formed on August 14, 1947 and the largely Hindu state, Union of India, was formed on August 15, 1947. In one of the largest instances of population transfers post World War II, over 11.2 million people moved from their homes as a result of the partition. Over 5 million Hindus and Sikhs moved to India, primarily from West Punjab, and about 6 million Muslims moved from India to present-day Pakistan. A poorly executed transfer resulted in violent communal disputes and caused about 500,000 deaths.

Simultaneously, India and Pakistan became embroiled a territorial dispute over Kashmir - an issue that was to poignantly mark the newly-formed neighborhood with hostility and distrust for times to come. Three major wars later, the two countries still nurture a legacy of conflict and hostility over the international boundary in Kashmir. It is estimated that the conflict has resulted in over 13,000 deaths in the Kashmir province in the past four decades. Insurgency has claimed a further 47,000 lives in the last twenty years alone. The history of political dissent in the Kashmir region does not, however, begin with the partition. To understand the background of the territorial claims we shall need to delve into the history of the state.

An Ancient Past

An in-depth study of the history of the Kashmir region reveals that the dispute goes way back in time. It precedes the creation of India and Pakistan as nations. References to the Kashmir Valley are replete in ancient Hindu mythology. According to legend, ancient Kashmir has long been under the sway of various rajas. The first raja was Adgonand, who ascended the throne in 4249 B.C. at a time when Egypt was said to have been ruled by demigods. He was succeeded by his son Danudar who was killed by the Yadhus, the tribe to which Krishna belonged.

The Kashmir region was ruled by the Kambojas and later by the Panchalas in the fourth and fifth centuries BC. With the spread of Mauryan dominion over most of the Indian subcontinent, Buddhism as a religion found a strong base in Kashmir. The Mauryan emperor Asoka is credited with the establishment of Srinagar. It comes as no surprise, then, that the valley has shared close cultural ties with China. A number of Buddhist thinkers used Kashmir as their base to spread the religion to China and Tibet during the reign of the Kushan kings.

ISLAM FINDS ITS FEET IN THE VALLEY

Through the first millennium, the Kashmir valley saw many alternating phases of prosperity and misery under the Hindu rulers. In 1320, the Kashmir valley was invaded by the Mongol ruler Zulquadr Khan (known as Dulacha) ending Hindu rule. He came to Kashmir through the Baramulla pass and plundered Srinagar. As there was no organized government, the local chiefs declared independence. Among those who took advantage of prevailing anarchy was Rinchana, the son of the Ladhak chief. Rinchana entered Kashmir through Zoji-La Pass. He converted himself into a Muslim and assumed the name Sadr-u-din. He died in the year 1323. From 1323 to 1338 the state was ruled by Udayanadeva. Shams-ud-Din Shah Mir, the first Pashtun ruler of the region came from the tribal Swat region of Afghanistan and established Muslim reign in the valley in about 1339. Some of the subsequent rulers such as Sultan-Sikandar persecuted the Hindus of the region and a mass exodus followed. The spread of Islam during this period was widespread. By 1586 the Kashmir Valley was annexed by the Mughal ruler Akbar. In 1589 AD, Kashmir became a province of the Mughal Empire. By the time Aurangzeb came to ascend the Mughal throne, the governors of Kashmir seemed to have taken to ravaging the natural bounty of the land and ruthlessly pursued religious fanaticism. By 1752, Kashmiri nobles invited Ahmad Shah Adbali of Kabul to invade and annex the land. Kashmir soon became part of the Pathan rule. It is generally agreed that despite the persecution of some rulers the Hindus and Muslims of the region lived in relative harmony and Kashmir evolved into a society where the intellectuals - both Kashmiri pandits and the erudite Muslims - were a dominant force.

Brokering A Kingdom

Through the early nineteenth century, religious despotism, cruelty, and poverty shrouded the Kahmir Valley and this lasted till the Sikh ruler Maharaja Ranjit Singh conquered the state in 1819. In 1822, Ranjit Deo's nephew Gulab Singh was designated "Raja of Jammu" by Maharaja Ranjit Singh. Gulab Singh successfully annexed the Baltistan and Ladakh regions. The death of Maharaja Ranjit Singh in 1839 accelerated the collision between the Sikh Empire and the British authorities. Gulab Singh, who had initially remained neutral, contrived to act as an advisor to Sir Henry Lawrence with the outbreak of the First Anglo-Sikh War in 1845. The conclusion of the treaties of Lahore and Amritsar left the Britishers in charge of the Sate of Lahore including all of West Punjab. Gulab Singh signed a separate treaty with the British, which gave him the status of an independent princely ruler of Kashmir. The Kashmir Valley was handed over to Gulab Singh by the Britishers for a payment of seventy-five lakh rupees. Having placed himself favorably with the British authorities, Gulab Singh found the opportunity perfect to orchestrate his ascendancy. Gulab Singh died in 1857 and was replaced by Rambir Singh (1857-1885). Two other Maharajas, Partab Singh (1885-1925) and Hari Singh (1925-1949) ruled in succession.

THE PRINCELY STATE OF JAMMU AND KASHMIR

The Princely State of Jammu and Kashmir, though ruled as a unitary kingdom by the Dogras (Gulab Singh and successors), remained divided by disparate religions and ethnic groups. While the Kashmir Valley was predominantly Sunni but both Baltistan and Gilgit regions were populated by a majority of Shi'a Muslims; Jammu, the traditional seat of the Dogra kings, was inhabited in equal measure by Muslims, Hindus, and Sikhs. The people of the Ladhakh region practiced Buddhism and shared close cultural ties with China and Tibet. The Poonch region was primarily inhabited by Muslims. The Kashmiri Pandits of the valley region wielded much influence in cultural and political matters.

Gulab Singh's demise in 1857 tied in closely with the Indian Rebellion, popularly known as the Sepoy Mutiny. The Dogras of Kashmir supported the British forces and subsequently ruled the state under the Paramountcy of the British Crown.

The Disputed Instrument of Accession

In 1947, Maharaja Hari Singh Dogra, the great-grandson of Gulab Singh, was offered a choice - the Princely State of Jammu and Kashmir could join either of the newly formed states of India and Pakistan or could remain independent. The undecided Maharaja entered into a Standstill Agreement with Pakistan allowing for continuation of normal trade and exchanges till a settlement was reached. In the meantime, a rebel faction from Poonch revolted against the Maharaja's rule and declared the formation of Azad Kashmir, an independent government. By the October of 1947, the Poonch rebel faction invited Pakistani guerilla troops to engage in a campaign to dissuade Kashmir from joining India. The guerilla troops left a trail of plunder and murder across Kashmir. Perturbed by the unsettling new development, Maharaja Hari Singh appealed to the British Viceroy Lord Mountbatten. As suggested by Mountbatten, the Maharaja agreed to accede to India on the condition that Indian troops would evict the Pakistani lashkars from Jammu and Kashmir. On October 26, 1947, the king executed the Instrument of Accession and Jammu and Kashmir was thus poised to join the Dominion of India. Mountbatten formally accepted the accession. With this, the Maharaja handed over the valley to India. By the instrument of Accession, the Maharaja of Jammu and Kashmir accepted three subjects as ones on which the Dominion Legislature can make laws. They are- Defense, External Affairs, and Communication. Lord Mountbatten remarked that the state's accession be eventually settled by a referendum. Pakistan contested the accession on the grounds that Kashmir's Standstill Agreement with Pakistan was still in force at the time. India has maintained ever since that the state has been irrevocable acceded to India following the Instrument of Accession, Pakistan has maintained that the people of Kashmir be allowed to participate in a referendum to settle the issue.

Three Wars and a Line of Control

Three major and bloody wars have been fought by the two countries over Kashmir since 1947. The Indo-Pakistan War of 1947 resulted from Maharaja Hari Singh's execution of the Instrument of Accession. When war escalated to vociferous levels India invited mediation by the international community and the United Nations. The war ended in December 1948 by which time the Line of Control (LOC) was established to demarcate the administrative segments of Kashmir. The international boundary dispute was still left pending. The war of 1965 ended after bleeding the two countries. Thousands of lives had been lost and the intervention of USA and erstwhile USSR had become necessary. India recorded a victory but the damages to both nations. On January 10 1966, the Tashkent Declaration was signed and the two nations withdrew forces to the LOC. The war of 1971 was unrelated to the Kashmir issue and centered on Bangladesh.

Later, in 1999, the Kargil War reopened raw wounds. Pakistani troops infiltrated the Kargil district across the LOC and assisted insurgents in the area. India retaliated and the war that ensued caused panic in the international community with the threat of a nuclear war becoming imminent. International pressure forced Pakistan to withdraw. Besides, with the Indian army having reclaimed the Tiger Hills and other strategic peaks in the Batalik, Pakistan had not much to gain by pressing on with the offensive.

Over the years, a number of clashes have marked the Siachen Glacier region where the Line of Control is not clearly chalked out.

DIFFERENT MAP VERSIONS

The Backstory

With the British decision to withdraw from the Indian subcontinent having become certain, it became imminent for India and Pakistan to agree on the terms of the partition and to decide on the fate of the 562 princely states that existed in 1947. On July 18, 1947, the Indian Independence Act received the Royal Assent of the British Crown and the Dominion of Pakistan and the Union of India came into existence on August 14 and 15 respectively. Of the princely states, Junagadh initially acceded to Pakistan but the geographic constraints made this untenable. After a brief struggle, Junagadh and Hyderabad joined India.

Why Pakistan?

Pakistan's claim stems from the fact that Kashmir had always been thought of as a natural territorial extension of Pakistan from the early 1930s when Choudhry Rahmat Ali, an Indian Muslim living in Cambridge, England, had in his pamphlet "Now or Never, Are We to Live or Perish Forever" created the name Pakistan from the five regions - Punjab, Afghan Province, Kashmir, Sindh, and Baluchistan. In Persian, Pakistan also means "land of the pure", an implicit gibe at the ritually "pure" high-caste Hindus who dominated the Indian National Congress. Despite having a Hindu ruler, the population of Jammu and Kashmir was predominantly Muslim. The terms of the Indian Independence Act, "the suzerainty of His Majesty over the Indian States lapses", made it possible for the princely states to choose either nation or remain independent. Pakistan had hence concluded that accession to Pakistan would be Kashmir's natural choice.

Why India?

Maharaja Hari Singh Dogra, the king of Jammu and Kashmir, delayed his decision to join either India or Pakistan possibly with an intention to remain independent. The king was soon under duress from the Muslim populace of Kashmir and threatened by the rebellion which broke out along the western fringes of the region. While the rebels of Poonch region came to be aided by the Pashtun tribesmen from the Dir region, a guerilla war broke out and left a trail of murder and destruction in Baramulla region. Maharaja Hari Singh Dogra appealed to India for military assistance. India and Pakistan had signed a non-intervention treaty which prohibited India from going up against Pakistan in a state which was not part of the Indian Territory. When the Pakistani guerilla lashkar had reached the outskirts of Srinagar, the Maharaja agreed to join India by signing the disputed Instrument of Accession in October 1947. Indian troops were dispatched to drive out the Pakistani lashkar from the state. India's claims on the state are the result of a legal accession executed by the king without any coercion.

UN Intervention

Pakistan contested the accession of Jammu and Kashmir to India. The ensuing Indo-Pakistan War lasted till 1948 when India invited mediation by the United Nations. With Resolution 39 (1948), the United Nations Commission for India and Pakistan (UNCIP) was established and with Resolution 47 (1948), both India and Pakistan were asked to withdraw their troops and create conditions conducive to holding a free plebiscite. On 1 January, 1949 the UN military Observer Group in India and Pakistan (UNMOGIP) was set up to observe and report on the ceasefire.

International mediation helped to the extent that war between the two nations ended in December 1948 but both countries did not endorse the withdrawal of armed forces and the recommended plebiscite was never held. India controlled over 60% of the territory and went ahead to hold state elections. The state constituent assembly was convened in October 1951. The Jammu and Kashmir Constituent Assembly and later the state Legislative Assembly ratified the accession to India on February 6, 1954. The state constitution was brought into effect on January 26, 1957. This Constitution also ratified the state's accession to union of India.

Pakistan, on the other hand, encouraged the establishment of Azad Jammu & Kashmir to the south of the Gilgit-Baltistan region as an independent territory but overseen by the authorities at Lahore. The northern tribal region, referred to as Northern Areas was incorporated into Pakistan. The constitution of Pakistan, however, did not make any reference to this province till the 1980s.

Since 1948, the United Nations has passed four resolutions revising the initial recommendations of Resolution 47. A further 11 proposals have been put forth by the United Nations, to demilitarize the region and facilitate the plebiscite. United Nations cannot, however, enforce its resolutions on member states and thus the two countries did not adopt the recommendations to withdraw forces.

More Wars

Three major and bloody wars have been fought by the two countries over Kashmir since 1947. The Indo-Pakistan War of 1947 resulted from Maharaja Hari Singh's execution of the Instrument of Accession. When war escalated to vociferous levels India invited mediation by the international community and the United Nations. The war ended in December 1948 by which time the Line of Control (LOC) was established to demarcate the administrative segments of Kashmir. The international boundary dispute was still left pending. The war of 1965 ended after bleeding the two countries. Thousands of lives had been lost and the intervention of USA and erstwhile USSR had become necessary. India recorded a victory but the damages to both nations were considerable. On January 10 1966, the Tashkent Declaration was signed and the two nations withdrew forces to the LOC. The war of 1971 was unrelated to the Kashmir issue and centered on Bangladesh.

Later, in 1999, the Kargil War reopened raw wounds. Pakistani troops infiltrated the Kargil district across the LOC and assisted insurgents in the area. India retaliated and the war that ensued caused panic in the international community with the threat of a nuclear war becoming imminent. International pressure forced Pakistan to withdraw. Besides, with the Indian army having reclaimed the Tiger Hills and other strategic peaks in the Batalik, Pakistan had not much to gain by pressing on with the offensive.

Over the years, a number of clashes have marked the Siachen Glacier region where the Line of Control is not clearly chalked out.

Gilgit-Baltistan

Gilgit - Baltistan is the northernmost province of Kashmir which is currently occupied and administered by Pakistan. Commonly referred to as Federally Administered Northern Areas (FANA), the area was formed by uniting Gilgit, Baltistan, Hunza, and Nagar.

The region is part of what India calls Pakistan Occupied Kashmir (POK). The mapping of this region poses a problem to most map-makers since both Pakistan and India consider Gilgit - Baltistan integral regions of their own respective territories.

Despite having occupied the Gilgit - Baltistan region, Pakistan had not officially assigned the region the status of a province due to the country's commitment to the United Nations Resolution 48.

The reluctance of the Government of Pakistan to establish constitutional authority caused much dissatisfaction among the inhabitants of the region.

In April 2008 an international conference was held in Brussels at the European Parliament.

The conference was overseen by the International Kashmir Alliance. Most members of the European Conference urged Pakistan to establish regulated administration in the region and to oversee the formation of a judiciary to deal with the human-rights violation concerns in the area.

Subsequently in 2009, Pakistan implemented autonomous rule in the province. Pakistan's President Zardari signed the Gilgit-Balistan Empowerment and Self Governance order on August 29.2009. Though the constitution of Pakistan does not yet officially recognize Gilgit-Baltistan as a province, the region has been provided a status comparable with other provinces. A Legislative Assembly is elected by the people and administration is overseen by the Chief Minister.

Currently Gilgit - Baltistan is a self-governing region administered through a representative government. The judiciary of the province is independent. Currently the office bearers of the Government of Gilgit-Baltistan, Pakistan, are -

Governor	Pir Karam Ali Shah
Chief Minister	Syed Mehdi Shah

Whose Kashmir Is It Anyways?

India's Position

The Government of India administers almost 60% of the state of Jammu and Kashmir and is unequivocal on its stand - "Kashmir is an integral part of India". The official map of the state, as approved by the Indian Government, shows the entire state of Jammu and Kashmir, including Gilgit-Baltistan, Azad Kashmir, and Aksai Chin, as part of Indian Territory. According to the Indian government the Instrument of Accession was a legal act executed without any deceit or coercion. Ever since the accession, Jammu and Kashmir has been given special concessions and is largely autonomous in deference to the Article 370 of the Indian Constitution.

Furthermore, the Instrument of Accession found the endorsement of the state's Constituent Assembly, say Indian authorities. The UN Resolution 47 could not be executed due to the refusal of Pakistan to withdraw troops at the time. India also claims that the formation of Azad Kashmir was illegal. The land ceded to China by Pakistan is also deemed illegal, as the land is officially claimed by India. Indian authorities have, however, issued statements from time to time expressing their willingness to settle the issue through bilateral negotiations.

The elections held in 2008 in Jammu and Kashmir by the Government of India had a high turnout. The United Nations regards the poll as free and fair. India was quick to point out that a high turnout of voters indicated that the people of the state endorsed the administrative governance of India.

But insomuch as Kashmir goes, India has remained unambiguous in its stand. In 2010, Government of India issued a statement that "We are very clear in our mind that Jammu and Kashmir is an integral part of India... And as a vibrant democracy,

India has sufficient mechanisms and constitutional safeguards to address issues raised by its citizens in any part of the country".

In January 2013, relations between the two nations took a sudden plunge as India accused Pakistani army of killing two of its soldiers and providing 'grave provocation' by beheading and mutilating one of them.

Pakistan promptly denied the claims and countered that India had violated the LOC. Tensions between the two countries escalated as the Indian Prime Minister Manmohan Singh in his Army Day address said, "After this barbaric act, there cannot be business as usual with Pakistan. What happened at LoC is unacceptable" Brigade-level flag meeting between Indian and Pakistani authorities at Chakan Da Bagh near the Line of Control in Poonch failed to ease the tensions between the two countries.

From time to time, demands for the liberation of Gilgit-Baltistan from Pakistani occupation have also resounded in the political circles of Delhi. This has further been fuelled by allegations of human rights violation, violence, and abuse by Pakistani troops in POK, especially in the Azad Kashmir region. The Indian Government abstained from giving in to these demands in conformity with the LOC drawn up by the Shimla Agreement. What remains to be seen if an amicable resolution is possible "within the ambit of the Indian Constitution".

Pakistan's Position

Pakistan authorities refer to the 1933 Pakistan Declaration and claim Kashmir to be one of the Indian units that were to secede from India and join Pakistan. Pakistan claims that the accession to India was unconstitutional since it violated the terms of the 'Standstill Agreement' between Pakistan and the Princely State of Jammu and Kashmir.

Pakistan was formed on the basis of the Two Nation Theory. Since most of the people inhabiting the Kashmir valley are Muslims, Pakistan does not recognize Indian claims to the state. Pakistan claims the entire Gilgit-Baltistan region, and the India administered Kashmir as its territory. The region made over to China is recognized by Pakistan as Chinese territory.

In the 1972 Shimla Agreement, the UN cease-fire line of 1949 was formally converted into the Line of Control (LOC). For more than four decades now it has been anticipated that the LOC shall eventually be converted into the international boundary. Pakistan, however, remains reluctant to cede control of the Kashmir Valley currently administered by India.

The Azad Kashmir issue has, however, elicited mixed responses from Pakistan. While on the one hand Pakistani officials have traditionally pledged to settle the issue of Kashmir in deference to the wishes of the Kashmiris themselves, there has been no indication that Pakistan is willing to cede its claims to either India or to an independent Kashmir.

In 2006 a controversy broke out about the circulation of a new "official map" by Pakistani embassies showing the Gilgit-Baltistan provinces as a separate region. The allegations were denied by Pakistan but the government declared that it had no change of stance with regard to the Kashmir issue.

In 2002, President Pervez Musharraf of Pakistan went on record to state, "Kashmir runs in our blood. No Pakistani can afford to sever links with Kashmir. We will continue to extend our moral, political, and diplomatic support to Kashmiris. We will never budge from our principle stand on Kashmir issue, which must be resolved through dialogue in accordance with the wishes of the people of Pakistan and in accordance with the UN resolutions". In 2011, Pakistan's Prime Minister Yousuf Raza Gilani said that Pakistan will continue to raise the Kashmir issue till its resolution.

Following the escalation of tensions across the LOC in January 2013, at an Asia Society talk in Washington DC, Pakistan's foreign minister Hina Rabbani Khar accused India of "war-mongering" and going on a "narrative of hostility" and denied the beheading incident at the LoC. She maintained that while Pakistan sought peace, India continued to seek war.

China's Position

China's position in the tripartite dispute is fairly straight. The PRC does not recognize the Princely State of Jammu and Kashmir. The country claims and currently administers the Aksai Chin region. The British demarcation of the region was a unilateral decision, says China. The Trans-Karakoram Tract, being strategically important for China was settled by the Sino-Pakistan Agreement in 1963. Neither Pakistan nor China acknowledges India's claims in this sector.

UN Stand

In 1949, following the first India-Pakistan War the UN Ceasefire Line was accepted as the line of administrative control for defense purposes. In 1972 the Shimla Agreement was signed by India and Pakistan and the Line of Control was recognized as the "line of Conflict', not an international border, but one that protects the recognized position of both nations.

The UN map of Pakistan clearly demarcates the LOC as per the Shimla Agreement and places a disclaimer that the international boundary as shown is not an endorsement by the UN. The map disclaimer also reads "The final status of Jammu and Kashmir has not yet been agreed upon by the parties".

All neutral agencies follow the UN lead and map the Gilgit-Baltistan and Azad Kashmir region as disputed territory. The United Nations' stand is not an official endorsement of the territorial authority by either nation, nor does the international community accept any demarcation till the two nations have reached an agreement.

CIA and Google Maps

The CIA Map of Pakistan includes all of Gilgit-Baltistan in Pakistan's territory. Most of Kashmir is still retained in the Map of India.

The map shows the 1972 Line of Control as the boundary separating the two countries. To the east of Kashmir, the CIA map designates Aksai Chin as territory claimed by India. The authenticity of this map has been disputed by many Indian agencies but has been endorsed by Pakistani groups.

Google Maps has designated the various regions without a clear international boundary demarcation and has not labeled the respective regions.

What is the history of the conflict?

Going back into history, the beauty and bounty of Kashmir to a lesser degree, and its strategic location to a greater degree, have been the reasons why the valley still remains highly coveted. The entire Jammu-Kashmir-Ladakh region has at different times been influenced by Hinduism, Islam, Sikhism, and Buddhism in terms of religion and culture. With the passage of time these influences translated into territorial claims nurtured by India, Pakistan, and China. The valley region has witnessed a number of bloody wars and political maneuvers, but no concrete adjudication of the conflict has come out of these. The idea of an independent Kashmir is also an alternative that is recurrently dredged up but is not acceptable to the nations embroiled in the issue.

Why was the Jammu & Kashmir issue not settled during the India-Pakistan partition? In 1947, with the withdrawal of the British, India and Pakistan came into existence. The princely states of the Indian subcontinent were given a choice - they could accede to either nation or could remain independent. The princely state of Jammu and Kashmir soon emerged at the center of a heated conflict between the two newly formed countries. The Maharaja of Kashmir, in an attempt to remain independent, had put off making a decision. When an internal rebellion in Kashmir came to be aided by Pakistani troops, the Maharaja agreed to join India by signing the Instrument of Accession on October 26, 1947. India claims the region as part of the territory annexed by a legally executed instrument of accession. Pakistan's claims stem from the religious demographics of the land, a Muslim-majority region. Pakistan upheld that the accession was a sham. It also blamed India of violating the commitment to hold a plebiscite on the future of the state. It maintained that India is cogently occupying a large part of the state.

Is war a real possibility? While both India and Pakistan are keen to avoid a war that could bleed the countries both economically and in terms of resources, Jammu and Kashmir has never failed to touch a raw nerve with the populace of both nations. A negotiated resolution seems difficult given the stubborn stance that both countries have adopted over the last six decades. Both India and

Pakistan are known nuclear powers. India is estimated to possess approximately hundred nuclear weapons and Pakistan between seventy and ninety nuclear arms. The prospect of war, therefore, is a debilitating one. Besides, given the background of a global economic recession, these developing nations can ill-afford war.

Headlinesindia brings to you a complete overview of the history, the issues, and the intricacies of the Kashmir conflict and a look at the various challenges faced while mapping the region.

Mapping Challenges

In India it is illegal to plot or circulate a map which excludes any part of Jammu and Kashmir.

The Survey of India's official version of the Indian map includes the Gilgit-Baltistan region, Azad Kashmir, Aksai Chin, and the Trans-Karakoram tract. The Criminal Law Amendment Act of 1961 makes it illegal for any Indian organization or individual to publish and/or distribute a map different from the official version.

Pakistan, on the other hand, has made it illegal to share a map of Pakistan which does not mark out the state of Jammu and Kashmir as a disputed territory.

This is in keeping with the practices followed by the United Nations. The popular version of the India-Pakistan map used across the world depicts both the Line of Control and the Line of Actual Control.

For over sixty years now Kashmir has been at the eye of a storm that threatens to erupt and ravage both India and Pakistan. Many violent protests, three full-scale wars, and the ongoing scourge of insurgency and terrorism have dissuaded the normalcy from returning to the valley. With accusations of human rights violation and gory bloodbath having been exchanged, both the countries are keen on settling the issue. But is an amicable negotiation possible? The more important consideration here is what the people of Kashmir want for their land and how India and Pakistan plan to negotiate in deference to the wishes of the Kashmiris.

INDIA-PAKISTAN: THE NEW VICTIMS OF AN OLD BORDER DISPUTE

India and Pakistan's decades-old territorial dispute is often portrayed as a dormant conflict, but for Zaigham Abbas it is anything but. His father Mumtaz Hussain was killed last August when India's Border Security Force (BSF) shelled the village of Bajra Garhi along the Sialkot Working Boundary in Pakistan.

"We were leaving the mosque after [morning] prayers when the Indians started shelling. The next thing I know, my father was hit in the ribs," Abbas said.

"By the time the shelling stopped, he was lifeless," Hussain's widow Shama Batool added. "I don't think much could have been done to save him."

In the street, the neighbouring homes still bear the scars of battle, with pockmarked walls and smashed glass.

STUCK IN THE MIDDLE

Abbas is one of around 80,000 Pakistanis who live in the 45 Pakistani villages regularly affected by fighting along the zigzagging 1,800-mile border with India.

Of that, a 124-mile stretch in Kashmir remains disputed between the countries – demarcated by a "line of control". Further south, the divide in the Sialkot-Jammu region operates on the basis of a "working boundary", meaning the Pakistani government considers the land on the other side occupied.

Three full-scale wars were fought over the border, the first in 1947 and the most recent in 1999. Tensions have heightened after the coming to power of Hindu nationalist Narendra Modi in India in May 2014. In August he called off peace talks, while in October fighting intensified, with Modi taking a more aggressive tone. On the Pakistani side, too, calls for moderation have increasingly been sidelined.

Violence continues to wreck lives – on December 31, a rare attempt at a flag meeting spiraled out of control, with two Pakistani rangers killed after clashes which both sides accused the other of starting. "The firing continued for five hours before the bodies could be retrieved," said Major Ijaz, a media officer of the Pakistan Rangers. He insisted that the Indians began the violence but Indian media denied the claim.

In January, at least four civilians were killed on each side of the border, while dozens of others were injured. Thousands in both countries have fled their homes. When IRIN gained rare access to the Pakistani border region in late January, there was intermittent shelling, with civilians describing how they live in fear of the next attack.

Sumaira Raza, a resident of the village of Jooyian, said that she has had to flee on multiple occasions. "Every few days, we leave and lodge with our relatives in neighboring villages. Others who do not have this option simply spend their nights in open fields. This winter, it was so cold that many families in neighbouring villages allowed women and children who are not their relatives to sleep in their homes."

Other residents describe having to leave elderly or disabled family members behind as they fled. There are no specialised medical facilities in the areas and basic health units are unable to treat the severely injured. Though there is no set pattern as to when the fighting begins, villagers say it usually starts after sunset. "The shelling is getting more intense with each passing day," Farid, a farmer from the region, added. Others say they live in fear of Indian drones, which they say often hover over the area shortly before an attack. "When the village has fewer people, the shelling doesn't happen even if the drone comes but when the village is full and a drone comes by, we know shelling will happen," one teenager said.

Other villagers reported similar tales, but Ijaz would not confirm or deny such claims. Late last year India committed to buying 49 more drones to patrol the border.

IDPs of the night

The effects of the conflict on the population can be drastic. Shama Bibi said she went into early labour during clashes and struggles with post-natal depression, which she blames on the violence. "There was firing every day and at times we had to run for cover. Then came the September [2014] floods. The shelling stopped but our mudhouse collapsed. I walked for miles with my family in that condition. When my son was born, I didn't look at him," she said.

Even when peace reigns, risks abound. Both the Pakistani Rangers and the BSF have laid thousands of landmines across the border region, with many dating back to 2002. Shama Bibi says she went into early labour during clashes between India and Pakistan During floods in September 2014, some landmines are believed to have been swept across the border into Pakistan.

One of Ehsan's sons was partially blinded and another two crippled in a landmine explosion a decade ago. "The government has abandoned us. No one came to offer us even medical help," he said. Residents claim the Pakistan government has made no arrangements to move the villagers to other areas and there are no compensation schemes for those relocating. Sometimes local politicians arrange some support for those killed or injured, but it is arbitrary and limited.

As such many are faced with a choice between leaving their land and livelihood for good and the safety of their loved ones. "I can either keep my family safe in another place or send my children to school," said farmer Ghulam Din who makes barely Rs8,000 ($78) a month. He moved his family from the border village Umeraanwali to a slum near Sialkot city where they are no longer in education. "I barely have money to feed them," he bemoaned.

Ironically the land he left behind could be some of the most valuable in Pakistan if the situation were different. Sialkot is among the most fertile parts of the country– yet the violence means there are few buyers for those seeking to flee.

PAKISTAN, INDIA SPAR IN KASHMIR IN WORST BORDER VIOLENCE IN YEARS

After a decade of relative quiet, Indian and Pakistani troops are shelling each other with vigor again along their disputed border, raising tension between the nuclear-armed nations and forcing hundreds of villagers to flee. Many fear there is worse to come. As the American military withdraws from Afghanistan, some Pakistan-based militants who had been fighting there have pledged to turn their attention to the Kashmir border region — and their old foe, India. Already, there are signs that militant activity is on the rise in this area, with graffiti appearing saying "Welcome Taliban."

In recent days, the disputed border that separates much of the Indian-controlled state of Jammu and Kashmir from Pakistan has turned into a virtual war zone.

A month of cease-fire violations by both sides has resulted in the deaths of at least 11 soldiers and two Pakistani civilians and the wounding of several residents.

"We can't sleep at night," said one village head, Lal Din, 38. "Whenever we hear gunshots and mortars we huddle together in the corners of our shacks. We are helpless to do anything to prevent it."

The two sides have fought for more than six decades over this hilly and verdant land, which has been at the heart of two of the countries' three wars.

While few people see the current skirmishes as exploding into a full-scale conflict, the fear of further deterioration is widespread.

"In three or four months, the people fighting in Afghanistan or Pakistan could come here," said Sheikh Younis, 42, who runs a mobile phone shop in a mall in downtown Srinagar, not far from the lotus-fringed lake where tourists take rides in colorful boats. "People are very concerned about it. What's going to happen after 2014?"

Militant incursions on rise

The current skirmishes began in August, when five Indian soldiers were ambushed and killed while on patrol in Indian-controlled Kashmir. That triggered near daily mortar and machine-gun fire from both sides along the Line of Control — some 460 miles of razor-wire fencing, surveillance cameras and heavily armed military posts snaking through the Himalayas. Although no major population centers have been hit, the exchanges of fire have renewed tensions as leaders of the two nations were to try and meet later this month during the U.N. General Assembly.

Kashmir, whose population is mostly Muslim, has been bitterly contested since the British granted India independence in 1947 and the land was split into Hindu-dominated India and Muslim-majority Pakistan.

In the late 1980s, an Islamist insurgencybacked by Pakistan emerged, seeking to end India's control over the disputed territory. Kashmir suffered more than 50,000 dead in that conflict. Over the last decade, India and Pakistan have crept toward normalcy, with easing visa restrictions and hopes for increasing bilateral trade. Violence along their disputed border ebbed, too, after a 2003 cease-fire agreement. Insurgent activity also declined dramatically, in part, experts say, because many of the fighters now had a far more compelling target nearby — American and NATO troops in Afghanistan.

Now, residents say the relative calm could be over. The army and police say cross-border incursions by militants are on the rise. In recent days, Indian army officials claimed they shot and killed five foreign fighters in Kashmir, including one from Pakistan's lawless North-West Frontier Province of Pakistan.

As the U.S. involvement in Afghanistan wanes, leaders of Pakistan-based militant groups such as Lashkar-e-Taiba — which carried out the 2008 Mumbai terrorist attacks — have publicly pledged to turn their attention again to Kashmir. On Friday, its founder, Hafiz Mohammad Saeed — who lives openly in Lahore despite a $10 million U.S. bounty offered for his arrest — gave a fiery speech laced with anti-India rhetoric to thousands in Islamabad, demanding the "liberation" of Kashmir.

Stephen Tankel, an assistant professor at American University and author of "Storming the World Stage: The Story of Lashkar-e-Taiba," predicted that Lashkar and smaller militant groups "are going to seek to ramp up as the U.S. draws down its forces in Afghanistan."

"It's pretty clear there is some sort of a strategy in place to slowly polarize the situation once again and do it in a way that looks as indigenous as possible," he added.

Local residents say they are worried by growing support for militants, with funerals of home-grown fighters drawing larger crowds.

Many young Kashmiri men — who consider the Indian army a brutish occupying force — are seeking to join insurgent groups like Lashkar and Hizbul Mujahideen to win an independent Islamic state, they say.

Yasin Malik, a former militant who is chairman of the Jammu Kashmir Liberation Front, a separatist political party, said that everywhere he goes in the region he hears from young men, many of them well-educated, who want to fight for Kashmir's independence.

Many of these youth, who resent India's presence but at that same time feel left behind by its growing prosperity, took part in civil protests in 2010 that degenerated into rock-throwing clashes with security forces that left more than 100 dead.

Now, instead of stones, some want guns. "I think if America leaves Afghanistan, the Taliban might come here, and a lot of Kashmiri youth would surely welcome this, including me," said Qadri Inzamam, 21, a soft-spoken college student.

"We have been born in a conflict zone. We have seen it from our childhood. It's in our veins to get liberated from this occupation."

Inzamam said he attended a funeral in December for one of those who threw stones in 2010, Aatir Yousuf Dar, a 19-year-old business major from the village of Sopore. He had dreamed of becoming an entrepreneur but instead joined Lashkar-e-Taiba. Dar was killed, along with five men from Pakistan, in a 30-hour gun battle with police and army forces in Kashmir, according to local press reports.

Thousands turned out for his funeral, Inzamam said. The women of the village showered his corpse with sweets and rose petals and painted his hands with henna, as if he were a bridegroom.

Politics get in the way

Few believe this month's talks between India and Pakistan — if they happen — will have much impact on the border clashes. Pakistan's newly elected leader, Nawaz Sharif, has pledged cooperation with India but must grapple with hard-liners within the military and the country's own Islamist insurgency, experts said.

On the other side, India is heading into an election season, with Prime Minister Manmohan Singh's government preoccupied with domestic issues as its once vibrant economy has slowed dramatically.

Stephen P. Cohen, a senior fellow at the Brookings Institution and the author of a new book on India and Pakistan called "Shooting for a Century," said that the relationship between the two countries is likely to remain hostile, but not flare into full-fledged war.

"Nuclear weapons play a paradoxical role — they make war too costly but they symbolize rivalry," he wrote in an e-mail.

The renewed fighting is already putting a damper on the few areas of cooperation that exist between the two rivals.

A plan for India to export electricity to its power-starved neighbor has stalled. At the spot on the border where Indians and Pakistanis trade almonds, dates and tomatoes, the number of trucks carrying goods has fallen by about half in the last month, according to a police official in the Poonch district, further south in the Jammu region.

Villagers up and down the Line of Control have found their lives suddenly disrupted by the cease-fire violations.

Masood-ur-Rehman, the administrator of the Kotli district in Pakistani-administered Kashmir, said that in recent days officials have had to move more than 500 people to temporary camps for their safety, and dozens more have fled to stay with relatives.

Before the cease-fire a decade ago, residents of the tiny village of Kirni in Jammu had been moved down the hillside into temporary quarters away from the violence.

In 2011, they finally decided to return to their ancestral homes. Villagers organized a big celebration with the savory turnovers known as samosas, sweets and dancing.

But their joy vanished on Aug. 22, when machine-gun and mortar fire again rained down on them from Pakistani positions up the hill. The firing — "like an earthquake," one said — lasted for four terrifying hours, wounding a six-year-old girl and a older woman. The village was shelled again Sept. 3.

Now village council head Mohammad Sayeed, 40, is pondering whether he will have to move all his people again.

"Unfortunately we are thinking there is no hope for us," he said.

6

India Faces off With Pakistan

In recent days, India has faced off with both Pakistan and China on its disputed Kashmir borders. Pakistani rangers opened fire on Indian border outposts along the Line of Control (LoC, the military border demarcating India-administered Kashmir from Pakistan-administered Kashmir) in what constituted a major ceasefire violation. Casualties included one Border Security Force (BSF) soldier and three more injured. Meanwhile, Chinese People's Liberation Army troops crossed the Line of Actual Control (LoAC, the boundary demarcating the India-administered part of Kashmir from the Chinese-administered Aksai Chin region) and were stopped by the Indian army, assisted by the Indo-Tibetan Border Police (IBTP). The stand-off lasted no longer than 30 minutes and was resolved peacefully with the PLA soldiers eventually returning to the Chinese side of the LoAC.

Both incidents demonstrate that despite positive diplomatic rhetoric from all three governments, the border situation in Kashmir remains tense. Ceasefire violations by Pakistan, in particular, proved highly destabilizing to bilateral relations between India and Pakistan in 2013. Meanwhile, the India-China Border Defense Cooperation Agreement (BDCA), signed in October 2013 between India and China in Beijing, was meant to prevent a recurrence of these sorts of incidents. According to the *Times of India,* the 30 minute stand-off involved Indian troops warning the Chinese troops to refrain from advancing furthers. The report further notes that the Chinese troops were on horseback. The incursion took place near Chumar.

By some measure, the BDCA may have proved successful in this instance as it prevented a prolonged episode like the April 2013 Daulat Beg Oldi incident when Chinese PLA troops spent over three weeks in India-administered Kashmir before retreating. That Indian and Chinese forces were able to resolve this latest stand-off without any perceivable central government interference from either side establishes that the BDCA's military-to-military mechanisms are working as envisaged.

The timing of the Chinese incursion is unfortunate as Indian Prime Minister Narendra Modi and Chinese President Xi Jinping declared their intention to negotiate a solution to their border disputes when they met in Fortaleza, Brazil earlier this week, ahead of the BRICS summit. Commenting on the border incident with China, Indian Home Minister Rajnath Singh commented that "Incursions along the border take place due to the difference of perception about boundary." Negotiations between the two sides will focus on ending ambiguities about what is perceived to be Indian territory and what is perceived to be Chinese territory in Kashmir.

INDO-PAKISTAN BORDER

India shares 3323 km long and complicated boundary with Pakistan. The India-Pakistan boundary is categorised under three different heads. The first is the international boundary also known as the 'Radcliff line'. It is 2308 km long and stretches from Gujarat to parts of Jammu district in Jammu and Kashmir. The second is the line of control (LoC), or the Cease Fire Line, which came into existence after the 1948 and 1971 wars between India and Pakistan. This line is 776 km long, and runs along the districts of Jammu (some parts), Rajouri, Poonch, Baramula, Kupwara, Kargil and some portions of Leh. And the third is the actual ground position line (AGPL), which is 110 km long and extends from NJ 9842 to Indira Col in the North. The LoC and the AGPL has been a scene of constant tensions with border skirmishes and firing between the armies and border guarding forces of both countries. The LoC has been vulnerable to constant infiltration by foreign terrorists, Kashmiri separatists and Pakistani army regulars for long.

Like the Bangladesh boundary, the India-Pakistan boundary also does not follow any geographical barrier. It runs through diverse terrain like deserts, marshes, plains, snow clad mountains, and winds its way through villages, houses and agricultural lands making it extremely porous. Porosity of this border has facilitated various illegal activities such as smuggling, drugs and arms trafficking, and infiltration.

Heroin and fake Indian currency are the two predominant items of smuggling along this border. Other items include saffron, textile, mercury, which are smuggled from Pakistan. The villagers adjacent to the border are alleged to be involved in smuggling in a big way. Money laundering is also quite rampant along the border. A large scale hawala network is flourishing in Punjab, especially in Ludhiana. In addition, the border population has also been subjected to hostile propaganda by Pakistan designed to mislead and sway their loyalties. The Sir Creek area, due to its peculiar terrain, makes the movement of border guarding forces very difficult and thus, provides scope for illegal fishing in the creeks.

Future Options For Declaration Of The Dispute

Over the past fifty years, besides the UN resolutions, observers and intellectuals have proposed various other options for resolving the Kashmir dispute time and again at the UN fora and at the bilateral India-Pakistan levels.

UN Resolutions: The Plebiscite Option

The UN Security Council resolutions of August 13, 1948 and January 5, 1949, proposed the plebiscite option for resolving the Kashmir dispute. However, it is important to note that the Government of India itself accepted *plebiscite* or *referendum* as a right of the Kashmiri people, when it filed the initial complaint against Pakistan before the United Nations on January 1, 1948, as pointed out in Part I of this paper. Beginning with Governor General Mountbatten, Indian leaders like Prime Minister Nehru also repeatedly made the commitment to 'the will of the Kashmiri people'.

After India filed its initial complaint, the UN Security Council passed the two important resolutions of August 13, 1948 and January 5, 1949. These resolutions laid down the principles and procedures for a free and impartial plebiscite under UN auspices. Broadly, the resolution of January 5, 1949, stated: '(a) the question of the accession of the State of Jammu and Kashmir to India and Pakistan, would be decided through the democratic method of a free and impartial plebiscite after the cease-fire and truce agreement provided for in the Resolution of August 13 had been carried out; (b) the Secretary General of the UN would nominate a Plebiscite Administrator, who would be appointed by the government of Jammu and Kashmir and given powers which he considers necessary for holding a free and impartial plebiscite; (c) on implementation of the ceasefire and the truce agreement, the Commission and the Plebiscite Administrator would determine, in consultation with the Government of India, the final disposal of Indian and State Armed Forces, as well as the Forces in Azad Kashmir (in consultation with the local authorities); (d) persons who had entered the State since August 15, 1947 would be required to leave the State, and citizens of the State who had left the State on account of disturbances would be allowed to return.'

Both India and Pakistan accepted the above UN Resolutions. However, later, differences arose over the interpretation of various clauses of the resolutions, especially on the issues of demilitarisation and disbandment/disarming of the 'Azad Kashmir' forces. India gave its own interpretation to the agreement and suggested that the Azad Kashmir forces be disbanded and the defence and administrative responsibility of the region be given to India and Indian Kashmiri authorities.

Pakistan, on the other hand, was in favour of a complete and simultaneous withdrawal of armed forces personnel by both the countries. On this issue, the President of the Security Council, General McNaughton, in his proposal of December 22, 1949, in para 2, clarified that the Resolutions of 1948 and 1949 called for demilitarisation of the whole State of Jammu and Kashmir and not merely Azad Kashmir: that 'demilitarisation should include the withdrawal from the State of Jammu and Kashmir of the regular forces of Pakistan; and the withdrawal of the regular forces of India not required for purposes of security or for the maintenance of local law and order.' The UN Security Council passed Resolution 80 on March 14, 1950, which called upon the Governments of India and Pakistan 'to prepare and execute within a period of five months from the date of this resolution a programme of demilitarisation on the basis of the principles of paragraph 2 of General McNaughton's proposal, or of such modifications of those principles as may be mutually agreed.' Pakistan accepted that Resolution as well, but India maintained its position as regards the demilitarisation issue.

The UN Security Council passed Resolution 98, in December 1952. The UNSC Resolution, regarding demilitarisation issue clarified that: (Article 4) 'the Governments of India and Pakistan to enter into immediate negotiations under the auspices of the United Nations representative for India and Pakistan in order to reach agreement on the specific number of forces to remain on each side of the cease-fire line at the end of the period of demilitarisation, this number to be between 3,000 and 6,000 armed forces remaining on the Pakistan side of the cease-fire line and between 12,000 and 18,000 armed forces remaining on the India side of the cease-fire line.' Though during the discussions Pakistan's representative to the UN, Mr. Zafrulla Khan, pointed out that the number of forces proposed was not fair, yet he said that Pakistan 'is prepared to go forward on the basis of this resolution.' The Indian representative, Mrs. Pandit, in her speech, however, categorically said, 'I should like to repeat that we reject the proposal in it and we are not prepared to enter into any talks on the basis suggested.'

Regarding the question of plebiscite, Pakistan was in favour of giving complete authority to the UN for holding, organising and supervising the plebiscite. India, on the other hand, only wanted the non-binding advice of the UN. Various UN mediators were appointed to resolve this issue, but no one was successful in convincing India on a compromise. Sir Owen Dixon, the UN mediator, in his report submitted in 1950, wrote: 'In the end I became convinced that India's agreement would never be obtained to demilitarisation in any such form, or to provisions governing the period of plebiscite of any such character, as would in my opinion, permit of the plebiscite being conducted in conditions sufficiently guarding against intimidation and other forms of influence and abuse by which the freedom and fairness of the plebiscite might be imperilled.' Dr. Frank P. Graham, appointed UN representative for India and Pakistan in 1951, submitted five reports, up to March 1953, but his efforts at mediation also proved to be unsuccessful as India would not agree on the size of the forces to be left on either side of the cease-fire line after demilitarisation. India, therefore, consistently refused to take recourse to all proposals of various statesmen and UN representatives for the holding of a plebiscite in Jammu and Kashmir. On the other hand, it is on record that Pakistan supported all such international mediation and UN efforts.

Defending the Indian position on plebiscite, Sisir Gupta, an Indian scholar, wrote: 'it became obvious even at the early stages of the Kashmir dispute that a plebiscite -an "ideal" solution according to some – because of the complexities in Kashmir was difficult to accomplish. Even as a democratic solution, it had loopholes. Kashmir, clearly, is not composed of one people: in religion, it has three major groups; in language, four. If there is a section which wants to secede from India, there are others who do not.' However, the fact of the matter is that, right from the beginning, India feared that if a plebiscite was held it would lose what it had already occupied. According to a Kashmiri activist, Prof. Mrs. Shamim Shawl, 'plebiscite is the most plausible solution of the problem. This has been accepted in the Resolutions of August 48 and January 1949. It is these resolutions, which confirm the disputed character of the problem and negate the Indian position that says Kashmir is an irrevocable part of India. India is in fact challenging the rightful and legal authenticity of the United Nations by delaying the implementation of UN resolutions.'

Keeping in view the basic genesis and nature of the dispute, the option incorporated in the then UN resolutions is still valid. The UN resolutions are not time-barred, as observed in 1956, by the UN Secretary General, Dag Hammarskjold, who clarified the important principle that 'the UN decision is valid until it has been invalidated by the organ which took it.'

The UN Trusteeship Option

Generally, this option proposes that Kashmir should be placed under UN Trusteeship and then plebiscite may be held for the final resolution of the dispute. It is argued that this will provide a face-saving for India, and will also give Kashmiris, on both sides of the Line of Control, enough time to come up with a joint option. The JKLF Chairman, Ammanullah Khan in December 1993, proposed: (1) complete, simultaneous withdrawal of Indian and Pakistani troops and civil administration, non-Kashmiri personnel from Jammu and Kashmir; (2) the reunification of Indian and Pakistani-controlled parts of Kashmir; (3) placement of the State under UN control for five to ten years; and (4) holding of a plebiscite. Well-known Pakistani economist, the late Dr. Mahbubul Haq, in an interview he gave to an Urdu Weekly *Hurmat,* in 1994, proposed that only the Kashmir Valley be placed under UN Trusteeship for ten years and then plebiscite be held in the Kashmir Valley.

As India regards Occupied Kashmir as its integral part, it is obvious that it will never voluntarily agree to the placing of the State, or the Kashmir Valley under UN trusteeship. *Secondly,* both the above trusteeship options support the plebiscite option under the UN auspices, an option that has been rejected by India even though in the early years of the dispute India committed itself to holding of the plebiscite.

As regards Pakistan and the Kashmiris, since the above proposals support a UN role and the option of plebiscite, in view of the already existing UN resolutions which provide the plebiscite option under UN auspices, the above proposal would mean unnecessarily prolonging the solution beyond five or ten years. Moreover, according to Article 76 of Chapter XII of the UN Charter one of the basic objectives of the trusteeship system is 'to promote the political, economic, social, and educational advancement of the inhabitants of the trust territories, and their progressive development towards self-government or independence, as may be appropriate to the particular circumstances of each territory and its peoples...' The case of Jammu and Kashmir does not require placement under UN trusteeship as the Kashmiris have, over the years, demonstrated their political will by waging an indigenous movement in Occupied Kashmir for their right of self-determination, underscoring the fact that their preferred option is self-determination.

The Partition Option

Regarding the option of the partition of Jammu and Kashmir, this has largely been an academic debate and various scholars have suggested different proposals. The *first* is a division-related option for Jammu and Kashmir, based on the holding of regional plebiscites. This proposal was first given by UN Representative, Sir Owen Dixon, in his report of 1950-51. Called the 'Dixon Report', it proposed the idea of holding regional plebiscites, instead of a general plebiscite as proposed in the UN resolutions. The Owen Dixon Plan proposed the division of the State of Jammu and Kashmir into four main regions: Jammu, Ladakh, the Vale of Kashmir including Muzaffarabad, and Gilgit-Baltistan. According to his plan the district of Poonch was to remain with Pakistan. He proposed that of the four regions, Jammu and Ladakh should go uncontested to India and the Northern Areas to Pakistan. He concluded that in the Valley a plebiscite might be held to decide about its future. Pakistan, did not outrightly reject the proposal, but was in favour of a general plebiscite in the whole of Jammu and Kashmir. India on the other hand regarded Jammu and Kashmir as a unit of the Indian Federation and thus was not in favour of any regional plebiscite.

The second partition proposal is an option based on a 'Trieste-type' solution. The Trieste issue, between Italy and Yugoslavia, arose as a result of the two World Wars. After World War I, Trieste and the adjoining areas, including the whole valley of the Adige river and Istria, went to Italy, but in 1945 it was claimed by Yugoslavia on the grounds that Italy was guilty of aggression against Yugoslavia. However, Trieste and its environs and the Gorzia region to the northwest (Zone A) remained under Anglo-

American control and the southern portion (Zone B) was under the control of the Yugoslav troops. Finally, in 1954, Italy and Yugoslavia agreed to a partition and Zone A (including Trieste) was given to Italy and Zone B to Yugoslavia. Italy agreed to maintain a free port at Trieste. Later, the agreement was given a *de jure* status by the 1975 Treaty of Osimo between Italy and Yugoslavia.

The 'Trieste'-type option for Jammu and Kashmir proposes that the Valley along with some adjoining parts of Jammu and the Pakistani side of Kashmir (Azad Kashmir), be made an autonomous units, under India and Pakistan, respectively. The LoC would be a soft border between the two autonomous units. The remaining areas on both sides of the LoC may be merged with India and Pakistan, respectively.

India and Pakistan would be required to withdraw their forces under UN supervision. Again, this proposal lacks viability, as it does not address either the genesis of the dispute, nor the complexities that have accumulated since then to date.

The struggle in Jammu and Kashmir is not for autonomy of any one region but for the right of self-determination to be expressed by the Kashmiris, as granted to them under UN resolutions. Also, India and Pakistan being parties to the dispute will continue to have a clash of interests in the proposed autonomous regions; therefore, this would certainly not result in any stability in the region. Moreover, the option implies that the existing Line of Control (LoC) may serve as the line of division. The LoC remains the UN-recognised ceasefire line (CFL) and was not drawn with any basis for serving as a permanent border, but with the intention of bringing about cessation of military hostilities.

The third partition proposal considers the conversion of the Line of Control (LoC) into an international border. This means maintenance of the prevailing *status quo*. This option is in principle supported by India. If it were accepted, India would take additional advantage by then propagating that it had conceded Indian territory to Pakistan and would try to emerge as a peacemaker in the region. As assessed by Robert Wirsing, 'by asserting the primacy of actual military *control* over punitive legal *entitlement*, it tacitly acknowledges India's dominant political standing in the region. By requiring Pakistan to relinquish its claim of the coveted Valley of Kashmir and the Kashmiri separatists their claim of independence, while at the same time entailing little or no detachment from India of territories now in its possession, it leaves existing political and economic arrangements essentially undisturbed. Thus, of the several conceivable forms of partition, it is clearly among the most generous to India.'

However, the 'the LoC as a border' option has to take into account the fact that the LoC is merely a ceasefire line, as well as take stock of the struggle for the right of self-determination that is going on in the Indian-held Kashmir. Moreover, Kashmiris do not recognise the LoC. Prof. Mrs. Shamim Shawl, a Kashmiri scholar from Srinagar, has argued that 'the proposal of division is in contravention of the basic principle that Jammu and Kashmir is an indivisible entity. It also violates the fundamental fact that the Kashmir problem is basically the problem of the people of Jammu and Kashmir. It is not a bilateral problem between India and Pakistan. Nor is it a territorial dispute.' Secondly, the present LoC is an altered ceasefire line, whereby India acquired territory through military aggression in 1971. Therefore, accepting LoC would mean legitimising Indian military aggression. Thirdly, the LoC as accepted by both Pakistan and India at Simla in 1972 does not exist anymore. Indian incursion into Siachen in 1984 has destroyed the sanctity of the ceasefire line.

Fourthly, some Western scholars have proposed the partition of Kashmir along ethnic/cultural, religious, and linguistic lines. For example the *Kashmir Study Group,* a US-based group comprising academics and diplomats from various countries as members, has made various proposals along these lines in its report entitled, *Kashmir: A Way Forward* (September 1999). The proposals suggested are as follows:

(a) Two hypothetical sovereign entities, self-governing in all aspects, established on both sides of the Line of Control on cultural and linguistic grounds. According to the study, 'On the Indian side of the LOC every tahsil in Kashmir proper and in Doda district in Jammu, and Gool Gulab Ghar tahsil in Udhampur district in Jammu would

seek incorporation in the proposed state. All these areas are imbued with "Kashmiriyat" or interact with Kashmiri speaking people. On the Pakistani side it is conceivable that the whole of Azad Kashmir would opt to have a sovereign status. This is predominantly Punjabi-speaking, wholly Muslim area';

(b) A new sovereign state on the Indian side of LoC with no territorial exchange between India and Pakistan. The state would include 'within its maximum potential area the whole of Kashmir proper as well as adjoining areas in which Kashmiri is either the majority language or that of a plurality of the population';

(c) Desirable territorial changes along and beyond the Line of Control in Jammu and Kashmir. Viewing that 'LoC is dysfunctional and has been violated innumerable times', it proposes that a new state be created with territorial exchanges between India and Pakistan. However, it proposes that Pakistan gives almost twice as much area (7,366 sq. km) to India, than India ceding territory (4,501 sq. km) to Pakistan. The rationale given for such an exchange is ' overall, the territorial adjustments should not be excessively disruptive of the established order and yet should appear significant and be of such a nature as to allow all parties to claim a victory.'

The above proposals are again not viable solutions, as they tend to complicate the situation in Jammu and Kashmir and result in a further division of the region, rather than leading to a stable solution. Moreover, the 'Kashmir Study Group's' proposals make no provision for the right of self-determination of the people of Kashmir to which presently a military struggle is underway by the Kashmiris in Indian-occupied Kashmir.

The Independence Option

An option gradually evolved as a result of the impasse on the Kashmir issue is that of independence, generally known as the 'Third Option'. Under this option, the pre-Partition status of the Jammu and Kashmir State is to be restored and an independent state established. The proposal is mainly advocated by the JKLF. Its Chairman, Amanullah Khan, in one of his articles says, 'the future independent Kashmir is to be neutral, like Switzerland, with friendly and trade relations with all its neighbours.'

According to Amanullah Khan's proposal, 'Independent Kashmir is to consist of five federating units: Kashmir Valley, Jammu province, Ladakh, Azad Kashmir and Gilgit-Baltistan, each enjoying considerable internal autonomy, having its own elected provincial government. At the centre there will be a bicameral parliament.'

He further says, 'the re-unification and independence of the state can be brought about without making any drastic changes in the existing socio-economic, political and administrative structures of any of the present three units i.e. Indian occupied areas, Azad Kashmir and Gilgit-Baltistan.'

According to Indian scholars 'independence, either for part or all of J&K, is equally unrealistic.

They maintain that although an artificial product of war, the Line of Control does follow a rough and ready ethno-cultural divide in some measure.

Further, "self-determination" within the two parts of J&K could result in the Balkanisation of a mosaic put together by history, with every new 'self-determined' minority being assailed for a newly-created majoritarianism, which lesser minorities refuse to accept. Such an unravelling would be a recipe for strife, insecurity, and destabilisation of the region.'

The option for an independent Jammu and Kashmir state does not seem to be a viable solution, as the State would be land-locked and, therefore, permanently dependent on its neighbours. For India the proposition would be unacceptable because it could lead to a similar unravelling in other areas where separatist movements are going on in India.

As regards Pakistan, the 'third option' can be advantageous. An independent Jammu and Kashmir state would have a preference for good relations with a neighbour that has consistently extended its support to the principles of self-determination. Pakistan's position on the 'third option' has been that it should not confound the existent problems further, and, therefore, it stresses the need to address the issue in the light of the Security Council Resolutions, as a first step in the resolution of the dispute.

The Irish Model

Recently, various scholars have suggested the Irish model, based on the 'Good Friday Agreement' signed in April 1998 between the Governments of the United Kingdom of Great Britain and Northern Ireland and the Government of Ireland, as a possible option for resolving the Kashmir dispute between India and Pakistan.

The main features of the 'Good Friday Agreement' are: (a) it recognises the consent principle: that change in the status of Northern Ireland can only come about with the consent of the majority of its people. It acknowledges that while a substantial minority in the North and a majority on the island want a united Ireland, the majority in the North currently wishes to maintain the Union. However, it says that if that situation changes, there is a binding obligation on both governments to give effect to whatever wish the people of the North express; (b) it recognises 'the birthright of all the people of Northern Ireland' to identify themselves and be accepted as Irish, British or both; (c) it proposes concrete legislative and constitutional changes; such as, the Government of Ireland Act, claiming British jurisdiction over all of Ireland is to be replaced, future polls in the North on its status are to be held on the order of the Secretary of State for Northern Ireland. Such polls must be at least seven years apart; (d) it proposes a 108-member Assembly elected by proportional representation; (e) it establishes a North-South Ministerial Council under legislation at Westminister and the Oireachtas, to bring together ministers from the North and the Republic; (f) it establishes a British-Irish Council consisting of representatives of the British and Irish Governments, devolved in situations in Northern Ireland, Scotland and Wales, the Isle of Man and the Channel Islands; (g) it establishes a new British-Irish Conference; (h) reaffirms commitment to the total disarmament of all paramilitary organisations, and confirms intention to work constructively with the Independent Commission on Decommissioning; and, (i) establishes an independent commission to make recommendations for future policing arrangements in the North.

Based on the Irish model, some Indian scholars have made suggestions supporting autonomy for various regions of Jammu and Kashmir. For example, Amit A. Pandya, an Indian scholar, has proposed the following steps: (1) An India-Pakistan commission to discuss boundary issues in Jammu and Kashmir, and to engage in joint monitoring of the LOC; (2) Phased demilitarisation at the LOC, contingent first on substantial cessation of 'cross-border' terrorism; (3) Three-way (Indian, Pakistani, Kashmiri) commission on internal law and order. Kashmiris to be chosen from Pakistan-occupied Azad Kashmir and all Indian-occupied segments—Valley, Jammu and Ladakh. (4) Indian and Pakistani commitments to proceed with a scheme of local government reform and strengthening of local institutions and local autonomy in respective areas of Kashmir. (5) Issue-specific consultative bodies (water, power, tourism, finance) comprising such local units, and Indian Jammu & Kashmir State and Azad Kashmir governments. (6) Regularly scheduled and publicity-free consultative mechanism for Indian government's talks with all parties, and with non-party civil society institutions, within Indian Kashmir on political issues. (7) Corresponding mechanism for Azad Kashmir. (8) Consultative mechanism for talks among all parties on ethnic and religious minority protections. (9) Consultative mechanism for dialogue between these processes on the Indian and Pakistani side of the LOC. (10) Indian commitment to allow free access, consistent with security requirements, to independent and credible Indian human rights monitoring organizations, and to Indian, and Pakistani press. Corresponding commitment by Pakistan for Azad Kashmir.

Another Indian scholar, Professor Sumantra Bose, basing his suggestions on the Irish model proposes three dimensions. *Dimension one: the New Delhi-Islamabad axis,* involving the 'establishment of a permanent India-Pakistan Intergovernmental Conference to promote the harmonious and mutually beneficial development of the totality of relationships between the two countries.' As suggested by Professor Bose, this body is to be chaired by the respective prime ministers, and its twice-yearly meetings to be rotated between Indian and Pakistani cities. *Dimension two: the New Delhi-Srinagar and Islamabad-Muzaffarabad axis,* here the 'objective in Kashmir would be the gradual, incremental normalisation of politics within Kashmir in both Indian-and Pakistani-controlled zones, and the devising and implementation of political frameworks which can foster a working degree of internal accommodation and cooperation between the representatives of communities holding radically different basic political allegiances.' *Dimension three: the Srinagar-Muzaffarabad axis,* proposes 'along with the progressive normalisation of the overall framework of India-Pakistan relations and the gradual normalisation of life and politics in both sides of the Kashmir border', that there is greater need to make the border porous. He further suggests 'the establishment of a cross-border Jammu and Kashmir Council for Cooperation, with representatives from inclusive, elected and autonomous governments from both sides of the line of control.'

These Indian proposals, selectively use the Irish model, but basically support autonomy for the regions of Jammu and Kashmir under the supervision of India and Pakistan. The central aspects focusing on self-determination and total disarmament after implementation of the agreement are ignored. The Indian proposals are similar to the idea of a condominium with dominant Indian influence. Also, the LoC has been proposed as the dividing line and a soft border. This is against the genesis of the Kashmir dispute, which is not for greater autonomy or 'self-government', as proposed, but for the right of self-determination to be expressed by the Kashmiris. However, as Dr. Mazari has suggested, it is the central aspects of the Irish model, which are relevant in case of the Kashmir dispute and could be used as guiding principles for a resolution of the conflict. For instance the underlying principle is *recognition of the right of the people as of Northern Ireland* to choose their political future through a referendum. Also, the principle of deweaponisation is linked to it, as following the implementation of the Agreement.

INDIA AND PAKISTAN: ON THE NUCLEAR THRESHOLD

This briefing book contains material from the National Security Archive's project on U.S. policy toward South Asia, which is documenting nuclear developments in India and Pakistan from the 1950s to the present. The archive is collecting U.S. government records that illustrate American policies and perspectives. Information is being collected from the National Archives and the presidential libraries, and through Freedom of Information Act (FOIA) and Mandatory Review requests, used to obtain the declassification of now-secret materials. A selective and focused collection of documents will be made available to researchers.

The project is creating a comprehensive history of nuclear developments in South Asia, including weapons programs in India and Pakistan, as well as international efforts to curtail proliferation in the region. Information about factors that influenced nuclear issues, such as the unresolved enmity between India and Pakistan, and India's perception of China as a security threat, will also be incorporated. The U.S. has generally opposed nuclear proliferation in South Asia, while seeking to preserve good relations with both India and Pakistan. At times, however, its commitment has been questioned, because it has seemed to subordinate nonproliferation policy to other concerns. During the Soviet occupation of Afghanistan, for instance, the U.S. provided massive levels of economic and military aid to its ally, Pakistan. The assistance was widely criticized, because Pakistan was demonstrably importing nuclear-related material, from China and other nations. Few doubted that it was engaged in an active nuclear weapons development program.

China's role as a leading provider of sensitive technology to Pakistan has repeatedly strained U.S.-China relations, and has complicated efforts to expand U.S.-China trade. The Archive's South Asia project is using the FOIA to seek the declassification of documents discussing this issue, and other contemporary and controversial topics. Materials collected for this project will, of course, reflect a U.S. perspective. As noted, nonproliferation policy is influenced by other concerns, including competition among the major powers. The Archive's efforts are directed toward enhancing understanding of U.S. decisions and the issues that influenced policy formulation. The analyst for the South Asia nuclear project is Joyce Battle, who prepared this briefing book. She is also the analyst for the Archive's documentation projects on the Persian Gulf and U.S. policy toward Iraq. Materials collected for the latter project were published in a document set, Iraqgate: Saddam Hussein, U.S. Policy and the Prelude to the Persian Gulf War, 1980-1994.

Briefing Book Documents

The documents in the briefing book date from 1961 to 1983. In 1961, India had an advanced civilian nuclear program, while Pakistan's was in its early stages. In 1983, nine years had elapsed since India's explosion of a nuclear device, and Pakistan's nuclear weapons program was well under way. During the early 1960s, India under Prime Minister Jawaharlal Nehru strongly advocated global disarmament, but was apprehensive about China's nuclear weapons program. India's concern increased following its October 1962 territorial war with China. The stakes were raised by China's first nuclear weapons test in October 1964. Many observers thought it increasingly likely that India would respond to China's actions by seeking its own weapons capability. War with Pakistan in 1965 further alarmed India: it was angered by China's outspoken support for Pakistan during the conflict, and disappointed by what it viewed as insufficient Western attention to its security needs. The U.S. considered various options that might dissuade India from developing nuclear weapons, including scientific cooperation aimed at enhancing India's national prestige. It also joined in cooperative arrangements with both India and Pakistan to monitor nuclear and missile developments in China and the Soviet Union. India, for its part, launched a campaign seeking security guarantees to shield it from Chinese nuclear attack, arguing that such assurances might make a nuclear weapons program of its own unnecessary. Various options were proposed: U.S. guarantees, joint U.S.-Soviet guarantees, guarantees from all the nuclear states, British guarantees, or guarantees in conjunction with the nuclear nonproliferation treaty, then being negotiated. U.S. policy makers seriously considered these proposals, although some doubted that they would deter India from developing a bomb.

The Embassy in New Delhi viewed India's overtures sympathetically, while the Defence Department opposed any commitment to India that would alienate Pakistan, a U.S. military ally. In 1967, both President Lyndon Johnson and Defence Secretary Robert McNamara supported the concept of guarantees during meetings with a visiting Indian representative.

Later that year, U.S. and Soviet officials were still discussing security guarantees, hoping to induce India to sign the nuclear nonproliferation treaty. No agreement was ever reached, however, in part because India itself concluded that such commitments would not guarantee its security in the event of actual nuclear conflict. In May 1974, India tested a nuclear device, although it called the event a "peaceful nuclear explosion."

Its terminology did not forestall censure, both within the international community and from domestic critics.

The test had serious consequences: India lost much of the foreign technical assistance that had till then sustained its civilian nuclear program.

A Pakistani reaction to India's test of a nuclear explosive was predicted, and confirmed within a few years. By the mid-1970s, intelligence reports indicated that Pakistan had an active nuclear weapons program, and in 1983 the State Department noted that it had "unambiguous evidence" of this fact. Documents in this briefing book illuminate aspects of the internal debate among U.S. officials, as they attempted to formulate effective policies toward nuclear proliferation in South Asia while protecting sometimes conflicting interests and objectives.

Nuclear Threat Reduction in India and Pakistan

The Carnegie Endowment for International Peace (CEIP) published a draft report, 'Universal Compliance: A Strategy for Nuclear Security', in June 2004. The report proposes a strategic blueprint for US leadership to rethink international nuclear nonproliferation and global nuclear security. In this report, the recommended measures for nuclear risk reduction between India and Pakistan include:

o Establishment of national risk reduction centres in both countries to administer agreed upon confidence-building measures.

- o Acommitment not to develop, produce, and use 'tactical' nuclear weapons.
- o Agreement not to flight-test missiles in the direction of the other country.
- o Agreement to flight-test missiles only from designated test ranges.
- o Provision of advance notification of the movement of missiles for training purposes.

The Henry L. Stimson Centre's report, 'Reducing Nuclear Dangers in South Asia', argues that: "The stability-instability paradox that was formulated in the West to characterise the dangers of nuclear deterrence is alive and well in South Asia. This paradox holds that, while offsetting nuclear capabilities might indeed prevent a full-blown conventional or nuclear war, the presence of these fearsome weapons could also encourage the use of violence at lower levels in the expectation that escalation would be contained by a mutual desire to avoid the nuclear threshold." And that, "Kashmir has been inflamed since the advent of covert nuclear capabilities on the subcontinent, and tensions have grown even more pronounced with the demonstration of overt nuclear capabilities in 1998. The region is now experiencing crises with greater frequency and severity."

The report includes extensive deliberations during two workshops, November 14-18, 2002, and May 20-23, 2003, with participants from the US, India and Pakistan, convened by the Stimson Centre to discuss escalation control and scenarios that could lead to crossing of the nuclear threshold. It provides the following 'doable' steps in the near term:

- o Establishment of national risk reduction centresto serve as focal points for the administration of confidence-building measures.
- o Missile-related measures to formalise and properly implement the agreement concerning prior notification of missile launches; to formalise and extend the time-line for such notifications; to forego missile flight tests in the direction of the other country; to flight test missiles only

from designated test ranges; and to provide advance notification of the movement of missiles for training purposes.

- o Clarifying terminology or developing common terminology on nuclear-related programmes, deployment, and doctrine could reduce misunderstanding and increase crisis stability.
- o Leadership declarations affirming responsible nuclear stewardshipcould help defuse nuclear dangers and facilitate an improvement in bilateral relations.
- o Increased awareness of nuclear dangers, particularly with regard to the possible acquisition of nuclear materials by terrorist groups, would be advisable.

In the Stimson Centre's report, the proposals collected in the workshops on escalation control are grouped in five categories: improving bilateral relations; nuclear risk reduction and strategic restraint; safety and security measures; and, improving intelligence through communication.

Both the reports, by CEIP and the Stimson Centre, have this presumption that 'deterrence' may not work between India and Pakistan as similar to the Cold War experience. Such assumptions are not completely invalid for the two countries did resort to nuclear rhetoric during the 1999 Kargil conflict and indulged in 'nuclear signalling' during the period of crisis in 2001-2. In addition, the absence of a doctrine without no-first-use policy and repeated calls from the Pakistani side to lower the threshold could have a certain bearing on the thinking of Western analysts. Already, the strategic debate had reached a slightly higher level than was normally prevalent in the subcontinent when the Indian Army Chief stated that a limited war with Pakistan is possible.

For any future war in the subcontinent, the two most likely scenarios discussed in the Cooperative Monitoring Centre Occasional Paper of Sandia National Laboratories, are: a breakdown along the common border in Kashmir, and failure of nuclear policy. The authors propose an alternative approach through which India and Pakistan can begin to cooperate in managing their common border to prevent a breakdown. The ultimate concern in the report about the existence of nuclear weapons is the possibility of their use in a time of conflict. The following are the enumerations in the Cooperative Monitoring Centre Occasional Paper that focuses on the monitoring of nuclear safety, security, and stability:

- o The ability to assess the current operational and deployment status of nuclear weapons is perhaps the most critical factor in near-term crisis prevention.
- o Developing measures to prevent escalation.
- o National decisions to include both technical and procedural mechanisms to restrict use of weapons and delivery systems will permit more time to attempt diplomatic solutions to conflict before initiating weapons use.
- o Another element of nuclear stability is determining the readiness of launch systems. There may be a number of indicators associated with launcher alert status. These include: Flight parameters loaded, other software updates (if appropriate); Vehicle fuelled (missile or aircraft); Crews readied; Delivery vehicle in launch location (moved to launch point); Transporter system in ready position (e.g., transporter erector launcher [TEL] in raised launch position); Weapon armed. While most of these indicators of launch preparation are difficult to monitor, some, such as missile fuelling and launcher movements, might be monitored through electronic sensors.
- o There is the possibility of use through miscalculation or misinterpretation.
- o Sharing information on any of the concerns for safety, security or accident will require an infrastructure of capabilities and procedures. These include methods for providing timely, reliable, secure, accurate, and authenticated communications.
- o Ensuring safety of nuclear weapons and materials will primarily be a state responsibility because of the highly classified nature of most safety issues. These issues involve detailed design, as well as material and handling details. An expanded mission for hotlines between the Directors-

General of Military Operations and between the Heads of State might be established to address this critical issue.

Acknowledging the fact that only the Indian and Pakistani governments can decide whether and on what basis, to establish new risk reduction measures, the 'Working Group Report of the Centre for Strategic and International Studies (CSIS)' recommends the following steps for nuclear risk reduction:

- o A new communications mechanism-nuclear risk reduction centres (NRRCs) in India and Pakistan-should be established to complement existing bilateral channels.
- o The main functions of the NRRCs would be to provide each party a dedicated, secure means of: (a) notifying the other side about activities or events on its territory that might be wrongly perceived or misinterpreted that could lead to conflict, (b) sharing information that the two countries are obliged to exchange under existing security agreements, and (c) seeking and receiving clarifications about ambiguous events on the other' sterritory. Other functions could include the conduct of joint exercises of certain NRRC notification procedures, technical back-up during crises, and support for consultations on the implementation of existing confidence-building measures (CBMs).
- o Adequate infrastructure already exists in South Asia to support a wide range of secure communication options, including data, voice, video, or a combination of these.

  The approximate cost for a dedicated cable permitting teletype and voice communication would be US$10,000-50,000 annually. For a dedicated satellite channel permitting teletype, voice, and video, the annual cost would be roughly US$560,000.
- o The centres would operate on a continuous, round-the-clock basis. Written messages using agreed formats would be the norm, although voice and video capability would also be desirable. It would be the prerogative of each government to decide where it would institutionally house its NRRC and to determine how its NRRC would relate

to other government organisations. The Indian and Pakistani solutions to these questions need not be symmetrical.

The Working Group Report concluded, that "the circumstances in South Asia today are very different from the circumstances surrounding the current US-Russian relationship and the relationship that existed when the US-Soviet Centres were brought into being. To tailor a new communications mechanism to the needs of South Asia, the mechanism could appropriately take on a wider range of functions than the US and Russian Centres."

Rodney W.Jones assumes that there lies intense political conflict over Kashmir and that the escalation in South Asia has the potential of becoming a nuclear war. In one of the papers presented during the fourth nuclear stability roundtable during March 12-13, 2002, in Washington on 'Military Asymmetry and Instability in Emerging Nuclear States: India and Pakistan,' he suggests the following conditions of nuclear stability in the region:

o High nuclear threshold (strong conventional defence)

o Secure second strike capabilities (robust C4I)

o Rough parity in size and defence space

o Neither falling behind the other's first strike edge (good early warning?) Supposing that "nuclear deterrence might provide the security that allows a general improvement in security relations" in South Asia, the UNIDR (United Nations Institute for Disarmament Research) research paper depicts various aspects of nuclear confidence-building measures between India and Pakistan. Commenting on the current conflict situation between the two countries, the authors of the paper subscribe to developing CBMs in connection with the 'central issue-Kashmir'. An interim suggestion is made to work on the possibilities of addressing the 'central sore-cross-border terror raids' from Pakistan.

With regard to nuclear CBMs, according to the UNIDR paper, India and Pakistan should share the development of respective nuclear doctrines and security concepts to have clarity over 'red lines'; develop mechanisms on notification of ballistic and cruise missile tests; create nuclear risk reduction centres with robust safety systems to deal with the issues of accidental or unauthorised use; and install a secure and dedicated line of communication including safe command and control systems between the national authorities (the nature or constitution of national authority remains undefined). The paper categorically puts the 'Kashmir issue' to be discussed as in the final stages of CBMs between the two countries.

The UNIDR study concludes that the two countries should seize the ripe moment (that has begun since the two countries agreed to peace talks during the sidelines of the SAARC summit in January 2004) in the context of possibility of conflict.

"Any future terrorist incident might provoke India into punitive action, which in the worst case might lead to uncontrolled or accidental responses, all the way to a nuclear exchange. This suggests that, although the nuclear aspects will have to be part of the general discussions on security, it might also be worth considering whether they can be made separable, in case the moment passes too quickly."

The aspect of geographical proximity of the two countries is also discussed in one of the reports dealing with nuclear threat reduction measures. Based on some hypothetical South Asian launch point-target combinations, the missile travel time between India and Pakistan is estimated between 8 to 13 minutes.

Taking account of the danger of false alarms and miscalculations, the Pugwash Discussion Paper of 2002 suggests that a posture of De-alert (most basic measures would be to keep the weapons de-mated from delivery systems; use of locking devices), and installation of best available safety measures into the weapons, like use of Insensitive High Explosive (IHE) and fire-resistant pits would significantly reduce the risk of inadvertent or unauthorised use of weapons.

From the above discussed strategic policy recommendations, there emerge two sets of proposals that could draw attention of the diplomats and strategic planners of India and Pakistan. In the first set, one can identify mechanisms for escalation control and nuclear force management within each state. The second set includes possible measures of nuclear CBMs by the two countries to work towards long lasting stability in the region.

"TERRITORIAL DISPUTE" IN KASHMIR DISPUTE

It is a "territorial dispute" only in the sense that the State of Jammu and Kashmir is disputed territory and is so recognized internationally. But the expression can be misleading. For it usually suggested contentious claims of two states to a territory, one party basing its claim on the validity of a de facto or de jure boundary demarcation and the other challenging it. That is why territorial disputes are hardly distinguishable from border disputes, amenable to solution through bilateral agreement, judicial determination or, more often, arbitration.

Kashmir is a case qualitatively different from border disputes. Here the territory involved is a whole country, a country larger than many member states of the United Nations, a country larger the major part of which has existed for more than a millennium as a sovereign political entity on its own, a country whose distinct physical environment, history and culture have shaped its people's individuality. Here the matter is not one of placing a few hundred square miles on one side or the other of an international frontier and thus settling a boundary conflict. It is a matter of the disposition of a country through the same process by which the two contestants, the Indian Union and Pakistan themselves emerged as independent states - the process of establishing sovereignties on the basis of popular consent. As long as the Kashmir dispute remains unresolved, the agenda of the independence of the South Asian subcontinent remains unfinished.

If this support had really rested on, and reflected, popular sentiment, then the history of the Kashmir dispute would have been entirely different. In that case, India would have been not merely willing but eager to have the United Nations conduct a plebiscite in Kashmir so that the accession would be speedily ratified and India's position vindicated for good. All that India would have required would have been sufficient safeguards against a breach of the Ceasefire Line or eruption of violence during the period of the plebiscite. These would have been easily obtained. Indeed, they were provided for in the plan drawn by the United Nations Commission for India and Pakistan (UNCIP). With a Plebiscite Administrator appointed by the United Nations and inducted into office, the freedom of the voters from coercion and intimidation would have been assured. Pakistan would have had no means to exert any pressure whatsoever on the voters nor would it have chosen to draw overwhelming international censure for disrupting the plebiscite process. If there has been popular support in Kashmir for joining India, the dispute over Kashmir would have lasted for a year or so at most. It would have dissolved long ago.

Let us here contrast the cases of Hyderabad, Junagarh and Goa - three areas that India annexed through what it called (a phrase reminiscent of Nazi ideology) "police action". In none of these cases did India have to bring in the resounding names of a local political organization or leader to justify the annexations. Yet, leader or no leader, organization or no organization, the overwhelming majority of the people in these areas wished to be part of the Indian nation and, though a certain arrogance on India's part raised some eyebrows, world opinion recognized the fact and the incorporation of the these areas in India met with international acquiescence. Pakistan's complaints in the cases of Hyderabad and Junagarh and the protest of the United States over the invasion of Goa were storms of the teacup variety; the controversies subsided in short time.

The presentation by India of Sheikh Abdullah and his National Conference as the embodiment of mass approval for the entry of Indian troops into Kashmir has itself provided an eloquent commentary on the nature of India's claim to Kashmir. The same Sheikh Abdullah was dismissed as Prime Minister in 1953, kept in prison for years and charged with treason because he insisted on complete autonomy for the State and stressed repeatedly that the accession was provisional. At one time, in 1957, he sent a hand-written letter from jail t the Security Council denouncing the Indian position. The National Conference formed what was called the Plebiscite Front, which demanded that the issue of accession be referred to the people's vote. The fact that later in 1975 Sheikh Abdullah turned a somersault and, signing on the dotted line, became Chief Minister again is an indicator more of his personal character than of the strength or consistency of India's political position in Kashmir.

A glimpse into Kashmir's political history might be apposite here. Kashmir was unique among all the Princely States of India in organizing a political movement on its own in opposition to autocracy.

This took the form of a mass agitation in 1931, which a year later, gave birth to the Muslim Conference. Sheikh Abdullah was undoubtedly the hero the agitation and no one equalled his appeal to huge Kashmiri gatherings. He was at the peak of his popularity from 1931 to 1933. As early as 1934, however, a streak of opportunism in him became visible when he stayed away from an agitation directed by his more steadfast and less theatrical colleague, Ghulam Abbas, against the limitation of the franchise for the legislative assembly and the restriction of the assembly's powers. From that time onwards, although he retained his unsurpassed capacity to arouse the emotions of the masses, his political position zigzagged and his popularity began to wane. When he succeeded in converting the Muslim Conference into the National Conference, he attracted the patronage of Jawaharlal Nehru, enlisted the support of the great propaganda machine run by the Indian Congress, gained some glitter in non-Kashmiri eyes but lost the cohesiveness of his Kashmiri following. Within a short period, the co-architect of the National Conference, Prem Nath Bazaz (Hindu) and the former President of Muslim Conference - both expressed disillusionment about Abdullah's integrity. The former established his own party and the latter revived the Muslim Conference. Non-Muslims regarded Abdullah as a Muslim chauvinist (what is called 'communalist' in India) and Muslims suspected that he had struck some kind of a deal with the Dogra regime despite its practice of open discrimination against the Muslims. Both were right not because Abdullah was taking the middle position but because he easily swung from one extreme to the other.

Two other things affected Abdullah's public standing. First, he betrayed pronounced fascist proclivities and frequently resorted to strong-arm methods in bullying his opponents. This became a scandal in the late 1930s and the early 1940s; he had to suffer physical reprisal for his hooliganism in places like Poonch and Rajauri. Second, while still employing his emotive rhetoric, he veered more and more towards cooperation with the Maharaja's autocratic regime. As if this was not enough, he broke the pledge he had made that he would not side with the Indian Congress against the Muslim League (the two major parties in British India).

In an attempt to recapture his following among Muslims, especially the intelligentsia, Abdullah joined prominently in the jubilant reception accorded to M.A. Jinnah on his visit to Kashmir in 1944. Jinnah tried to reconcile Abdullah and Abbas and put the question squarely to Abdullah. "How much significant support have you obtained from Hindus for the objectives of the National Conference?" When Abdullah could cite only the names of a few individuals, Jinnah queried, "The what is the point of dividing the Muslims into two camps, the Muslim Conference and the National Conference?" Abdullah thought he had a answer to that. "But the National Conference is in reality the Muslim Conference in a better guise," he said. Came back the forthright rebuke, "That means you are committing a fraud on Hindus." This left Abdullah only with one course: vituperative speeches against "outsiders" like Jinnah. (In private remarks, he, however, disowned the speeches.) This was the nadir of Abdullah's position in Kashmir.

When he felt the ground slipping from under his feet, Abdullah sought the counsel of a group of very able communists from Lahore. They drafted the manifesto called 'New Kashmir' for him in 1944 and then produced a most impressive declaration about the sale deed miscalled the Treaty of Amritsar to which the Maharaja owed his title to Kashmir. Armed with this and a stirring slogan, Abdullah launched his 'Quit Kashmir' campaign against the Maharaja in May 1946. He was jailed on a charge of sedition and Jawaharlal Nehru felt impelled to enter the fray. Considerable publicity was generated as a result, but apart from small groups (mostly the cadres of the National Conference, better-trained than those of the Muslim Conference) the masses, both Muslim and Hindu, stood aloof. The Maharaja demonstrated his triumph by arranging to be driven in a spectacular motorcade through the main street of Srinagar on his birthday in September. It was not the respect and sympathy for the Maharaja on the part of the great Muslim majority but the distrust of Sheikh Abdullah that made this possible. The wrong medium had eclipsed the right message.

After the partition of British India in August 1947, Abdullah wrote letters to his friends from jail recommending Kashmir's accession to India, making sure that the letters would be seen by the Maharaja's officials. This reinforced the assurances that the Maharaja had received from the leaders of the Indian Congress, including Mohandas Gandhi, that Abdullah would help him to join India. Abdullah was granted "royal clemency" and released from jail in return for colluding with the Maharaja in maneuvering accession to India. He flew immediately to Delhi to confer with the Indian leaders, as did the Maharaja's courtiers. Abbas, the leader of the Muslim Conference, languished in jail.

At the time, Abdullah's constituency in Kashmir, in the estimate of impartial observers, had shrunk to a few districts of Srinagar. That, in essence, was the reality of the popular backing for India establishing sovereignty over Kashmir. The estimate, of course, was not shared by Jawaharlal Nehru, nor perhaps by Gandhi, but when doubts began to grow in Delhi whether Abdullah's presumed popularity would swing the vote in India's favour, did India begin to wriggle out of its pledge to a plebiscite. The doubts about success turned to certainty of defeat when Abdullah, had to be ousted as Prime Minister and jailed in 1953. From that time, Indian policy was set dead against any ascertainment of the wishes of the people of Kashmir on the accession issue. Nehru did make a promise to the Prime Minister of Pakistan to cooperate in the holding of a plebiscite by April 1954 but, as the ensuing correspondence between the two showed, it was done only to palliate an aroused public opinion in both Kashmir and Pakistan.

No invasion of one country by another encounters an immediate insurrection. There were no popular uprisings in the capitals of Western Europe when they witnessed the victorious march of the Nazi troops. Nor did the Soviet forces when they were triumphant, face mass upheavals and defiance in Eastern Europe. There was no immediate revolt in Kabul against the Soviet invasion of Afghanistan. Resistance against foreign occupation requires organization and takes time to develop.

If in Kashmir, India did succeed in dampening the sentiment of revolt for a number of years by co-opting the section of the people represented by the National Conference which was joined by a whole lot to careerists, it nor more belies the claim of popular loathing of Indian occupation than the existence of the Vichy regime belied French resistance to Nazi occupation. If Sheikh Abdullah who in 1947 supported India taking over Kashmir by force had been at one time the most popular leader in Kashmir, Marshall Petain, who capitulated before Hitler and cooperated with him, had been the most respected war hero of France. All occupation regimes find collaborationists in the occupied countries; there are Quislings and Lavals and Najibs in every society. Kashmir could not be in exception. There were some added circumstances in Kashmir.

First, simultaneously with sending its troops into Kashmir, India made a solemn declaration that the accession of Kashmir was provisional and subject to the people's verdict. She gave this solemn assurance to the people of Kashmir, to Pakistan, to Britain and to "the whole world", in Jawaharlal Nehru's words. This created the reasonable expectation in the mass mind that India's annexation of Kashmir was a temporary affair and would be reversed by a peaceful process. Arzi Ilhaq (temporary accession) became a common expression. A mass uprising seemed unnecessary.

Second, at the time of the entry of Indian troops, the leaders of the Muslim Conference were in jail or in exile from the Vale. The organizing force of resistance was dispersed.

Third, fighting ensued between the Indian army and the Azad Kashmir forces in extensive parts of the State. Though vastly outnumbered, ill equipped and poorly organized, and hence unable to reach Srinagar and Jammu, the two capitals, the Azad forces did hold some ground and, even before Pakistan provided them regular military support, they had prevented India from overrunning the whole State. Newspapers in India itself at the time reported a number of incidents of a few guerrillas holding at bay large companies of Indian troops with all their armour and air support. This along with the proceedings of the Security Council and the dispatch of a United Nations Commission in 1948, created the kind of expectancy that inhibits a people's revolt.

First, it is open to question who in Pakistan count on an insurgency in the Vale of Kashmir at the time. There are different versions, none wholly plausible. However, if anyone in authority did, his thinking must have been at the adolescent level. He must have thought that insurgencies are made like instant coffee; he must have lacked education in rebellions. Uprisings, as distinguished from acts of sabotage, rarely go with inter-state wars; when they do, they end in disaster. Of the first of these two lessons, the Vietnam War provides a good illustration: throughout that war, no uprising took place in Saigon. Of the second, the genuine Shiite uprising in Iraq at the time of the Persian Gulf War in 1991 has been another graphic example. Even when Saddam Hussein's retreating troops, waving white flags, were being bulldozed with the earth, he still had the means to reduce the rebellion to cinders.

If a state at war defeated but not yet admitting defeat, does not make a suitable target for rebellion, far less does an undefeated state. Indian troops would have to be forced by Pakistan's military offensive to begin a retreat from Karachi before a civilian uprising against the remnants of Indian authority and welcoming the entry of Pakistani forces could take place. This had nothing to do with passivity or docility in the Kashmiri character - that myth has been shattered now. It has everything to do with the dynamism of popular uprisings. They need their own impulse and are sustained by their own strategy; they abort if they lack native political guidance. To ignore this principle is to plan for failure.

Second, the situation in Kashmir in 1964-65 has been misrepresented in both Pakistan and India for opposite psychological reasons. India feels the compulsion to prove Kashmiri acquiescence in Indian occupation, Pakistan to account for the miscarriage of its plans. Neither acknowledges the fact that Kashmiris did rise on their own against Indian rule in 1964.

When Jawaharlal Nehru sent a senior intelligence official who was his confidant to Srinagar to make a report on the situation, the man returned and candidly said to him, "Prime Minister, from what I have seen, Kashmir is not a part of India."

Even Lal Bahadur Shastri, who had not yet become Prime Minister, remarked significantly after his visit to Kashmir that the situation would have to be resolved ultimately in accordance with the people's wishes. The agitation was intelligently directed by the indigenous Committee of Action set up in Srinagar. There is evidence that Nehru had accepted the need "radical rethinking" about India's policy with regard to both Kashmir and Pakistan.

Nehru's death at that delicate point, Sheikh Abdullah's trip abroad during which he met some world leaders, including Zhou En-Lai, his consequent re-imprisonment, Shastri's political inferiority when stepping into Nehru's shoes, the frequent military probing and exchanges across the Ceasefire Line, the worsening of Indian forces by Pakistani troops in the Rann of Kutch (distant from Kashmir), the crescendo of belligerency on both sides, and finally the entry of commandos from Azad Kashmir and Pakistan uncoordinated with a native plan for a guerrilla campaign - all tangled the plot and arrested its denouement.

Nevertheless, besides rendering help to commandos wherever physically possible in August 1965, Kashmiris hardly showed themselves as resigned to Indian occupation since the world media had their attention riveted on the fighting between India and Pakistan, non-military happenings in the Vale of Kashmir itself went rather unnoticed.

Still, a number of major western newspapers, including the New York Times carried stories about what was called "the children's revolt": young boys and girls showing defiance of Indian authority. It was then that the slogan (unacceptably abusive but betraying the people's exasperation) "Indian dogs, go home" gained currency in Srinagar and was blazoned by the letters I.D.G.O. painted on walls and pavements. There was not - there could not be, as we have seen - an organized revolt. Nor was there the quiescence that Indians like to believe and Pakistanis prefer to complain about.

It is no more unrealistic that it was to expect Algeria to cease to be a department of France, Namibia to be detached from South Africa or Estonia or Lithuania to become independent of the Soviet Union. France had ruled Algeria, South Africa had held Namibia and the Soviet Union had annexed Estonia and Lithuania for longer periods than the Indian Union has occupied Kashmir. What belongs to a State and cannot be pried loose from it is what feels itself to be part of that State, some discontent notwithstanding. Kashmir never felt itself to be part of India before 1947 and feels even less so after its forcible seizure by the Indian troops. The de-annexation process is inevitable in the post-colonial age. The only question is whether it is accomplished by armed struggle, resulting in a spiral of violence and counter-violence or through negotiation and/or other means of peaceful settlement. The choice always lies with the occupying power. Until now, India has pre-empted negotiation by its adamant assertion that the status of Kashmir is not negotiable.

Is this adamancy an insuperable obstacle, considering that it is backed by the military power of the Indian Union, one of the most formidable in the world? The question invites reflection. Even as recently as the mid-1980s, the idea of the liberation of Estonia and Lithuania was regarded as a pipe dream. So was the institution of majority rule in South Africa. The military and technological arsenal at the disposal of the Soviet Union was mightier than what the Indian Union possesses. The same could be said of the apartheid regime proportionately in the context of the South African subcontinent. Yet military power did not bring political strength to the Soviet Union nor immunize South African because the rest of the world did not bend its knee to it. It is the deference down by the West to India's military power that reinforces India's obduracy. It also weakens the liberal section of Indian opinion that would prefer a sensible and human policy with respect to Kashmir. Unwittingly, the West contributes to the depletion of the already small but the most promising resource in India's political society, the resource of self-criticism, and to the encouragement of that sanctimoniousness which the more thoughtful Indians regard as a bane of their country's attitudes in international affairs.

We have spoken of countries that were liberated from the Soviet Union. Since their release was followed immediately by the collapse of the Soviet Union itself, the suggestion might seem to lurk that Kashmir's freedom is envisaged in the prospective context of the disintegration of the Indian Union. Quite the contrary. It has been brought out elsewhere in these pages that the liberation of Kashmir would strengthen the cohesion and solidity of the Indian Union. It would cure India of what was called "a frontier sore" by Lord Ismay who advised Lord Mountbatten, one of the men chiefly responsible for the invasion of Kashmir by India.

The impression is not groundless but, on a more serious examination, it turns out to be superficial. For some years now, Pakistan's leaders have not displayed qualities or care and sensitivity in certain statements they have made on Kashmir. A couple of these statements, blithely citing the Indian Independence Act passed by the British Parliament in 1947, directly contradict the position clarified by the Founder of Pakistan himself who, besides being the redoubtable constitutionalist that he was, had vetted the Act before it was adopted (the Indian Congress leaders had done the same). In his characteristically straightforward manner, he published his view that the British government or Parliament had "no power or sanction" to restrict the freedom of the Princely States to remain independent, if they so desired. It must be noted, in passing, that he spoke of 'States' not of 'Princes'. The viability of independence, of course, was a separate issue; it could not be judged by legal criteria and it could not be regarded as the same in all cases.

But occasional crude utterances by Pakistan's present-day spokesmen do not affect the validity of Pakistan's traditional position in the Kashmir dispute. The dispute is on the agenda of the world organization as the India-Pakistan question. Pakistan cannot in fairness be expected to relinquish its position as a party to the dispute and assume instead the lesser role of a supporter of Kashmir in the India-Kashmir conflict. The military occupation of Kashmir by India violates not only Kashmir's self-determination but of Pakistan's as well.

For Pakistan came into being as the successor state of the British Indian empire comprising Muslim-majority areas as India did comprising Hindu-majority areas. This happened on the basis of a tripartite agreement arrived at by Britain, the Indian Congress and the Muslim League. It followed from the agreement that, unless the State of Jammu and Kashmir chose to remain independent, its Muslim-majority area would be incorporated in Pakistan exactly as the Muslim-majority area of the province of Punjab was. In fairness and in accordance with the principle of the settlement to which both the Indian Union and Pakistan owe their independence, there were only two options for Muslim-majority Kashmir: either to remain independent or to join Pakistan.

The pre-emption of both these options by India's military action had made Pakistan as much the wronged, aggrieved party as Kashmir itself. In Pakistan's eyes, Kashmir is not just another country whose self-determination is to be promoted in the way Pakistan championed the cause of the freedom of Morocco or Tunisia (in the early 1950s), for example, or of other peoples under colonial rule.

Kashmir is potentially a part of Pakistan and its society is intertwined with Pakistan's. If matters had been allowed to take a straight course in 1947, Kashmir would have been one of the provinces of Pakistan (the sentiment for Kashmir's independence at that time was very weak). This is not Pakistan's self-view.

Not to speak of all impartial observers, even Lord Mountbatten, who played a crucial role in engineering India's annexation of Kashmir, has conceded that but for a certain "basic mistake" by Pakistan, "Kashmir might well have eventually acceded to Pakistan, either with or without a plebiscite or might conceivably have been peacefully partitioned between India an Pakistan". The "basic mistake" he mentions is questionable but even if it were admitted, neither Pakistan nor Kashmir would merit permanent punishment for it in the form of a an unnatural disposition of the State. Mountbatten's statement recognizes Kashmir's place in Pakistan.

7

China on Disputed Kashmir Borders

INDIAN, PAKISTANI AND CHINESE BORDER DISPUTES

Disputed borders are both a cause and a symptom of tensions between big neighbours in South Asia. When the colonial power, Britain, withdrew from India it left a dangerous legacy of carelessly or arbitrarily drawn borders. Tensions between India and China flare on occasion, especially along India's far north-eastern border, along the state of Arunachal Pradesh. In recent years Chinese officials have taken to calling part of the same area "South Tibet", to Indian fury, as that seems to imply a Chinese claim to the territory. A failure to agree the precise border, and then to demarcate it, ensures that future disagreements may flare again. Pakistan, too, is beset by difficult borders. Afghanistan, to the north, has long been a hostile neighbour. This is largely because Afghanistan refuses to recognise the frontier—known as the Durand line—between the countries, drawn by the British.

Most contentious of all, however, are the borders in Kashmir, where Pakistan, India and China all have competing claims. By the time of independence, in 1947, it was clear that many Indian Muslims were determined to break off from Hindu-majority India. It fell to a British civil servant, who knew nothing of the region, to draw a line of partition between territory that would become Pakistan and India. Pakistan was given Muslim dominated areas in the far north west, plus territory in the east (which itself got independence as Bangladesh in 1971). The rulers of some disputed areas, notably Kashmir, were told to choose which country to join.

While Kashmir's Hindu rulers prevaricated, hoping somehow to become an independent country, Pakistan's leaders decided to force the issue. Since Kashmir was (and is) a Muslim majority territory, Pakistan felt justified in seeing Pushtun warlords charge in from the north-west of Pakistan, late in 1947, to seize control of Kashmir. In response India, apparently invited by Kashmir's rulers, deployed its national army and stopped the invaders taking Srinagar, Kashmir's capital, located in the Kashmir valley, the most coveted part of the territory. The resulting line of control, by and large, remains the de-facto international frontier within Kashmir and, in effect, is accepted by Paksitan and India. Huge numbers of Indian and Pakistani soldiers remain in Kashmir today as both countries profess to be the rightful authority for the rest of Kashmir. Complicating matters, China has also extended its influence, and control, over portions of Kashmir, largely with the support of Pakistan, an ally.

CHINA, INDIA MUST STOP PEDDLING MYTHS ABOUT THE LINE OF ACTUAL CONTROL

Political commentators have been gushing over the possibilities of strengthened economic and strategic relations between China and India, but the unresolved border dispute remains alive and can always play spoiler in the future. A border is, after all, more than a line on the map or a series of military posts on the ground; it is a reflection of how the political elite of a nation-state thinks about its security.

Chinese-controlled Aksai Chin is claimed by India as part of Jammu and Kashmir, and Indian-controlled Arunachal Pradesh is claimed by China. The only feasible solution is to accept the status quo and transform the Line of Actual Control into an international boundary. There have been several rounds of talks since the 1990s, but a resolution remains distant. Despite its parliamentary majority, Prime Minister Narendra Modi's government will be unable to sell a permanent boundary settlement without being accused of ceding territory in Aksai Chin, though in reality it will only be giving up its claim over a territory India never controlled.

This raises a pertinent question: what precisely is the border upon which India and China cannot agree?

New neighbours

Through history, China and India have not been neighbours. The current de facto border has its genesis in a line drawn on a map by Henry McMahon during a secret treaty between Britain and Tibet in March 1914. Both entities, British India and Tibet, are no more: one has been transformed into postcolonial India and the other was occupied and colonised by communist China. Yet India and China, both of whom have overthrown the mantle of Western imperialism, are jostling over the same imperialists' line – and have completely militarised and destroyed the traditional zone of contact that the border regions were.

The border is a legacy of a few dynamics, including the expansionist policies of the British in the Himalayan regions of India, the disappearance of the traditional Tibetan state, which had political and sacral hegemony over much of the region, and the modern nationalisms in postcolonial India and revolutionary China, which are keen on implementing a rigid notion of sovereignty in the border regions and legitimising the primacy of militarised security over the religious, cultural and human rights of the people inhabiting the region.

Stuck in the middle

The primary loser in the dispute is neither India nor China but Tibet. China has occupied most of Tibetan territory, while India has occupied the Tawang tract, which was historically part of Tibet. The Tibetan state had given up the Tawang region to British India in 1914 on the understanding that they would get friendship and assistance to protect their independence from China. When China went on to occupy Tibet in 1949-'50, India reneged on that understanding, preferring the diplomatically attractive Hindi-Chini-bhai-bhai rhetoric over a strategically sound and morally defensible Indo-Tibetan friendship.

Despite reluctantly hosting the Tibetan exile community today, India did not offer any tangible help to the Tibetans in their struggle for independence. Today, as Modi and Xi plan collaborations on various fronts, Tibetans are reminded that in this world of realpolitik, morality and human rights are subservient. Tibetans are perceived as strategic assets or liabilities in bargaining with China, not people of an occupied land for whom India should raise its voice. For India, it is the border that matters, not the border inhabitants.

Myths peddled by India

The popular as well as strategic approach of many in India towards the border dispute is jaundiced by the myths the Indian state peddled about the humiliating war of 1962. After the 1962 defeat, there was no credible reflection at the policy level in India. Indians accepted as real the myths that Indian territorial claims were legitimate and sacrosanct, and that the Chinese were duplicitous and stabbed gullible India in the back. The reality could not be further from this. The first Survey of India Map in 1950 showed the boundary as undefined in Aksai Chin and as undemarcated in the north east. It was only in the summer of 1954 that Jawaharlal Nehru gave personal orders for all old maps to be withdrawn and destroyed and to remove qualifiers and show the McMahon Line in bold, as if that was the de jure boundary.

Nehru later claimed innocence, insisting that there was no boundary disagreement and that Chinese claims were surprising. Since 1959, India rejected all the diplomatic overtures of Zhou Enlai and said negotiations could only take place if China withdrew from Aksai Chin, though India would not offer anything in return. Since 1961, the Indian military followed a "forward policy" in the border regions that was not only provocative but based on the assumption that China would not retaliate.

A great unresolved mystery from the time is why the best Indian minds working in intelligence, military and diplomacy accepted this assumption without a murmur of protest. It can be explained by Nehru's hubris in his own capacity as a statesperson, bureaucracies subservient to him, and the inability of the civilian and military elite to be independent-minded. Macho posturing was the order of the day. The Indianisation of the top brass in the military occurred only after independence in 1947, so they were inexperienced as leaders. Faced with an army that had its genesis in revolutionary wars, the Indian army, which had been servant to an imperial power, failed to perform its basic duty of protecting the country.

Henderson Brooks report

The post-war military report is still confidential, though an excerpt from it was leaked online earlier this year by Neville Maxwell. This Henderson Brooks Report shows that the Indian military barely put up a fight in the north east. There was a total failure of command and control at every level. The only thing that saved India from losing more territories was the unilateral ceasefire declared by China and the Chinese withdrawal back to the pre-war LAC. Had China not withdrawn, India could not have done much.

Rather than reflect upon its own follies, India embarked on militarisation and refused to negotiate. While the fantasists may be waiting for China to collapse one day, the fact is that China is here to stay and India has an option of either being sincere in negotiations or letting the dispute fester. It took the border dispute and a revolt in Tibet and the exile of the Dalai Lama in 1959 to destroy the camaraderie of early 1950s. Unless China manages to put an end to the Tibet issue by reaching a settlement with the Tibetans led by the Dalai Lama, and both India and China resolve their disagreements over the border, the newfound bonhomie could unravel once again.

CHINESE INTRUSIONS ACROSS THE LINE OF ACTUAL CONTROL TELL INDIA

A number of Chinese border intrusions across the Line of Actual Control have been reported in recent months. One such event near Mount Gya in the Chumar sector of Ladakh saw Chinese troops intruding 1.5 kilometres inside Indian territory and writing "China" on the rocks with red paint. The intrusion was first noticed by an Indian patrol team on July 31, 2009. An earlier incident of Chinese intrusion in this area reportedly took place on June 21st, when two Chinese M1 helicopters violated the Indian airspace and air dropped canned food at Chumar. While admitting that such an intrusion has indeed taken place, Army Chief General Deepak Kapoor played down the episode saying that the intrusion might have taken place because of navigational error. He also went on to state that such intrusions are not new and have been taking place for years. Minister of External Affairs, S. M. Krishna, also said that the border between India and China in the Ladakh sector is 'most peaceful' and such cases of intrusion would be sorted out through the 'inbuilt mechanism'.

This 'inbuilt mechanism' is the Border Personnel Meetings/ Flag Meetings, which take place at regular intervals. The establishment of this mechanism for resolving such border transgressions can be traced to the Agreement on the Maintenance of Peace and Tranquillity along the Line of Actual Control in the China-India Border Areas of 1993. As far as the recent case of intrusion is concerned, it is reported that the regiment posted in the area under 14 Corps had taken up the matter with their Chinese counterparts during such a border meeting in August and had also lodged a formal protest.

The Chinese side, however, denied the charges and maintained that border patrols by Chinese troops were 'strictly conducted according to the law' and they had never violated India's land or air space. Despite Chinese denials, the fact remains that China has been intruding inside the Indian territory all along the LAC. The Indian Army has reportedly recorded 270 border violations and nearly 2,300 cases of "aggressive border patrolling" by Chinese soldiers last year. The point to note is that earlier such intrusions were frequently reported from Arunachal Pradesh, while lately incidences of Chinese border transgression are increasingly being reported from Sikkim and Ladakh, hitherto considered as peaceful sectors of the LAC.

The reason behind the heightened Chinese incursions has been falsely attributed by many to the on-going strengthening of Indian military capability along the LAC – the deployment of

Sukhoi-30 MKI fighter jets in Tezpur, raising of two additional mountain divisions for the defence of Arunachal Pradesh, the landing of AN-32 transport plane at Daulat Begh Oldhi, the proposed deployment of an AWACS (airborne warning and control systems) plane as 'force multiplier' in the Ladakh sector, and the construction of 27 strategic roads along the India-China border. It is being argued that Chinese border intrusions are a reaction to these developments. The reality is, however, quite different. China does not need any of these excuses to transgress the LAC. It has been doing so in the past and will continue to do so in future. The unsettled border and these incursions are nothing but a manifestation of the uneasy relationship which the two countries share. The slow and steady emergence of India as a strong power in Asia is not looked upon favourably by China. And this sentiment also adversely impacts on the attempts to resolve the border dispute amicably.

China has had serious border disputes with many of its neighbours, and it chose to resolve those disputes only when it felt that the concerned neighbour was weak or when the latter acknowledged China's superior status. In the early 1960s, in a bid to demonstrate to the world that it was a responsible country and a good neighbour, China concluded border agreements with Burma, Nepal, Afghanistan and Pakistan. These countries were militarily weak neighbours and did not have any serious ideological or political differences with China. Notably, many of those border agreements were preceded by Chinese propaganda and border incursions by Chinese troops. At this time, however, China did not settle its borders with India, Bhutan, Soviet Union, Vietnam and Laos. It even engaged in wars with India in 1962, Soviet Union in 1969 and Vietnam in 1979.

As is often said, the best indication of strained relation between two countries is tensions across their shared borders. In the case of India, China felt threatened by India's standing in the international forums and especially by its leadership role among the third world countries. This feeling of unease was compounded by the Khampa rebellion in Tibet and the subsequent flight of the Dalai Lama to India in 1959. The strained relations between the two countries were manifested by Chinese territorial claims and increased skirmishes along the border, which culminated in the border war of 1962.

As regards the Soviet Union, the ideological split and China's attempt to supplant the USSR as the leader of the communist movement led to deteriorating relations, heightened border tensions and border clashes in 1969. Vietnam's closer affinity for the Soviet Union gradually led to the souring of relations with China, which eventually culminated in the 1979 border war. China could not settle its borders with Bhutan and Laos, which chose to be guided by India and Vietnam, respectively, on the border issue.

The second phase of Chinese border settlements with its neighbours started with the break-up of the Soviet Union in 1991. Negotiations to settle the border with Moscow began in 1987, and China and Russia concluded the border agreement in 1991. China also negotiated separate border agreements with Tajikistan, Kyrgystan and Kazakhstan. Border negotiations with Vietnam had resumed almost immediately after the 1979 border war, and a final agreement on their land border was signed on December 30, 1999. Incidentally, the text of the Land Border Treaty is not available in the public domain. China also signed a border agreement with Laos in 1992. The point to note is that all these border settlements resulted only in minor territorial changes, despite China's extravagant territorial claims.

Now, India and Bhutan are the only two countries with which China is yet to settle its border. In the case of Bhutan, news reports hinted that during the border talks in July 2005, Bhutan might have relented to Chinese pressure tactics and accepted a package deal. In 1996, Beijing had proposed the exchange of the 495 square kilometre area of Pasamlung and Jakarlung valleys in the northern borders of central Bhutan (which China claims) for Sinchulumpa, Dramana and Shakhtoe with an area of 269 sq km in north-west Bhutan. China has also been applying pressure tactics like large scale intrusions by Tibetan herdsmen and also by the PLA to keep Bhutanese border guards in tenterhooks and has also resorted to construction of roads inside Bhutanese territory. It appears that

Bhutan is under pressure both from China and its own people to arrive at a final solution to the festering border problem, but till now there is no indication that it has been successful at arriving at an acceptable solution.

Intrusions by Chinese troops into Indian territory are signals meant to assert China's growing political and military stature as well as means to test India's resolve. Given India's gradual emergence as a powerful military and economic power in Asia, China is unlikely to be keen on settling the border issue till such time India slumps into a period of weakness. Thus, for the foreseeable future, the India-China border is likely to be characterised by tensions, incursions and skirmishes, interspersed with endless border negotiations. Given this, India needs to be prepared for any eventuality and calibrate its responses to Chinese intrusions.

LINE OF ACTUAL CONTROL CLARIFICATION AND CBMS IMPLEMENTATION

The eight rounds of border talks demonstrated that their conflicting border versions, based on historical-legalistic arguments, could not find common ground because no mutually acceptable border treaties or agreements existed.

The eight rounds of border talks raised the hope for a political solution to the border dispute. In 1991, Premier Li peng visited India and signed the Sino-Indian Joint Communique on December 16, 1991. In the joint communiqué, they reaffirmed their independent foreign policy and the five principles of peaceful co-existence. The two sides appealed for the joint efforts for the establishment of a new international political and economic order. India reiterated its position that Tibet is an autonomous region of China and it does not allow Tibetans to engage in anti-china political activities in India.

After the two summit meetings in 1988 and 1991, China-India interactions shifted from the border dispute to the identification of a mutually acceptable lie of actual control along the China-India border. In 1993, Indian Prime Minister Rao visited China and signed an agreement on maintaining peace and tranquility along the line of actual control and reduced military forces in the border areas. This peace pact, under which both sides agreed to respect and observe the LAC, is a big step forward in exploring a lasting border solution, eliminating concerns about events such as the Sumdurong Chu incident which nearly sparked another border war in 1987.

Under the LAC agreement in 1993, the two sides agreed that the boundary question shall be resolved through peaceful and friendly consultations. Neither side shall use or threaten to use force against the other by any means. Pending an ultimate solution to the boundary question, the two sides shall strictly respect and observe the LAC.

Each side will keep its military forces in the areas along the LAC to a minimum level compatible with the friendly and good-neighborly relations between the two countries. Both sides shall work out effective confidence-building measures (CBMs) in the areas along the LAC. However, the two sides agreed that references to the LAC in this agreement do not prejudice their respective positions on the boundary question.

Under this agreement, both sides agreed that each side of the China-India Joint Working Group on the boundary question shall appoint diplomatic and military experts, advising the Joint Working Group on resolution of differences on the alignment of the LAC and address issues relating to military redeployment in the border areas along the LAC. In 1996, the Chinese president Jiang Zemin visited India and both sides decided to develop a cooperative and constructive partnership, further raising political level of bilateral cooperation between the two countries. However, the Indian nuclear tests in 1998 and its leaders indicated India's nuclear tests for counter-China's nuclear threat dashed the healthy momentum of China-India relations in the late 1990s. Apparently, China-India interactions in the 1990s focused on political and security fields. The line of actual control, the CBMs in the areas along the China-India border, and emphasis on the establishment of an international political and economic order and even India's nuclear tests are all pointed to political and security dimension of the China-India relations.

Shift Back to the Settlement of the Border Dispute in the New Century

Ushering in the new 21st century, China and India, the two Asian giants, are rising at the same time. Their bilateral relationship has its regional and global significance. As the two largest emerging powers in Asia and the world, their roles have been played far beyond the bilateral context. Certainly, their bilateral dispute, particularly the border dispute, has constrained each other's capability to play their responsible role in the regional and global affairs.

If they focused on stabilizing their relations and securing their border areas in the 1990s, they have shifted their attention to the settlement of their border dispute by developing their political and economic relations while taking concrete and substantive measures to resolve the border dispute. They understand that their bilateral problems have complicated their policy coordination and cooperation in the regional and global issues. Their bilateral differences have tended to be manipulated by other powers to serve their geostrategic interest.

For the past decade, in terms of the border dispute, they have taken three substantive steps to intensify their efforts to resolve it. The first step is that India has accepted Tibet is an autonomous region of China, implying that India has given up the intention to use Tibet as a buffer zone between China and India and recognizes China's sovereignty overTibet. However, although India does not allow the Tibetans in India to engage in Anti-China political activities, it still hosts the Dalai Lama's government-in-exile. China has recognized Sikkim's status as a state of India's federation by signing the agreement on the cross-border trade with India.

The second step is that China and India signed an agreement on political parameters and guiding principles on the settlement of the China-India border dispute. This document is regarded as a big breakthrough in the joint efforts for resolving the border dispute. The third step is that the two governments have appointed their special representatives to promote the negotiations on a framework of the border settlement. The two governments have paid importance to the annual meetings of the two special representatives. The Chinese special representative is State Councilor Dai Bingguo and The Indian special representative is India's National Security adviser M. K. Narayanan.

After the two special representatives were appointed, they started to work together for a framework settlement of the border dispute according to the agreed political parameters and guiding principles. Under the current circumstances, although the two governments continue to work on the settlement of the border dispute, peace, stability, and tranquility in the border areas have remained. No armed conflicts or even skirmishes happened although some media has played up such noises of China's invasions into India's territory dozens or hundreds of times.

INDIA'S RELATIONS WITH CHINA: THE GOOD, THE BAD AND THE (POTENTIALLY) UGLY

Later this month, Indian Prime Minister Manmohan Singh will travel to Beijing. The visit will cap a year that has been full of ups and downs in India's relations with China. The tale of three trips is representative. One in May by Chinese Premier Li Keqiang, his first abroad, was intended to signal the importance Beijing placed in the Sino-Indian relationship. But it took place in the aftermath of—and some would say was overshadowed by—a border standoff between the two countries' militaries. In July, the Indian defense minister visited Beijing to rebuild trust and defense ties. Media coverage, however, focused on warnings to India issued by a PLA general, which Chinese officials had to rush to dismiss.

And Singh will be travelling from a country that is largely preoccupied domestically. When discussions do turn to China, they have focused on concerns about Indian capacity vis-à-vis that country, Indian politicians accusing the government of being soft on China and Chinese scholars labeling India's border infrastructure upgrades as provocative. These and other developments have highlighted what Indian policymakers acknowledge—that there are elements of cooperation, competition and concern in the China-India relationship.

There have been good signs for those interested in stable, cooperative Sino-Indian relations.In the spring, just after he'd formally taken office, Chinese President Xi Jinping proposed a five-point formula to improve ties between the two countries. "Positive vibes" were detected at Xi's subsequent meeting with Singh on the sidelines of the BRICS summit in Durban in March. There have been numerous public Chinese declarations of the importance of the relationship—perhaps not seen since the first half of the 1950s.

The Chinese ambassador to India unusually took to the editorial pages of an Indian newspaper to emphasize, "To strengthen good-neighbourly and friendly cooperation with India is China's strategic choice and established policy which will not change." Chinese officials have indicated that greater efforts should be made toward a boundary settlement.

The two countries have strategic and economic dialogues in place. They restarted their defense dialogue earlier this year and are expected to resume joint military exercises shortly. China and India also have specialized dialogues on issues like Afghanistan, Central Asia and counterterrorism. The agreement to discuss Afghanistan was considered a departure from previous Chinese policy; Beijing had earlier been reluctant to add it to the agenda because it would have likely meant talking about Chinese ally Pakistan. Along with regional discussions, China and India have also cooperated in the multilateral realm, including on issues like trade and climate change.

Premier Li chose India as his first overseas stop, with the Chinese government indicating that the choice was very deliberate. Hosting an Indian youth delegation, Li put a personal spin on the choice, noting the "the seeds of friendship sown" when he visited India 27 years ago—a trip that he said left a "lasting impact." During the May visit, he stressed the need to build trust and especially emphasized the economic benefits of greater ties.

Those economic ties have already grown. China is one of India's largest trading partners. Bilateral trade in goods has gone from less than $3 billion in 2000 to $66.57 billion in 2012. While investments haven't kept the same pace, they have also grown. In

India, the interest in doing business with China is evident beyond the private sector and the central government—along with visits by a number of Indian CEOs, China has also seen visits from chief ministers of a number of Indians states, including Andhra Pradesh, Bihar, Karnataka and Madhya Pradesh. Narendra Modi, current chief minister of the state of Gujarat and prime ministerial candidate for the forthcoming national election for the BJP (India's largest opposition party), has also traveled to China. While Modi has expressed hawkish views on China on the geopolitical front, he has expressed admiration for that country's economic achievements.

The governments of both countries have reasons for wanting stable ties: the desire for a peaceful periphery in order to focus on domestic socio-economic objectives; the need for stability in South Asia, especially with the impending American drawdown of forces from Afghanistan; existing and potential economic ties; and the prospect for cooperation in the multilateral realm. For Delhi, in addition, a stable relationship with China opens up the possibility that Beijing might use its leverage with Islamabad to shape Pakistan's behavior in a way that might benefit India. For Beijing, there's desire to limit India's burgeoning relationships with the United States and Japan, as well as with other countries in what Beijing considers its backyard. Moreover, as China is preoccupied with eastern maritime disputes and the North Korean situation, stable relations on its southern and southwestern flank would also help the Chinese leadership.

This year has, however, also shown how quickly the bad in the relationship can steal the spotlight from the good—with the potential to turn ugly. In April, less than two weeks after an Indian observer commented on the "upswing in relations" between China and India, their long-standing boundary dispute flared once again. While the two countries communicated through the crisis and resolved it diplomatically, and Li's visit proceeded as planned, the border incident reinforced the mistrust that many in India feel toward China and its intentions. Furthermore, it was a reminder that despite increased engagement, bilateral differences have the potential to stall, if not reverse, progress toward more stable relations.

Differences are not restricted to the boundary dispute. Tibet remains a key source of tension between the two countries though the two countries have found a way to manage their differences on the issue for now. In addition, China's relationship with Pakistan has been a major source of concern in India. Its role in strengthening Pakistan's conventional, missile and nuclear capabilities is especially highlighted. India also disapproves of China's assistance to Pakistan in developing projects and infrastructure in area disputed between India and Pakistan.

China's growing political and economic ties with India's neighbours are also a subject of concern. Delhi watches warily increasing Chinese interactions—political and commercial—with and involvement in countries like Afghanistan, Bangladesh, Myanmar, Nepal and Sri Lanka. Concern about a military dimension being added persists. Beijing's increasing interest in operating in the Indian Ocean, which India has traditionally considered its backyard, has also not gone unnoticed. While China emphasizes that these activities have benign goals—economic development, security for its ships, etc.—some in India who tend to take a hawkish position are not convinced; others are taking a wait-and-see attitude. Even beyond the neighbourhood, there are concerns about competition with China for markets, influence and resources across the globe.

Closer to home, water is the resource that has become the subject of tension—specifically Chinese dam construction on its side of the Brahmaputra River. Indian officials have publiclycalled for Beijing to reassure India on this matter. Domestic critics, however, perceive the Indian government as being too tolerant of the construction. They argue that China has not respected information sharing agreements on this front and warn of more ambitiousChinese river diversion plans.

Economic ties, which many envisioned as the driver of good Sino-Indian ties, have also not escaped trouble. Bilateral trade in goods actually fell almost 10 percent from 2011 to 2012. In India there's much concern about the trade imbalance. The overall trade deficit has gonefrom $28 billion in 2010-2011 to $40.8 billion in 2012-2013. While investments have grown, they remain limited compared to the investment relationships that both China and India have with other countries. In India, there have also been complaints about market access in China and the treatment of Indian labor there, concern about Chinese investment in "strategic" sectors in India, accusations about visa abuses by Chinese companies and restrictions on Chinese labor. Indian companies also privately express concerns about cyber-espionage. Overall, reports of cyber-attacks on Indian government and military networks—allegedly emanating from China—have done nothing to decrease distrust that persists, especially among the public.

There is also an overall sense that China does not respect India and/or that it will seek to prevent India's rise. As evidence, critics point not only to China's relationship with Pakistan, which is seen as driven by a desire to keep India tied up in South Asia, but also note China'sreluctance to endorse India's demand for a permanent seat on the U.N. Security Council or its objections to India being given membership in the Nuclear Suppliers Group.

Another overarching problem: the lack of trust in China and its intentions. This is especially evident among the public. According to a Pew poll last year, more Indians have an unfavorable view of China than a favorable view. In a more recent Lowy Institute poll, China ranked only second to Pakistan in terms of countries that people considered threatening to India, with 60 percent indicating China would be a major threat over the next decade (an additional 22 percent identified it as a minor threat). 73 percent of those surveyed identified "war with China" as a big threat over the next ten years. Almost three-quarters believed that China wants to dominate Asia. 58 percent felt that China's growth had not been good for India. This reinforces what the Pew poll found last year. In that poll, two-thirds of urbanites who expressed an opinion on the subject believed that China's growing economy was a bad thing.

Overcoming this mistrust continues to be a major obstacle. The legacy of history remains a problem. Every time there is a border incident it reinforces the narrative that has prevailed in many quarters in India since the 1962 China-India war: that China only understands strength; that while Beijing's leaders say China and India "must shake hands," they cannot be trusted—that one hand held out might just be a precursor to the other stabbing one in the back. This problem is made worse by limited connectivity and communications, and little knowledge about the other country—even though these have improved. Media coverage about China and the relationship can also get quite heated, with a tendency to focus on the negative. All these problems are exacerbated by the lack of transparency when it comes to Chinese decision-making. This has led to uncertainty about Chinese behavior and motivations, which was evident in the debate about why the border incident in April occurred—and this uncertainty exists even among policymakers.

Thus, Indian governments have tried to follow a multi-pronged strategy. The emphasis might have differed somewhat, but for the last two governments in India—one a coalition led by the BJP and the current one led by the Congress—the general approach towards China has been to co-operate, if possible, and to compete, if necessary.

Indian officials have joined with Chinese counterparts to increase ties, build trust and improve communications. Simultaneously, policymakers note that competition in and of itself is not all bad. As former Indian Prime Minister Vajpayee noted in Beijing, "a sense of competition between two close and equal neighbours" might indeed be natural. There is also, however, a realization that beyond cooperation and competition, there is a potential for conflict. Thus, while hoping and working for the best, there has been some attention on planning and preparing for the worst—i.e. the possibility that China will emerge as an explicit threat. There is a desire to do this cautiously, however, with policymakers quite conscious of the potential for provocation, miscalculation and exacerbation of the security dilemma.

In practice, this overall approach has meant increasing engagement with China—political, economic and even military-to-military—at the bilateral, regional and multilateral levels. Simultaneously, this approach has translated to a series of actions including strengthening India's military, as well as its border infrastructure and border regions, maintaining a nuclear deterrent, and consolidating or expanding ties and influence in India's near abroad.

India has also tried to step up its game in China's neighbourhood. Indian policymakers underplay the strategic aspects and goals of India's "Look East" policy—which the Indian foreign ministry describes as "oriented towards deepening India's engagement with the countries of East and Southeast Asia"—and emphasize its cultural and economic aspects. However, these elements and the link to China have not been entirely missing in action. The Indian government and companies are increasingly interested and engaged in the region, especially focusing on countries like Indonesia, Japan, Singapore, Thailand and Vietnam. In recent months, India-Japan ties have probably been in the spotlight the most, with another round of the U.S.-India-Japan trilateral dialogue and Singh's visit to Japan in May. India has also sought to be more engaged with multilateral fora in the region. Officials from some Southeast Asian countries, however, want India to do much more. Channeling some of their frustrations, Hillary Clinton, when she led the State Department, called for "India not just to look east, but to engage East and act East as well."

Another key aspect of India's approach has been the pursuit of closer relations with the United States. Of course, these ties with the United States are not solely driven by China. India indeed has no desire to make a choice between its relations with China and the United States. However, the United States plays a useful role as an offshore balancer. Furthermore, Indian policymakers believe that a strong U.S.-India relationship gives them leverage with China and sends a signal to that country. Some also note that China takes India more seriously because the United States does. India, however, still has doubts about U.S. reliability as a potential partner, especially given the level of Sino-U.S. engagement, and prefers to maintain a diversified portfolio of partnerships.

So, where do India's relations with China go from here? In the near term, during the Prime Minister's visit, the two sides might sign a border defense cooperation agreement. The accord would essentially be a way to manage rather than resolve the boundary question, which the Indian foreign secretary has noted continues to be "a particularly difficult issue." The trans-border rivers question is also likely to be discussed. In addition, given the two countries' priorities, bilateral and global economic and financial issues will be high on the agenda. Potentially, there also might be agreements that could facilitate greater people-to-people ties, including a cultural and visa pacts. Regionally, developments vis-à-vis Afghanistan and the Middle East that concern both governments are likely to be discussed. Finally, on the multilateral front, trade and climate change issues might be on the agenda, given upcoming international summits in those two areas.

As for the longer term, the scenarios usually outlined are deepening cooperation, increasing competition that might lead to conflict, or continuity with both competition and cooperation in evidence. There is a debate in India—inside and outside government—about China, which scenario might prevail, the future of the relationship and what approach to take with China. The differences are evident in the Lowy poll—almost equal numbers of those surveyed believe that India "should join with other countries to limit China's influence" and "should cooperate with China to play a leading role in the world together."

How the relationship plays out will depend on a number of internal, bilateral, regional and global factors. In the meantime, Shyam Saran, a former foreign secretary and currently chairman of the National Security Advisory Board, has called for India to manage relations with China "with prudence but firmness." An air force chief described the way forward as "play cool and continue to develop capabilities."

BEIJING'S RESPONSE TO INDIA-PAKISTAN TENSIONS AFTER 9/11

Since the late 1990s, China had become increasingly concerned over the gradual shift in the regional balance of power in South Asia, driven by the steady rise of India coupled with the growing US-India entente and the talk of "India as a counterweight to China" in Washington's policy circles, and by Pakistan's gradual descent into the ranks of failed states. Since the end of the Cold

War, a politically dysfunctional and economically bankrupt Pakistan's flirtation with Islamic extremism and terrorism, coupled with its nuclear and missile programs, had alienated Washington.

However, the 11 September 2001 attacks changed all that. Pakistan saw an opportunity to revive its past close relations with the United States, shed its near pariah status, and enhance its economic and strategic position vis-à-vis India by instantaneously becoming a "frontline state" in the international coalition fighting global terrorism. In return, Washington lifted sanctions and agreed to provide Pakistan with billions of dollars in aid and debt rescheduling. From Washington's perspective, courting Musharraf made geopolitical sense because the Pakistani military not only knew a great deal about the Taliban, Osama bin Laden, and al Qaeda, but also because any US military operation against Afghanistan could not be successful without the bases, logistics, personnel, and airspace in neighbouring Pakistan. In Beijing, as a result, there were great expectations of a sharp downturn in US-India relations, because in many ways what happens on the Indian subcontinent is unavoidably a zero-sum game and Pakistan's new relationship with the United States did affect India negatively.

However, tensions between South Asia's nuclear-armed rivals rose sharply after the terrorist attacks at the Kashmir Assembly in October 2001 and the Indian Parliament on 13 December 2001. The attack on the Indian Parliament triggered a major deployment of Indian troops along the border with Pakistan, with Islamabad responding in kind. New Delhi warned of retaliatory, punitive military strikes against terrorist camps inside Pakistani-controlled Kashmir. Although the Chinese Foreign Ministry spokesperson condemned these attacks, Chinese leaders and South Asia watchers were much more circumspect and ambivalent while lauding Pakistan's contribution to the war against terrorism. A South Asia specialist from China's National Defence University, Wang Baofu, noted with satisfaction that under the new circumstances, "The United States, considering its own security interests, readjusted its policies toward South Asian countries and started paying more attention to the important role of Pakistan in the anti-terrorism war, therefore arousing the vigilance and jealousy of India." Wang criticized India for "defin[ing] resistance activities in Kashmir as terrorism by taking advantage of the US anti-terrorism war in Afghanistan, thus putting more pressure on Pakistan through the United States," and praised General Musharraf for his "clear-cut attitude toward fighting against international terrorism)." Such a stance was not unexpected. For almost a decade, China had rejected India's proposal to issue a joint declaration against terrorism lest it be interpreted as a condemnation of Pakistan. Pakistan President General Musharraf made three trips to Beijing in less than a year (in December 2001, January 2002, and August 2002) for urgent security consultations with President Jiang Zemin and Premier Zhu Rongji and reportedly obtained "firm assurances of support in the event of a war" with India. At the time of heightened tensions in mid-January 2002, General Zhang Wannian, Vice-Chairman of China's Central Military Commission, met with General Muhammad Aziz Khan, Chairman of Pakistan's Joint Chiefs of the Staff Committee, and was quoted as telling Khan: "For many years the militaries of our two nations have maintained exchanges and cooperation at the highest and all levels and in every field. This fully embodies the all-weather friendship our nations maintain." Zhang's reference to "cooperation... inevery field" (meaning the nuclear and missile fields) was a thinly veiled warning to India to back off. Later, Beijing matched words with deeds by rushing two dozen F-7 jet fighters, nuclear and missile components, and other weapon systems to shore up Pakistani defenses in the tense border face-off.Asecret "futuristic arms development cooperation" agreement was signed during General Musharraf's five-day visit to China in December 2001 to construct, among other weapons, an all-solid-fuel Shaheen III missile with a range of 3,500-4,000 kilometers to target all major Indian cities. The People's Liberation Army (PLA) troops from the Military Regions of Chengdu and Lanzhou and their respective subdivisions, the Xizang (Tibet) and Wulumuqi (Urumqi), along China's southern borders, were also put on alert in January to test their war preparedness should the conflict in the Indian subcontinent spill over onto Chinese soil.

The Chinese leaders had reportedly conveyed the following message to Musharraf: "China hopes Pakistan will not initiate any assault. Pakistan should not get involved in wars and instead focus on economic construction. However, if a war does break out between India and Pakistan, Beijing will firmly stand on the side of Islamabad." Soon thereafter, President Musharraf in a televised speech on 12 January 2002 announced a crackdown on extremist organizations waging jihad from Pakistani territory, and as a result, Indo-Pakistani tensions somewhat subsided. The Chinese media claimed some credit for "mediating" between the two sub-continental rivals despite the Indian government's aversion to the dreaded "m" word: "Mediated by the United States, China, Britain, and Russia, leaders of India and Pakistan recently expressed their desire to try to control the tense situation." 12 Interestingly, this stance contradicted then Indian Foreign Minister Jaswant Singh's statement during Premier Zhu's visit to New Delhi in January 2002 that "China has neither any intention, nor shall it play any mediatory role between India and Pakistan." Not only that, the Chinese Foreign Minister also succeeded in persuading his Russian counterpart to issue a "Joint Declaration on the India-Pakistan Situation," signaling to New Delhi that, for the first time, Beijing and Moscow had a unified stand on the dispute. In concrete policy terms, it meant that New Delhi could no longer count on the Russian veto in the UN Security Council in the event of a war.

Then came the 14 May 2002 terrorist attack on a military base in Jammu that killed 34 people, mostly women and children, once again escalating tensions along the border where more than one million troops backed by heavy armor, warplanes, and missiles were deployed. There was renewed tough talk of war, including nuclear war, on both sides of the border. Beijing called for restraint from both India and Pakistan and emphasized the need for peaceful dialogue to settle outstanding disputes. Chinese Defence Minister Chi Haotian also urged both countries to desist from a military conflict and not to threaten each other with nuclear weapons. Describing the US diplomatic moves (i.e., the dispatch of Deputy Secretary of State Richard Armitage and Defence Secretary Donald Rumsfeld in early June 2002) to defuse the India-Pakistan military stand-off as "too little too late," the state-run media accused Washington of showing "no genuine desire to resolve the Kashmir issue." It noted that Washington had clearly not taken the tensions very seriously when it went on with a ten-day joint military maneuver with India on 16-26 May 2002, thereby implying that the Indo-US joint military exercise had emboldened India to up the ante against Pakistan. On 15 May, a Chinese official accompanying Foreign Minister Tang Jiaxuan during his visit to Islamabad told Pakistani journalists that China would back Pakistan in any conflict with India. Concerned over the "one-sided nature of public appeals" from Washington, Moscow, London, Paris, and Tokyo to General Musharraf to halt "cross-border terrorism" into Indian Kashmir, Chinese Foreign Minister Tang Jiaxuan told US Secretary of State Colin Powell on 27 May 2002 that "the international community should encourage direct dialogue between India and Pakistan in a more balanced and fair manner, which is the most effective way to lead South Asia towards peace and stability." Apparently, the growing threat of nuclear war and the prospect of Pakistani nuclear weapons falling into the hands of Islamic terrorists have made Washington lean heavily on Islamabad. In contrast, Beijing repeatedly asked New Delhi to do more to end the military stand-off while publicly calling for restraint by both sides and claiming to be even-handed. China continued to covertly side with its long-term ally, however, and is providing military wherewithal to Pakistan.

Meanwhile, in yet another television address on 27 May, Musharraf pledged that all militant infiltration across the Line of Control (LoC) would end, and he announced the banning of Lashkar-e-Toiba, the Jaish-e-Mohammad, and the Harkat-ul-Mujahideen—the three "*jihadi*" outfits at the forefront of terrorist activity in Indian Kashmir. From New Delhi's perspective, India's military deployment had succeeded in bringing the international focus on Pakistan as the home of pan-Islamic *jihadis* after the war in Afghanistan.

At the Conference on Interaction and Confidence Building Measures in Asia held in Kazakhstan in early June 2002, Chinese President Jiang Zemin pressed Indian Prime Minister Vajpayee to enter into direct talks with Pakistani President Musharraf to prevent the Kashmir conflict from exploding into a full-scale war. But the Indian government was so irked over Musharraf's playing of "the

China card" that Vajpayee refused to budge. Later, in an interview with *The Washington Post*, the Indian Prime Minister complained that he saw "no basic change in China's policy. China continues to help Pakistan acquire weapons and equipment." In an article titled "Beijing as Guarantor of Pakistan's Security," a Russian weekly, *Nezavisimoye Voyennoye Obozreniye* (Independent Military Review), had reported that new security commitments have indeed been made to Pakistan by China since 9/11.18 New Delhi expressed its displeasure with Beijing by postponing scheduled visits by Indian Army Chief Padmanabhan and Prime Minister Vajpayee to China in October and November 2002.

The Nuclear Connection

There were other grounds for the cooling of relations between Beijing and New Delhi. In his testimony before the US Senate governmental affairs subcommittee in early June 2002, the Assistant Secretary of State for Nonproliferation, John S. Wolf, revealed that "China recently provided Islamabad with missile-related technologies, which include dual-use missile-related items, raw materials, and other accessories essential for missile manufacturing." In a sense, China's nuclear and missile assistance to a volatile Pakistan over the last two decades has now created the risk of a conventional conflict swiftly escalating into nuclear war. Beijing has not only provided Islamabad with nuclear bombs, uranium, and plants (all three Pakistani nuclear plants—Kahuta, Khushab, and Chasma— have been built with Chinese assistance) but also their delivery systems: readyto-launch M-9 (Ghaznavi/ Hatf), M-11 (Shaheen), and a number of Dong Feng 21 (Ghauri) ballistic missiles.

This cooperation has continued despite Beijing's growing concerns over the "Talibanization" of the Pakistani state and society. When Islamabad carried out a series of missile tests amidst heightened tensions apparently to warn New Delhi to back off, the Indian government drew the international community's attention to the Pakistani missiles' China connection. "We are not impressed by these missile antics, particularly when all that is demonstrated is borrowed or imported ability.... The technology used in the missiles is not their own but clandestinely acquired from other countries," said a spokesperson of the Indian External Affairs Ministry.

Pakistan's test of its nuclear-capable, medium-range, Shaheen ballistic missile in early October 2002, just days before the parliamentary elections, once again provoked India to level accusations of missile technology proliferation by China. India's outspoken Defence Minister, George Fernandes, long a critic of China, said that Pakistan's military had always depended on support from China ever since it was carved out as a homeland for South Asia's Muslims in 1947 following decolonization of British India. "Everyone knows what Pakistan will be without China. Its ego is boosted purely by the support it gets from China," Fernandes said at a party convention in Mumbai. Earlier, when India weaponized its nuclear capability through a series of tests in May 1998, Fernandes had described "China [as] the mother of Pakistan's nuclear bomb" and claimed that India's aim was to counter China's capability rather than Pakistan's, drawing protests from Beijing. When Pakistan came in the firing line following revelations in the US media about the missiles-for-nukes barter deal with North Korea, New Delhi argued that blame should also be put on China for making Pakistan a nuclear weapons state.

For New Delhi, Beijing's military alliance with Islamabad remains a sore point because the Sino-Pakistani nuclear nexus has introduced a new element of uncertainty and complexity in sub-continental strategic equations. While the attention of world leaders and the media has been focused on the nightmarish scenario of a nuclear Armageddon in South Asia and large-scale mutual assured destruction leading to the deaths of 12 to 30 million people, strategic circles in Islamabad and New Delhi have been discussing the pros and cons of a short, limited nuclear war in Kashmir. Media reports based on intelligence leaks have revealed the forward deployment by the Pakistani military of low-yield (five kilotons or less) tactical nuclear weapons (TNWs). Such small battlefield nuclear weapons have a one-mile destruction radius and could be used effectively against large troop concentrations and advancing tank formations along the LoC in Kashmir.

The Pakistanis seem to have taken a page out of China's book on tactical nuclear warfighting capability. Just as persistent Sino-Soviet disputes and the Soviet Union's conventional military superiority during the 1970s and 1980s gave China strong incentives to develop and deploy TNWs, the decade-long India-Pakistan border tensions and India's conventional superiority may have added momentum to Islamabad's efforts to deploy TNWs. Most of Pakistan's missiles acquired from China, such as the M-9, are short-range, solid-fueled, mobile, nuclear-capable missiles and can be used in a tactical mode. Asked to comment on reports that Pakistan has acquired TNWs, the Deputy Chief of the Indian Army, Lieutenant General Raj Kadyan, was quoted as saying that the "Indian Army has trained itself to cope with a tactical nuclear strike in the battlefield." Tactical nukes can be launched over an unpopulated area from field artillery guns or aircraft to halt an enemy advance or in an effort to intimidate a numerically stronger enemy. Since the damage is localized or confined to a certain area, the danger of affecting the civilian population is greatly reduced as compared to a strategic nuclear weapon of the Hiroshima kind and therefore need not evoke massive retaliation by enemy forces. The mountainous terrain in Kashmir provides the perfect setting for their use.

In addition to the United States and Russia, only China is believed to have a large stockpile of about 120 TNWs or "baby nukes." Some of these were apparently delivered to Pakistan following the visit of PLA Deputy Chief and military intelligence boss General Xiong Guangkai (arguably China's most important military figure and the man who calls Pakistan "China's Israel") to Islamabad in early March 2002.27 If the reports of China's transfer of TNWs to Pakistan are indeed true, the question then is: Would India, which does not possess TNWs but has strategic nuclear weapons in abundance, keep a nuclear conflict limited or escalate it to the strategic level and respond with massive retaliation? Though New Delhi has long maintained that even a tactical nuclear strike on its forces would be treated as a nuclear first strike, and would invite massive retaliation, some Pakistani generals believe that a tactical strike would circumvent retaliation from India, since such an attack on an advancing tank regiment or infantry battalion (in contrast to a strategic strike killing millions of civilians), would not be provocation enough for all-out retaliation. They contend that the many layers of bureaucracy surrounding India's nuclear capability, the strength of world public opinion, and the fact that strategic command remains in civilian hands places severe doubts on India's willingness and ability to retaliate with a massive nuclear strike against an opponent, particularly in the face of only a limited tactical strike from Pakistan.

Some analysts attribute the recent lessening of tensions to the belated recognition in India's strategic circles that New Delhi cannot afford to dismiss Pakistan's repeated threats of using nuclear weapons as "mere posturing" or "bluffing" on Islamabad's part. They point to the Pakistani military's strong aversion to fighting a 1965-or 1971-type conventional war with India and offer this as the rationale behind Islamabad's decision to pull back from the brink on several occasions in recent history (in 1987, 1990, 1999, and 2002). Others believe that the tendency of Indian strategic planners to discount the threat of nuclear escalation may well be based on some fundamentally erroneous assumptions:

- That the United States cannot allow Pakistan to be the first Islamic country to use nuclear weapons to settle a territorial dispute, as it would mean the end of the global nonproliferation regime and encourage other countries to go nuclear to settle their territorial disputes as well.
- That the presence of US forces in Pakistan will be a constraining factor.
- That the international community (the United States, United Kingdom, China, or the United Nations) will intervene in time to prevent such a catastrophe.
- And that India can count on American and Israeli military support to seize or take out Pakistan's nuclear and missile infrastructure. These assumptions do not seem to be based on cold, clear-headed calculations of the strategic interests and influence of major powers (especially the United States and China) and may well be a sign of wishful thinking on India's part. It is worth noting that new strategic and

geopolitical realities emerging in Asia since 9/11 have put a question mark over Beijing's older certainties, assumptions, and beliefs.

China's Concerns

Much to Jiang and his Politburo's chagrin, the US-led war on terrorism has developed in ways that could not have been foreseen, with potentially disastrous consequences for China's core strategic interests. A major unintended (and unsettling, from Beijing's standpoint) consequence has been not only to checkmate and roll back China's recent strategic expansion moves in Central, South, and Southeast Asia, thereby severely constricting the strategic latitude that China has enjoyed since the Cold War, but also to tilt the regional balance of power decisively in Washington's favour within a short period. The supposedly brief Unipolar moment in history seems to have turned into a long-lasting Imperial moment—a Pax Americana *par excellence*. More important, recent developments show how tenuous Chinese power remains when compared to that of the United States.

The fast-changing strategic scene not only undercuts Chinese ambitions to expand Beijing's power and influence in Asia, but also hems in the one country in the world with the most demonstrable capacity to act independently of the United States. Not surprisingly, the beginning of 2002 saw Chinese leaders and generals shedding their earlier inhibitions about publicly expressing concern over the growing "southern discomfort"—that is, ever-expanding US military power and presence in southern Asia after 9/11. China's Chief of the General Staff Fu Quanyou warned the United States against using the war on terrorism to dominate global affairs by saying "counter-terrorism should not be used to practice hegemony." On an official visit in April 2002 in Iran, Jiang Zemin openly repudiated the US stance against the Iranian and Iraqi regimes, saying, "Our opinion [on terrorism] is not the same as the United States." In Germany, he told the *Welt am Sonntag*: "We all want to fight terrorism. But the states involved in the fight against terror each have their own specific viewpoint." China's initial optimism that new Sino-US-Pakistan triangular cooperation in the aftermath of 11 September 2001 would wean Washington away from New Delhi turned out to be wishful thinking as Bush Administration officials went out of their way to assure India that America's intensifying alliance with Pakistan would not come at India's expense. If anything, the current crisis has strengthened the American commitment to building stronger relations, including defence ties, with South Asia's preeminent power. However, China does not want to see India increasing its power, stature, and profile regionally or internationally. Beijing shares Islamabad's deep mistrust of India's strategic ambitions and seeks to prevent India's emergence as a peer competitor and a major strategic rival in Asia. That is why Chinese strategists have long argued that China's pursuit of great power status is a historical right and perfectly legitimate but India's pursuit of great power status is illegitimate, wrong, dangerous, and a sign of hegemonic, imperial behaviour. For its part, New Delhi has long accused Beijing of doing everything it can to undermine India's interests and using its ties with other states to contain India. Beijing is also alarmed over the growing talk in some con-servative policy circles in Washington and New Delhi of India emerging as a counterweight to China on the one hand and the fragile, radical Islamic states of West Asia on the other.

Earlier, when President Bush unveiled his missile defence plan, New Delhi responded far more positively than did most US allies. Some Indian strategic thinkers even see in the emerging US-India quasi-alliance an opportunity for "payback" to China. As G. Parthasarthy, former Indian Ambassador to Pakistan and Burma, put it: "Whether it was the Bangladesh conflict of 1971, or in the Clinton-Jiang Declaration in the aftermath of our nuclear tests, China has never hesitated to use its leverage with the Americans to undermine our security." Growing Chinese strategic pressure on the Malacca Straits has already led to maritime collaboration between India and the United States, with their navies jointly patrolling the straits. More significantly, US-India strategic engagement has scaled new heights with the announcement of a series of measures usually reserved for close US allies and friends: joint military exercises in Alaska that would boost India's high-altitude warfare capabilities in the Himalayan glaciers of northern Kashmir where it faces Pakistan and China; sale of military hardware including radars, aircraft engines, and surveillance equipment to India; joint naval exercises and the training of India's special forces; and intelligence sharing as well as the joint naval patrols in the Straits of Malacca. Washington also reportedly gave the green light for Israel to proceed with selling the Phalcon airborne early warning and control system (AWACS) to India—something that was earlier denied to China for fear of enhancing Beijing's air surveillance and early warning capabilities in the Taiwan Strait.

All of these measures send an implicit signal to China of India's growing military prowess. In a cover story in the authoritative *Beijing Review*, one of China's noted South Asia specialists expressed concern over the US sale of arms to India which "enables it to become the first country to have close military relations with the world's two big powers—the United States and Russia." To make matters worse, in early May 2002 Prime Minister Koizumi of Japan, Beijing's other Asian rival, which sees China representing a clear and future threat to its security, called for a broadening of Japan's security cooperation with India.

Many Chinese strategists believe India is using the war on terrorism as a pretext to militarily subdue Pakistan or to destabilize and dismember the country. Pakistan is the only country that stands up to India and thereby prevents Indian hegemony over the region, thus fulfilling a key objective of China's South Asia policy. 39 As South Asia watcher Ehsan Ahrari points out: "India may end up intensifying its own rivalry with China by remaining steadfast in its insistence that Musharraf kowtow to its demands, especially if China calculates that US-India ties are harming its own regional interests. China, though still concerned about the continued activism of Islamist groups in Pakistan and contiguous areas, is not at all willing to see the regional balance of power significantly tilt in favour of India." Though Beijing welcomes the new US commitment to prop up Beijing's "all-weather friend" after a decade of abandonment and estrangement, most Chinese strategists worry about the destabilizing consequences of a prolonged US military presence in Pakistan and increased influence on the future of Sino-Pakistan ties as well as on Pakistan's domestic stability. The Chinese are also believed to be "highly uncomfortable" with the four US military bases in Pakistan. Of special concern to Beijing is the US presence at Pasni in the Baluchistan region of Pakistan, where China is constructing a deep-water naval port at Gwadar, the inland Makran coastal highway linking it with Karachi, and several oil and gas pipeline projects.

Beijing has long been eyeing its construction of the naval base at Gwadar, at the mouth of the Strait of Hormuz in the Persian Gulf, as a bulwark against the US presence and India's growing naval power. Furthermore, the US military presence in Pakistan could sharpen the divide within the Pakistani military into pro-West and pro-Beijing factions, with China supporting the latter to regain ground lost since 9/11.44 The pro-Beijing lobby within the Pakistani military is reportedly getting restive and waiting to strike if and when General Musharraf falters. The pro-China faction within the Pakistani military could also join hands with the pro-Islamic fundamentalist faction opposing the US military presence on Pakistan's soil. Alternatively, it could throw its support behind those nationalist elements that find Pakistan's loss of its "strategic depth" in Afghanistan for elusive diplomatic gains very hard to digest. The US arms sales to India and joint US-Indian military exercises may further sour China's and Pakistan's willingness to assist Washington in its war on terrorism.

War Scenarios

It is said that each conflict simply prepares the ground for the next one or every war contains the seeds of another. The Afghan War of the 1980s against the Soviet occupation culminated in the war on terrorism in 2001. Whether the war on terrorism will lead to another war or a clash of civilizations or a nuclear jihad in South Asia, only time will tell. Pakistan is, in the words of former Italian Foreign Minister Gianni De Michelis, "the fuse of the world." The provinces close to the Afghan border and home to the US military bases are now controlled by Islamic parties that created the Taliban and are openly sympathetic to the aims and ideals of al Qaeda.

The rising anti-American sentiment in Pakistan as demonstrated in the recent elections has made the country increasingly unstable. Violence levels in Indian Kashmir also continue to rise. Many observers believe that Washington may have to rethink its strategy vis-à-vis Islamabad if the war on terrorism is to be won decisively. The complete dismantling of the al Qaeda terrorist infrastructure in Pakistan seems unlikely because of the apprehension within the Pakistani military that doing so would devalue Pakistan's importance in the US security strategy and once again make the United States turn its back on the country and make the country vulnerable to Western pressure and sanctions. It would also deprive Pakistan of invaluable Western aid and leverage vis-à-vis Washington and New Delhi.

One Chinese national security analyst argues that "what worries China more is the possibility that it could be drawn into a conflict, not between Pakistan and India per se, but between Pakistan and the United States, with the latter using India as a surrogate." With the top al Qaeda and Taliban leadership fleeing into Pakistan's Wild West and Pakistani-held Kashmir, Beijing knows full well that Pakistan is no longer the "frontline state" in the war on terrorism that it once was; it is, in fact, the battlefield in the war on terror. Should the India-Pakistani conflict escalate into a nuclear one, neither the geopolitical nor the radioactive fallout will remain limited to South Asia. Indeed, the most worrisome scenario would be one where Pakistan is losing a conventional conflict and uses tactical nuclear weapons in a desperate effort to win or to salvage a face-saving defeat that would allow the regime to survive. (The risk-taking nature of the Pakistani military leadership suggests that such a scenario cannot be completely ruled out.) Should India respond by launching strategic nuclear strikes resulting in the complete destruction of the Pakistani state, China would find it difficult to sit idly by. The next India-Pakistan war also could bring the United States and Pakistan on a collision course, with or without India acting as a US partner. Such a development would obviously present China with difficult choices. Open support for its closest ally would jeopardize China's relations with the United States and India. But nonintervention on Pakistan's behalf could encourage India to solve "the Pakistan problem" once and for all, with or without a nuclear exchange, and thereby tilt the regional balance of power decisively in its favour. As Zhang Xiaodong put it: "There is the real possibility that a new Indian-Pakistani war will take place in the future. This war would be disastrous, as it would change the whole political balance in Central and South Asia," which is currently tilted in China's favour. Unrestrained Indian power could eventually threaten China's security along its soft underbelly—Tibet and Xinjiang.

Should post-Musharraf Pakistan disintegrate or be taken over by Islamic extremists, a new level of instability would rock the region and increase tensions among Pakistan, India, and China. Another dreadful scenario is one in which Chinese-made Pakistani nuclear weapons fall into the hands of the United States, Israel, or even India in the event of a civil war should al Qaeda or the Taliban declare jihad against Pakistan—the weakest ally in the US-led anti-terrorism coalition. 51 India would be tempted to militarily intervene in Pakistan if Islamists gain control over the nuclear weapons of its neighbour, either through a coup or civil war. Such a scenario could reveal information regarding China's own nuclear program and the extent of help provided by Beijing to Islamabad. The scenario of Pakistan in splinters, with one piece becoming a radical Muslim state in possession of nuclear weapons, can no longer be simply rejected as an alarmist fantasy.

Difficult Choices

These scenarios put Beijing on the horns of a dilemma. Some Chinese strategists see in the current South Asian crisis an opportunity to recover lost ground and thwart India's ambitions to challenge China's future economic and military primacy in Asia. Should another war between India and Pakistan break out, New Delhi's high hopes of an India-US alliance to counter China may never materialize, a welcome development from China's perspective. Some hawks in the PLAsee China even benefiting from an India-Pakistani nuclear war. Hideaki Kase, a former special advisor to Japanese Premiers Takeo Fukuda and Yasuhiro

Nakasone, believes that "China wants an Indo-Pakistan war, possibly a nuclear conflict, to weaken India." At the time of the 1999 Kargil War, one Chinese military official had reportedly told a Western diplomat that "should India and Pakistan destroy themselves in a nuclear war, there would be peace along China's southwestern frontiers for at least three decades, and Beijing needs 20 to 30 years to consolidate its hold over restive Tibet and Xinjiang provinces." However, this remains a minority viewpoint, as a nuclear war would have worldwide repercussions in terms of global economic depression, humanitarian crises, WMD proliferation, and China's developmental priorities.

Most Chinese analysts and policymakers believe that Beijing should have absolutely minimum involvement in a situation where there can be no clear winners. Some argue that Beijing should seize the opportunity to coordinate its South Asia policy with Washington as it is in the interests of both countries to avert the world's first nuclear exchange and to use India-Pakistan tensions to strengthen Sino-US ties.

While the Pakistanis are confident that if war comes with India, China will throw its weight behind Pakistan, diplomatically as well as militarily, the Indians remain adamant that the Chinese would not do so for fear of India playing "the Taiwan and Tibet cards."

Interestingly, on 31 May 2002, the day Pakistan's new UN Ambassador, Munir Akram, issued an explicit nuclear warning to India, a Chinese Foreign Ministry spokesman denied a *Times of India* report that Chinese President Jiang Zemin had assured a US congressional delegation that China would not favour Pakistan in the existing tensions, and claimed that the report was "not based on facts." A Chinese South Asia analyst at Fudan University in Shanghai, Shen Dingli, told *The Wall Street Journal*: "China needs to send a message: For my own security I will intervene." Though Beijing may not overtly intervene in a limited war, China's geopolitical imperative requires it to come to Pakistan's defence if the latter's existence as a nation-state is threatened by India. Clearly, there is a great deal more to the Chinese role in South Asia than meets the eye. In the final analysis, Beijing's response to the next India-Pakistan war will be shaped by its desire to protect Chinese national interests, no matter what the cost.

Geostrategic concerns require China to covertly side with Pakistan, while publicly calling for restraint by both sides and appearing to be even-handed. In the triangular power balance game, the South Asian military balance of power is neither pro-India nor pro-Pakistan, it has always been pro-China. And Beijing will take all means possible, including war, to ensure that the regional power balance does not tilt in India's favour. Even in the absence of a war, Pakistan hopes to continue to reap significant military and economic payoffs not only from the intensifying Sino-Indian geopolitical rivalry in southern Asia but also from what many believe is the coming showdown between China and the United States, which will further increase the significance of China's strategic ties with Pakistan. In the meantime, a major consolation for Beijing is that a stronger Pakistan aided by the United States, Western Europe, Japan, and international financial institutions would be better able to balance and contain rival India.

8

India's Border Dispute with Nepal

BACKGROUND

Nepal is situated in between India and China. China is located on the northern border, whereas all three sides are surrounded by India. India and China are the neighbours of Nepal and it has very good relations with both of the countries. There are so many fellow-feeling in so many items due to close and neighbourly relations. At the same time there may have some issues, dialogues and debates in some extent because of closeness and inter-related with each others. It is natural that sometimes there might have some issues and problems in between the close neighbours. And border issue is one of them.

INDO-NEPAL BORDER

India and Nepal have shared an open border since 1950. The conception of such a border can be found in the Treaty of Peace and Friendship that the two countries signed that year. Provisions in the treaty, wherein citizens of both countries are given equal rights in matters of residence, acquisition of property, employment and movement in each other's territory, provide for an open border between the two countries. Although there is a general perception that the Indo-Nepal border has always allowed unrestricted movement, it has been argued that the concept of an open border started only after signing of the Treaty of Sugauli in 1815. Under the Treaty of Sugauli, Nepal ceded Sikkim, along with territory west of river Kali and east of river Teesta. However, some territory in Terai was restored to Nepal after the revision of the treaty in 1816. Further in 1865, the British India government returned additional territory to Nepal in recognition of its support to the British government during the 1857 revolt. After the restoration of Naya Muluk to Nepal, the India-Nepal border was finally settled.

During colonial times, the British had an interest in keeping the border open for two reasons. Firstly, impressed by the fighting skills of the Gurkhas, the British wanted to recruit them into the Indian Army. Secondly, Nepal was seen as a market for finished goods from India. To achieve these objectives, it was necessary to provide unrestricted cross border movement for both goods and people, and hence the idea of an open border. Independent India also followed the British tradition of an open border with Nepal. The open border between the two countries has facilitated close social, cultural, and economic exchanges and led to a special relationship between the two countries. People from both countries are free to enter the other's territory from any point on the border, while the movement of goods is allowed along 22 designated transit points. The unrestricted movement of people across the border over the centuries has led to the development of well-entrenched socio-cultural linkages. These linkages have, in turn, facilitated greater economic interdependence and political ties. There is no denying the fact that an open border has been a great facilitator of strong and unique bilateral relations. At the same time, it has given rise to many irritants and problems that raise serious concerns.

There are many points of dispute along the Indo-Nepal border, mostly a result of the constantly shifting courses of the turbulent Himalayan rivers. Prominent among these are the ones relating to Kalapani and Susta. The submergence, destruction and removal of border pillars and encroachment into no-man's land by people from either side add to the problem. Allegations of excesses such as intimidation, and forcible grabbing of land by either side along the disputed border also surface from time to time. The disputed border has created lots of unease not only between the two countries but also among their local populations.

An open border allows easy egress to terrorists and insurgents. In the late 1980s, Sikh and Kashmiri terrorists sneaked into India via Nepal. In later years, many insurgent groups from the North East, such as the United Liberation Front of Asom (ULFA), the National Democratic Front of Bodoland (NDFB), and the Kamtapur Liberation Organization (KLO), also misused the open border.

In recent years, it has been reported that many terrorists have sneaked into India through the porous and poorly guarded Indo-Nepal border. Earlier, Maoists reportedly often escaped into India when pursued by Nepalese security agencies.

Apart from insurgents and terrorists, many hard-core criminals pursued by Indian and Nepalese security forces escape across the open border.

These anti-national elements indulge in illegal activities, such as smuggling of essential items and fake Indian currency, gun-running, and drugs and human trafficking. Unrestricted migration over the years has produced territorial pockets dominated by people originating from the other country. The net effect of such migration, in extreme cases, is the clamour for a 'homeland', as was witnessed in the hill district of Darjeeling adjoining the Indo-Nepal border. A similar situation might arise in Madhesh region of Nepal. These adverse consequences of an open border have led from time to time to demands for its closure.

Boundary in the Constitution of the Kingdom of Nepal-1990

The Constitution has a provision that any treaty or agreement related to the boundary and the territory of the country must be approved and implemented by a two-thirds majority of the members of parliament present in both Houses of the Parliament. But what is more important is that the Constitution completely prohibits the territorial division of the country even if it is passed by the absolute majority of the parliament...........

The following clauses are mentioned under the title 'Kingdom' of Article 4:

(1) Nepal is a multi-ethnic, multi-linguistic, democratic, independent, and indivisible sovereign Hindu and Constitutional Monarchical Kingdom.

(2) The territory of Nepal shall comprise: a) the territory existing at the commencement of this Constitution; and b) such other territory as may be acquired after the commencement of this Constitution...........

Indian Military Check-posts in Nepal

In keeping with bullying attitude, India established its military check posts on the Nepalese frontier of the Nepal-China borderline. This happened during the premiership of Matrika Prasad Koirala, beginning 9 June 1952, at 18 points of the Nepalese frontier. In each of the checkpoints, 20 to 40 Indian army personnel equipped with arms and communication equipment were deployed, together with a few Nepali army and civilian officials. The Indian army deployment was completed in two trips to Nepal.

Ever since their deployment, Nepal's political parties and civil society members kept on voicing their strong opposition to this issue. Once in 1959, a loud protest was launched, but the check posts remained as they were. At long last, the issue was again raised, this time more sharply, during the premiership of Kirti Nidhi Bista, and consequently, on 20 April 1969, the check-posts were removed and the Indian army personnel sent back home. But what is to be remembered here is that the Indian para-military forces stationed at Kalapani in Darchula district of Nepal ever since 1962 during Sino-Indian war are still not withdrawn. As a result, Indian military camps can still be seen in and around the Kalapani-Limpiyadhua area. The talk has been going on between Nepal and India regarding this "encroached and occupied" land of Nepal as well, but to no avail and the problem remains as it is, mainly because of no concrete dialogue and negotiation...........

Viewed from Nepal's security perspective, the current strategy of keeping southern border open and northern border controlled is not in tune with the changing requirements of time. However, a careful and scientific balance needs to be maintained in managing border systems on both sides. For this to happen, Nepal should begin opening the northern border points for the regional balance of economic development. It is to be recalled that a Cabinet decision has been made on 25 April 2002 for opening some previously prohibited tourist destinations. Whatever it was in the past, Nepal must not tolerate the military activity of the countries of any part of the globe, within the nation.

Border Management

Different countries have adopted different systems of managing their border vis-à-vis their neighbours. Among them, following three systems are mostly in practice in international arena:

- Open Border System..........
- Controlled Border System..........
- Close Border System..........

In normal situations, the four levels mentioned above are implemented one after the other. But sometimes, these procedures may overlap each other or there could be a long gap between the two procedures.

Such as the political decision on allocation of border and boundary delimitation can be carried out simultaneously but demarcation of boundary could take years to complete after boundary delimitation. For example, boundary demarcation of western Nepal, along the river Mahakali, where the Sugauli Treaty of 1816 did boundary delimitation, has not yet been carried out. Some borders may remain without administration for years while some may be under the administration of one or the other state before the demarcation is completed.

Nepal-India Border Management

Nepal-India Joint Border Management Committee was formed on 28 February 1997 to perform the new activities concerning the management of border between the two countries. Joint meetings of the Committee were held three times till this date: Whatever may be the history but an open border system exists between Nepal and India. Citizens of both the countries can cross and enter each other's border any time and without any restrictions.

Implications of Open Border System

If we make a list of both positive and negative implications of the open border system between Nepal and India, Nepal shares certainly most of the negative aspect.

Positive implications :

1. Convenience in movement and travel
2. Strengthening mutual ties
3. Quick emergency response and assistance
4. Medical service facilities
5. Immediate supply of food-grains and daily consumer goods
6. Competitive market
7. Supply of local labour
8. Others:

Another positive aspect of the India-Nepal open border is the opportunity for enhancing economic benefits for the residents along the border, as they can easily access to each other's weekly open-air markets (*hat bazaar*) for selling and buying their goods such as vegetables, dairy products, domestic cattle, etc. Such markets are organised at different place seven days a week on both sides of the frontier.

Negative implications :

1. Encroachment of border and no-man's land
2. Cross-border terrorism
3. Illegal arms transaction
4. Women trafficking
5. Peace and security
6. Drugs trafficking
7. Trans-border crime
8. Theft and robbery
9. Smuggling of goods and machinery
10. Kidnapping of individuals
11. Plane hijacking
12. Distortion of historical facts

13. Migration
14. Entry of Bhutanese refugees
15. Deforestation
16. Degeneration of political values
17. Others:

Distribution of fake educational certificates, fake citizenship certificates, abduction of children and businessmen, smuggling of petroleum products, kerosene and food grains, leakage in the revenue collection of customs and excise duty, fake currency notes circulation, adverse effect on Nepali culture and tradition, smuggling of drugs, illegal transport of wildlife, illegal hunting, trafficking of unauthorized medicines, illegal import of below standard chemical fertilizers, smuggling of high quality fertilizer, export of cattle, poaching, transporting audio blue-video materials causing deformity by theft, the loss of Nepali identity due to the disappearance of traditional Nepali culture, the rise in anti-social activities, rape, cheating and dacoit, etc. have also resulted due to the open uncontrolled, unregulated, porous, wanton, vagabond, blurred and unquiet border between Nepal and India

NEPAL-CHINA BORDER

Nepal has had border business and some issues with both of the countries, India and China. So far as the issues and border business with China is concerned, it is settled and resolved with signing the Boundary Treaty of 5 October 1961 by His Majesty the King of Nepal and Chairman of the People's Republic of China, after delineating and physical demarcation of the boundary line. However, there were disputes, conflicts, debates and controversies in 35 places including the question of Sagarmatha (Mount Everest) during the joint boundary demarcation on the Sino-Nepal borderline. But it was settled forever in accordance with the principles of equality, mutual benefit, friendship and mutual accommodation. Besides, it was adopted by both the parties, the Five Principles of Peaceful Co-existence and in a spirit of fairness, reasonableness, mutual understanding and most importantly respecting each other as Nepal and China have the equal rights and status in the international arena. Regarding the question of

Sagarmatha, it was agreed to take the Nepalese map drawn with its historical facts, which depicted the highest part of the peak on Nepal side. As a result, the dispute of Sagarmatha was settled and ended while the visiting Prime Minister Chou En-Lai made a statement in Kathmandu on 28 April 1960 that "Sagarmatha belongs to Nepal." Finally the border line was demarcated and erected border pillars with watershed principle, determining the water-parting line to connect snow-capped high altitude mountain peaks, passing and crossing through mountain passes and spurs, saddles and cols, rivers and rivulets, pasture land and river basin or valleys. With the basis of these entire mutual understanding, Nepal-China border demarcation was successfully completed within the period of two and half years. Consequently, three Joint Boundary Protocols have been signed as the last one in 8 December 1988. However, it is high time to make the fourth protocol, because fourteen years have been elapsed since the third protocol was signed.

NEPAL-INDIA BORDER

So far as the Indo-Nepal border demarcation is concerned, Nepal-India Joint Technical Level Boundary Committee is working for the last 21 years (since 15 November 1981). But the boundary business is not yet completed. There may be so many reasons the boundary business not to be completed in due time, though it has the target to complete it by 2003. However, this type of target had been fixed many times in the past as in 1993, 1998 and 2001. But the target was not materialized. The main reasons and issues of the boundary business with India is the border encroachments, disputes on certain segments, divergence of opinion on basic materials such as maps and old documents for demarcation, slackness in joint survey field teams and so on and so forth.

Nepal and India has two broad issues concerning border business :

BORDER DEMARCATION

The Treaty of Sugauli of 4 March 1816, Supplementary Treaty of 11 December 1816 and Boundary Treaty of 1 November 1860 delineate the boundary of Nepal with India. British East India

Company made treaty of Sugauli on 2 December 1815 and it was provided to Nepal to make the counter signature by fifteen days. But Nepal did not make the signature in due time, because of unwillingness. It was finally ratified after 92 days under pressure and compulsion enforced by the British regime that they will invade Kathmandu, the capital city of Nepal. Eventually, it was not signed by the King or Prime Minister/Maharaja but by only the courtier Chandra Shekhar Upadhaya. So there were disputes and conflicts and controversy on the borderline even after the ratification of the Treaty.

Historical Border Disputes

There were so many issues of disputes just after the Sugauli Treaty. Some of the disputed areas are cited as examples as follows:

1. Disputes on Siwalik Range : whether the borderline runs from the crest (ridge) of the Siwalik Range or northern or southern foot-hill of the range!
2. Origin of the river Mechi : whether it is originated from north-east of Antoo Hill or from north-west!
3. Dunduwa Range : India had claimed that the border line should be followed on the northern foot from Arrahnala to Talbagauda, whereas Nepal denied it.
4. Dispute on ownership of the village and settlements of Ramnagar Zamindari area.
5. Dispute on the lands adjoined with the districts of Tirahoot and Sarun.
6. Land area of Sharada Barrage constructed by India on the river Mahakali.
7. Disputes on the borderline of the river and rivulets, whether it has to be taken on the old course or the new channel.
8. Disputes on the demarcation of borderlines in agricultural land, forest area and village areas, where there are not conspicuous features.

Some of the above mentioned disputes were settled with mutual discussions. For example, identification of the origin of the river Mechi was solved by Campbell, taken as the origination from north-east, though Captain Lloyd had judged in 1827 that the area falls under the jurisdiction of Sikkim. Similarly, the dispute of Dunduwa range was solved jointly by Lieutenant Col. Mac Andrew and Siddhiman Singh Rajbhandari on 7 January 1875 that the borderline shall be demarcated on the southern foot-hill of Dunduwa Range from where the plain area begins. Regarding the disputes of Ramnagar Zamindari area, it was settled on 2 January 1841 with an Ikararnama of 95 people of village-heads, gentlemen, Chautaria and Guru Gharana. As far as the matter of the exchange of lands of Sharada Barrage is concerned, Nepal has not yet received 36.67 Acre of land from India. These are some of the examples of the then border issues between Nepal and East India Company. The main problem lies that Nepal's southern borderline on the Indo-Gangetic plain with India does not run from the prominent natural features such as mountain peaks, passes, crests etc.

BORDER DISPUTES AFTER INDIA'S INDEPENDENCE

The disease of border demarcation issues and disputes have not been cured even after the independence of India from the British rule in 1947. Encroachment on the Nepalese frontier have been rather increased. It is due to population boom across the Indian frontier. Secondly, dense forest of Charkoshe Jungle of the Nepalese frontier was being cut-off and cleared-up, so that encroachment of the Nepalese land from Indian population pressure was much easier, where there were not boundary pillars and demarcation of ten-yard width No-man's land.

By this time, there are 54 places and spots of encroachment, dispute, conflict, controversy and debate along Indo-Nepal borderline, especially in the plain area of southern border of Nepal. There are number of cases of disputes and encroachments in the Nepalese frontier of 21 districts among 26 districts which are adjoined with India. The area of encroachment consists of from a few hundred square meters of a small patch or strip of land to a big chunk of 372 square kilometers. There are frequent border disputes and debates in the borderline, on which it is not yet demarcated and erected border pillars. Surprisingly, disputes have been raised even on that spots where the boundary pillars have been installed. It is due to pull out of the pillars and cultivate the land and construction of houses, disfiguring the no-man's land. It has created the problems on either side of the borderline.

Places of Encroachments and Disputes

There are not less than 54 places of encroachments, disputes, debates, controversy, differences and conversations on the Nepalese frontier and even inside the depth of the frontier. The most noted places and spots are Kalapani-Limpiyadhura area, Susta area, Mechi riverian sector, Balmikinagar, Thori, Sandakpur, Manebhanjyang, Chiwabhanjyang, Bhantabari, Jogbani, Sakhada-Lalapatti, Kunauli, Sunauli-Belhi, Krishnanagar, Santalia, Bhadanala, Biranala, Luna river area, Laxmanpur dam area, Rasiawal Khurdalotan dam area etc. etc.

1. After the independence of India, the issue of dispute was raised in Susta area along the river Narayani on the Nepalese frontier. The area is consisted of near about 14,850 hectares. The main reason of dispute is change of course by the river Narayani. During heavy floods of 1845, 1954, and 1980 the river changed its course dramatically some kilometers westward to the Nepalese territory. After the flood, Indian peasants used to encroach and cultivate the Nepalese land supposing that the new river course is the boundary line between the two nations. The river is changing its course more and more westward to Nepal side nearly every year but bluntly during flood havocs. And Indian nationals are encroaching the Nepalese land more when the river shifts it course.
2. The largest chunk of encroachment by India is Kalapani-Limpiyadhura area. It consists of 372 sq. km (37,800 hectares). It was encroached just after the border war of November 1962 between India and China. After the defeat with the Chinese army, Indian troops retarded back and set up a camp in the Nepalese territory of Kalapani area. Indian army men judged the Kalapani area as a strategic point to watch the Chinese activity and to check the attack / infiltration of the Chinese army via Lipulek Pass. There is a most strategic and highly sensitive spot with 6,180

meters high in Kalapani area, from where it can be visualized with the help of a binocular, whether horse or mule/ sheep or goat/ white or fair complexed men are crossing the Lipulek Pass to and from Taklakot of Tibet. At first, there were some Indian armed policemen with some tents and hand operating wireless and binoculars in Kalapani camp, as they had named Indo-Tibetan Border Post (ITBP). But these days there are more than eight buildings constructed having bunkers, deployed battalions of Indian army men with modern arms and ammunitions and means of satellite communication. Some of the buildings have central heating system, not to let freeze the expensive arms and ammunitions during winter season. Presently, the crux of the matter of dispute in Kalapani area is the determination of the river Kali, whether it is originated from nearby Lipulek Pass or Limpiyadhura or an artificial pond, south of Pankhagad Khola.

3. Mechi riverian sector is one of the notable disputed areas in the recent times since 1995. There are disputes in various places along 20 kilometer of the river Mechi. The main reason of the dispute is that Joint Boundary Survey Team erected new and small boundary pillars, ignoring the old Masonry Pillars (Junge Pillars), whereas Urdu written map of 1874 was taken as the basis of the demarcation of the course of river Mechi. The most illogical aspect of the dispute on this segment is that it tried to demarcate the old river course, instead of counting century old masonry Junge main boundary pillars, which have been standby along the river. These Junge pillars are the live guards in the border of Nepal, erected by the British Surveyors themselves during 1816-17, just after the Treaty of Sugauli. What needs the solid and live proofs more than these live and standby Junge Pillars? Paradoxically, these Junge Pillars have been categorized as the Reference Pillars, but not the main boundary pillars. So there are cases of encroachments and disputes in near about 1,600 hectares of Nepalese land from Bahundangi, Nakalbanda to Kakarbhitta, Pathamari, Bhadrapur, Maheshpur etc.

4. Border pillars and ten-yard width no-man's land have been disappeared due to the construction of Laxmanpur dam and 22 km embankment by India on the river Rapti, only 350 meter apart from the Border pillar No. 19. Small rivers flowing from Nepal have been blocked and Nepalese land of 5 Village Development Committees (VDCs) have been submerged.
5. The other construction by India is the Rasiawal Khurdalotan Dam on the river Danab-Ghongi in Marchawar area of Nepal. The three kilometer long dam has been constructed just 40 meter apart of Border Pillar No. 30, so that 20 km long no-man's land have been encroached. As a result, paddy land of 11 VDCs of Nepal have been submerged during the monsoon season. Besides, Lumbini, the birthplace of Lord Buddha will surely be inundated, if the water of the river is blocked by closing down the shutters of the dam and by further constructing the embankments.
6. 222 hectares of Nepalese land have been encroached in connection to the construction of Afflux Bond of Tanakpur Barrage by India. In connection to the construction of Sharada Barrage, Nepal has yet to get 14.84 hectare (36.67 Acre) of land. Furthermore, most recently India has encroached the area of six households and one government office of Nepal in Hile area of Pashupatinagar Ward-4. This is due to the erection of new Pillar No. 71/22 by Indian side in 8 July 2002. Similarly, part of Sandakpur (3,336 meter high) hill area of Ilam has been encroached. Sandakpur is a touristic place, from where Mount Kanchanjunga can be visualized majestically. There are various cases of encroachments in 21 districts of Nepal out of 26, which are adjoined with Indian States.

NEPAL-INDIA JOINT TECHNICAL LEVEL BOUNDARY COMMITTEE

Nepal-India Joint Technical Level Boundary Committee is working for the last twenty-one years. It is going to relocate the missing pillars, reconstruction of the damaged and dilapidated pillars, clear ten-yard width no-man's land and preparation of strip-maps of both the sides of borderline. But it has not resolved the issues, such as Kalapani-Limpiyadhura, identification of the source or river Kali, Susta dispute, Mechi controversy etc. These are the major issues and problems of demarcations of border between two nations, which should be settled in higher level (most probably in head of the government level) with diplomatic and political level talks.

The issues climb slowly up to the ministerial level but it is instantly pushed back to the technical level, which has its limitations as the nature of the problem. In such a fashion, major issues have not yet given yield by the higher level decision making authorities.

BORDER MANAGEMENT

There is an open border system between Nepal and India, whereas Nepal has its controlled border system with China. It needs passport and visa to go to China and recently Hongkong, after China regained it from Britain. If we have a look back on the border management system between Nepal and India, anyone entering into Nepal particularly to the Kathmandu valley and towns of Tarai in general, had to get Rahadani or visa from the district administrations.

It was prior to the restoration of Naya Muluk by Nepal in 1860, as the controlled border system was prevalent during that period. Afterwards, it was started slowly to keep the border open for recruiting the Nepalese hill and sturdy boys in British Gurkha regiment. The second factor was to have easy and free access of British and Indian goods and material into Nepal and Tibet (via Nepal). Next was to secure raw materials from Nepal to India such as timber, forest products, herbs and medicinal plants, hides and skins etc.

Open Border System

Nepal-India Peace and Friendship Treaty of 31st July 1950 motivated for the openness of border between two countries. After the installation of democracy in Nepal in February 1951, it became major turning point in reinforcing the Nepal-India border open with the accelerated movement of Indian nationals into Nepal. Indians used to come to Kathmandu as politicians as advisors to the Nepalese ministers, overseers as technical experts, unemployed citizens as teachers, retailers as whole seller businessmen etc. Similarly, Nepalese were also free to go to Indian cities in search of jobs and works as guards, domestic workers and restaurant waiters. All these phenomena can be cited as Nepal India open border as it is unique in the world in the sense that people of both countries could cross the international borderline from any point / any time. Single citizen could cross the frontier of both the sides without any record running to and fro so many times a day.

Controlled Border System

In other aspect, if we have a look back on the Nepalese perspective, Rahadani or controlled border system was on practice till four and half decades ago. This system was unknowingly relaxed after the construction of Tribhuvan highway, which linked Kathmandu to the Indian town Raxaul.. Before the completion of this highway, Nepalese people even going from Nepal to Nepal via Indian territory had to obtain Rahadani permit from Rahadani Goswara, Kathmandu or local / district office (Gadhi-Gaunda-Goswara). For the foreigners and even emigrant Nepali residing in India should have obtained Rahadani (visa) to enter into Nepalese territory either from Nepal Embassy or counselor or Alainchi Kothi of Patna, according to Rahadani Regulation- 2009 BS (1952 AD). But it was relaxed slowly, however Nepalese have not forgotten the then Rahadani System.

Impact of Open Border System

Every object has its two aspects as every coin bears two faces. And every item has its negative and positive impacts. Similarly, Nepal-India open border system has its negative and positive impacts for both the nations. But Nepal has experienced a large percentage of negative impacts in many cases, as compared to India. If we make an inventory, negative impact outnumbers the positive one for Nepal. Followings are the impacts of open border system :

Positive Impact

As we make a list of positive impacts, it may be the followings:

1. *Easy access:* The most positive aspect of open border system is the easy movement of people of both the countries.
2. *Strengthens relationship:* People to people relation on the frontiers of both sides has been maintained and strengthened due to free movement of people on either side of the border.
3. *Rescue operation:* Prompt services have been offered and provided on either side during calamities and disasters.
4. *Health service:* When there is an epidemic, health services can be offered from both the sides.
5. *Instant supply of labour:* When there is a shortage of local labour in one side it can be supplied instantly from other side.
6. *Competitive Market:* There is always a competition between the businessmen of the cross-frontier towns to be benefited to the consumers..
7. *Prompt Supply of food grains and daily stuff:* Unrestricted border has made comfortable for the prompt supply of food grains and daily foodstuffs from either side of the territory, where there are shortages.
8. Open border has economically benefited the inhabitants of both sides of the border from the sell and purchase of livestock products, vegetables and daily kitchen stuff in *Hat Bazars* (open-roof markets) taking place regularly in various days a week in different parts on either side.

Negative Impact

Current open and unrestricted border system between Nepal and India has created so many adverse impacts and it has emerged many problems. Some of the issues have been mentioned as follows:

Border Encroachment: Aggression of boundary line and encroachment on the Nepalese territory is the by-product of the open border system. People are free to cross the border without any restriction. Some of the inhabitants who reside in the frontier area do not hesitate to destroy and pull off the main boundary pillars.

Cross-border terrorism: Open border has provided as safe passage to the terrorists. India has been blaming Nepal that Pakistani ISI agents are infiltrating into India via Nepalese territory. But it is the fact that Pakistanis must travel to India at first to come to Nepal, if they use the land route. Most recently Nepalese Maoist terrorists are creating havoc and they are making war with the Nepalese army men and policemen killing so many innocent local people, especially in the hill districts of Nepal. Those Maoist fighters who have been saved as casualties use to cross the borderline and they are taking shelter in the Indian settlements. The Indian policemen have arrested most recently five wounded Maoist casualties, who were under treatment in the private hospital at Lucknow. Besides, Lucknow Police officer D.B.Bakchhi arrested eight Nepalese Maoist terrorists (with one woman), including the leader Aakash Darlami (Nischal) and handed over them to the adjoined Nepal police post on the 8th of April 2002. Local inhabitants of India believe that Maoist terrorists are taking shelter at Kauwapur, Bishanpur, Balarampur and Baharainch of India as they think safe and secure (Gorkhapatra Daily, 22 April '02). American Assistant Secretary of State Christina Rocca expressed her worrines during her recent visit to India that the Nepalese Maoists are taking shelter in India. United States under its military assistance has proceeded to provide equivalent to 20 million dollars to control the Maoist terrorism in Nepal. (Gorkhapatra Daily, 25 April '02)

Trafficking of girls: More than five thousand Nepalese girls have been sold annually in the Indian brothels. U.N. Women Development Fund, UNICEF Nepal field office mentions that there are near about two hundred thousand Nepalese girls and women in total in India. They are as the consuming commodity in the red-light and prostitution areas of Bombay, Calcutta, Darbhanga, Betia, Siligurhi and some other cities of India.

Illegal import of arms and ammunitions: Various types of guns, fire arms, gun-powder, grenades and its raw-materials, used by the Maoist terrorists have been confiscated by the army men, especially in the western hill districts. These unregistered and unlicensed arms and ammunitions might have been transported illegally because of the weakness of unrestricted border.

Smuggling of goods, material and machinery: There is always a possibility to be transported market goods and merchandise through the illegal entry points of the border, where there is no custom or police post.

Smuggle of archeological artifacts: Archeological materials such as ancient bricks and materials of Lumbini area (birthplace of Lord Buddha) have been smuggled to Piparhawa of India. Because India is going to construct duplicate structures to draw attention of the world, saying as Buddha was born in India. They are trying to distort the historical facts due to lack of the controlled border system between two countries.

Cross-border crime: Criminal activities such as murder, theft, and rape cases have been increased on the frontier of both the countries due to open border.

Kidnapping: Kidnapping of businessmen and children of well to do family is due to unrestricted movement in the borderline.

Highjacking: Indian aircraft IC 814 to Delhi was highjacked from Tribhuvan international airport on 24 December 2000. It was ultimately landed at Kandhar, Afganistan and the aircraft with the passengers were stranded for complete one week. People realized that open border is the cause of highjacking. It is to be noted that passport / identification card or controlled border system was introduced for the air passengers at Tribhuvan international airport Kathmandu and New Delhi Indiragandhi international airport after the Indian aircraft highjacking incident.

Robbery and theft: Two Indian motorcycle men looted Rs. 200,000 from the local money change counter at Malangwa of Sarlahi district in 5 February 2000. After snatching the money, they rushed and entered into Sonbarsha of Indian territory.

Infiltration of Bhutanese refugees: Nearly 100,000 Bhutanese refugees infiltrated into Nepalese territory five years ago via India. It was the cause and effect of open border between Nepal and India.

Deforestation and exploitation of medicinal plants and herbs: Smugglers have exploited Nepalese forest resources illegally due to open border.

Peace and Security: General people of Nepal are experiencing that peace and security in the nation is being weak due to free movement of people on either side of the frontier. Third country nationals, as similar face to the Nepalese and Indian may cross the border in the form of Indian / Nepalese national. It is creating problems to maintain peace and national security in both the nations.

Migration: Density of population in the adjoining districts of India is higher than in the frontier areas of Nepal. So some of the Indian people resembling with the Nepalese faces have migrated to Nepalese territory, being benefited by the unmanaged open border.

Trafficking of narcotic drugs, encroachment on the Nepalese culture and traditions, leakage in revenue collection, distribution of fake academic certificates, prevalence of anti-social activities, rape cases, construction of dams and embankment submerging the borderline are also the result of thorough passage from the uncontrolled and wanton border

Concluding Remarks

Nepal and India has a long and traditional relation. It has naturally promoted social and cultural relationship among the general people of both the nations, through matrimonial relation as well. Nepalese boys are the son-in-laws of the Indian nationals. Similarly, Indian daughters have been the daughter-in-laws of the Nepalese, being Nepalese and Indian fathers as the father-in-laws each other. So the border demarcation issues and the problem of border management can be solved through from the level of the general people to the levels of intellectuals, diplomats and politicians, if they make lively interactions with each others. They can highlight the issues, make convince to others by discussions. It can be made good understanding to solve the problem and issues, segment by segment grasping the difficulties of other side.

But the most important thing is the dedication and willingness to resolve the issues, since border business is a matter of equal participation from both the parties. Nothing can be happened if only one nation is willing, eager and hurried. It needs the equal spirit from both sides. Nextly, it must have time bound programme and monitoring of work from upper level is also important. Effective instruction from higher level to the lower and grass-root level field teams must flow in due time. Particular problem of particular segment of the border must be solved in such a fashion that this is resolved forever and no question will be raised in future.

So far as the border management is concerned, Open border system has created so many problems and it has affected in social and economic aspects for both Nepal and India. The most sensitive issues these days are the free movement of the terrorists and transportation of illegal arms and ammunitions across the open border. This is quite harmful for both the countries. An uncontrolled, unrestricted and opened border constitutes the breeding ground for terrorism, criminal, illegal and anti-social activities. Keeping in view the welfare and development of general people of both the nations, there is an urgent need to manage and regulate the free movement of people. It needs to check and stop transportation of smuggled goods across the unpatrolled open border. The time has been changed much from peacefulness to disturbing and troublesome. General people of both the countries are feeling panicky and fearfulness due to current circumstances in the South Asian region. It has to be made joint efforts to review the impact of open border system through dialogues and negotiations. It must come to the conclusion jointly to make the border restricted for the terrorist, controlled for smugglers, obstructed for the girl traffickers, checked for the criminals, stopped for narcotic holders but managed for the genuine passengers and regulated for legal export and import.

LAND DISPUTES BETWEEN INDIA AND NEPAL

Nepal is at the brink of historical transition. The civil war has ended and so has the 240 year old royal institution. The Maoists have left the jungle to join the parliament. The amalgamation of Maoist guerrillas into the national army has been a success. Communist hardliners have finally agreed that the only way to win the hearts of the people is through democratic practice. The heyday of drawing power out of the barrels of a gun is over. The rise of Maoism in Nepal is a political epiphany. It is an upshot of age old practice of feudalism, poverty, inequality, untouchability and other socio-economic factors that had choked the Nepalese society.

The wound was further idealized by communist dreams. Due to the drastic reform within the party, the Maoists have written a new history in the soil of Nepal. Flexibility of thought and the right timing, both have contributed to make it a successful party.

Looking back at the sacrifice of nearly 17,000 lives, Nepal's political situation should have been better. Nevertheless, the present imbroglio suggests a different direction. The ritual of democratization has been painful. Newer difficulties have cropped up. Federalism issues have stirred the nation. Questions of social and political inclusion of various ethnic groups in mainstream politics have created a concern.

In the backdrop of these vibrant political transactions, India's role has been phenomenal. Back from the days of the Sugauli treaty in 1950, India has dominated the scene; sometimes drawing water out of the Nepalese river and sometimes constructing dams on Nepalese soil. When the British quit India in the late 1940's, Nepal did not have strong leaders to ask back for her lost territories.

One of the crucial setbacks in the India-Nepal relationship has been the issue of land grab. India still occupies 37,000 hectares of Nepali land in Kalapani. The encroachment has been ongoing since November 1962. It is estimated that the claims of land-grab extends to over 23 districts covering 60,662 hectares.

The second major land grab is in the Susta area where India has seized 14,500 hectares of Nepali land. The Narayani River changes its course every year leaving a substantial portion of dry land. These areas are in turn possessed by Indian farmers. Various prime ministers have tried to settle the dispute during their times including late G.P.Koirala, however, no solution has been reached.

In addition to Kalapani and Susta; other occupied areas lie in Mechi, Tanakpur, Sandakpur, Pashupatinagar and Hile Thori. The

Indian border security force had carried series of operations in the past. In May 2009, the case in Dang in which Indian forces seized Nepali land and carried out atrocities is still not stale. Thousands of Nepalese were displaced.

The Indian base camp at Darchula is another example of encroachment. Forceful border penetration seriously questions India's attitude towards Nepal. This geographical bully will strain the historic kinship between the two countries. In an interview on February 18, 2009, Indian Foreign Secretary Shiv Shankar Menon said, "I think 98 percent of the boundary problem in Nepal had been resolved. " Although Menon has recently visited Kathmandu, the boundary problem has not budged. Will India be happy to return the occupied land in Kalapani and Susta?

Although Nepal failed, she has fought on all levels to regain occupied land

International intervention should be sought to resolve the dispute. India's territorial hegemony has to stop once and for all. The annexation of Sikkim in 1974 should not be forgotten. As a strong preacher of democracy, India should respect territorial harmony and resolve the issue once and for all. India's dormant role during the Bhutanese refugee crisis also serves as a burning example of how its foreign policy functions in regard to Nepal. If it had sincerely wanted, the refugee problem would have been solved many years ago.

Nepal does not share a common border with Bhutan. However, more than 100,000 refugees came to Nepal via India. The Indian government did not allow them to settle. Professor Surya Subedi has said in his article that, "Indo-Nepal relations are marred by mistrust, confusion and dogmatism." Is Nepal paying the price of being India-locked from three sides? Or is it the sheer negligence of the Nepalese leaders who are lost within the vicious circle of blame-game?

This intimidation will not stop unless Kathmandu stops looking towards New Delhi for its political solution. Had the Nepalese leaders been confident and bold enough to make their own decisions, the Indian government would not have intervened.

Why do our political leaders rely so much on India? These are questions that have to be considered in order to deal with this crisis.

The only way to resolve this territorial dispute is through the willingness and efforts of Nepali politicians. Timely awareness and proactive measures can save the borders of Nepal from shrinking in shape and size.

Kalapani: A Bone of Contention Between India and Nepal

The Kalapani, is a 35 square kilometer area claimed by India and Nepal. It has been embroiled in controversy since mid-1996, shortly after the ratification of the Mahakali treaty with India by Nepal 's Parliament.

The 1816 Segauli treaty between the British Raj and Nepal provided that the Kali river would mark the western border between India and Nepal. Kalapani is on its east bank. The pilgrim-cum-trade route here from India to Tibet runs for the most part on the west bank of the Kali, but, at Kalapani it crosses briefly to the east bank. India asserts that old British surveys and maps show this section as part of India. But Nepal points to other maps and documents to support its claims.

Nepal has laid claim to all areas east of the Lipu Gad—the rivulet that joins the river Kali on its border, a tri-junction with India and China. The tributaries of the Kali River comprise a number of streams, including the Lipu Gad, which merge into the main river at the Kalapani temple near the tri-junction. The Nepalese contention is that the Lipu Gad is, in fact, the Kali river up to its source to the east of the Lipu Lekh Pass.

According to Nepal , after the India-China war in 1962, Nepal allowed Indian troops to occupy some posts in Nepal as a defensive measure. India has withdrawn from all of them, except Kalapani. It apparently wants to hold on to that post.

Nepal has long complained about minor Indian encroachments into other parts of the border, mainly when rivers shift their course from time to time. But Kalapani is different, with Indian soldiers in possession, and this has raised nationalist hackles in Nepal. Nepal claims that the Kalapani area lies within its Darchula district and, therefore, the Indo-Tibetan Border Police (ITBP) presence there amounts to "Indian encroachment of Nepal 's territory." It has therefore demanded that the border post be removed and the area restored to it.

Nepal 's claims first surfaced during the negotiations resulting in the Sino-Nepal Border Agreement (1961), Sino-Nepal Border Protocol (1963) and, the subsequent 1979 Border Protocol, and it continues to seek adjustments on the western extremity of the border, about 5.5 kms. westwards towards the Lipu Lekh Pass.

Official sources in India claim that the administrative and revenue records dating back to 1830s (available with the UP state government), show that Kalapani area has traditionally been administered as part of Pithoragarh district. A State Police post was established by the state government at the now disputed site in 1956 and operated from here till 1979. Since 1979, the Indo-Tibetan Border Police (ITBP) have been manning a post for surveillance over the area, which is on the tri-junction of the international boundaries of India, Nepal and the autonomous region of Tibet in China. According to India , vide Article 5 of the Segauli Treaty (1816), Nepal had renounced all claims to areas 'lying west of the river Kali'. The Kali (now Mahakali) river thus evolved into a well-identified border demarcation in the west. Before claiming some area around the Kalapani tri-junction, Nepal had disputed even the source of the river Kali, as claimed by India.

India has contradicted Nepal 's claim that Lipu Gad is in fact, the Kali river upto its source to the east of the Lipu Lekh Pass. India holds that the river Kali begins from the meeting point of the Lipu Gad with the stream from Kalapani springs. In the Survey of India Maps, the border thus leaves the mid-stream of the river Kali below Kalapani turning eastwards away from the river, to follow the high watershed.

Significantly, British India conducted the first regular surveys of the upper reaches of the river Kali, in the 1870s. A map of 1879 vintage shows the whole Kalapani area as part of India. India has refuted Nepal 's proposal that the map sketched by the British-

Indian government in 1850 and 1856 should mark the basis for the origin of Mahakali river. Instead, India has pressed for the map sketched by it in 1879 and 1928/29 being utilised.

These differences amount in reality to differences in the maps that each country possesses, which is further exacerbated by the shifting course of the Mahakali river in the area that was earlier accepted as the boundary.

The Indian government has suggested that the two sides should discuss this matter in a Joint Working Group. Though, a Joint Technical Boundary Committee (JILBC) was formed 18 years ago, which meets twice a year in Nepal and India consecutively to discuss this issue, nothing concrete has come of its deliberations so far. Technically, it may be possible for India to shift its post from Kalapani to the west bank of the Kali. But what is technically feasible may not be possible politically and from the strategic point of view.

India has been apprehensive of Nepal's intentions, particularly after the reverses it suffered in its conflict with China in 1962; it is often thought that Nepal has been trying to play China and India off against each other. A section in Nepal, hostile towards Delhi and pro-Beijing, has been involved in precisely such activities. This is further authenticated by the fact that following its border agreement with China, Nepal has suggested that the sensitive western extremity along the Kalapani tri-junction be discussed trilaterally between China, Nepal and India, adding yet another dimension to the dispute.

Both Delhi and Kathmandu fear that the continuing border dispute might endanger the safe movement of trade and pilgrims along the strategically located Lipu Lekh Pass —the all-weather and reliable entry point into Tibet from Almora.

During Prime Minister Mr. Koirala's visit to India in July-August 2000, there was a convergence of views between Mr. Koirala and Prime Minister Vajpayee on matters of far reaching import relating to political, security and development co-operation. It has been agreed that field-work for the demarcation of the boundary will be completed by AD 2001-2002 and final strip maps will be prepared by 2003. Significantly, the Joint Boundary Committee also agreed, that in case both sides were unable to reach a mutually acceptable agreement on specific segments (referring to two pockets on the boundary-Kalapani in the west and West Champaran in the east, which have defied resolution), detailed reports including a compilation of available evidence would be submitted to the two governments for consideration. The External Affairs Ministry in India , however, is rigidly opposed to the withdrawal of troops from Kalapani and maintains that the issue has been exaggerated. According to New Delhi , "such a withdrawal will have adverse bearing on India 's security."

INDIA AND NEPAL TACKLE BORDER DISPUTES

On the heels of Indian Prime Minister Narendra Modi's reinvigorated regional diplomacy, representatives from the Indian and Nepali survey offices sat down this week in Kathmandu, Nepal to work out border disputes that have risen as the frontiers between the two countries become increasingly blurry.

India's commitment to keep an open and accurate border is another indicator of Modi's interest in regional security. Modi's attaché arranged the talks when they visited Kathmandu in August.

The two countries are revisiting the issue after seven years. The previous mandate, which was in effect from 1981 to 2007, saw the countries settle 97 percent of border discrepancies using modern technology.

The topic of the border with India is a hot-button issue in Nepal; many feel that the current border does not protect Nepali sovereignty. There are a couple swathes of land that both countries claim.

But with renewed talks comes new hope that India will focus its attention and investment in its backyard. Earlier this month, the two countries signed the Indo-Nepal Power Trade Agreement, which appears more favorable to water-rich Nepal than previous agreements.

"[Modi] was speaking the language people wanted to hear," Nepali journalist and commentator Drubha Hari Adhikari said. "He thinks it is significant to have a neighborhood in good humor."

And an emotional issue for Nepal is to have a respected border. Nepalese are conscious of the fact they lost nearly a third of their land to the British Raj in the 1816 Sugauli Treaty, according to Buddhi Shrestha, former Surveyor General of Nepal.

Two areas in particular strike a chord in Nepal: Kalapani and Susta, which lie on the western and eastern border of Nepal, respectively.

Kalapani, which is where India, China, and Nepal meet, has a strategic military position and has been held by India's Indo-Tibetan border security forces since the 1962 war with China. The Mahakali River defines the border in Kalapani, but India and Nepal each claim the river originates in different places, thus the conflict.

In eastern Susta, the Narayani river forms the Indian-Nepali border. But several large floods have re-shaped the river, causing a 14,500 hectare Indian encroachment into Nepal. Here, again, Nepalese are sensitive to the perceived threat to their sovereignty. According to reports, lands disputes among locals are usually won by Indian nationals who have the support of the armed Indian Border Police Force (Seema Sashastra Bal) SSB.

But the renewed border talks are a start. The surveyors concluded the meetings on Friday with a tentative schedule for inspecting the current border and clearing the 20-yard "no-man's land," onto which shops and farmers have encroached. They are also developing a system to address cross-holdings and local land disputes. As a result of the redefined border, people living along the frontier may soon find their land has changed countries. Families who find their land has switched nationalities will be given options to accept compensation for their land and move, or switch nationalities.

The Boundary Working Group also may pave the way to settle disputed lands once and for all. It will provide technical support if diplomatic-level talks happen. But the disputed areas would require more than just the surveyors from the two countries meeting. Buddhi believes these disputes are above the jurisdiction of the surveyors. "They need to be settled at the prime ministerial level," he said.

During his visit, Modi indicated he is willing to hear Nepali Prime Minister Sushil Koirala on issues like this. According to Adhikari, the Indian prime minister's "early indicators are encouraging." In a speech he gave to Nepali politicians, he indicated he would be willing to consider just about anything for his neighbors, even mentioning the 1950 Treaty of Peace and Friendship, which is widely resented in Nepal for the many liberties it gives to India. He also promised to stay out of the internal affairs of Nepal, a promise that many in Nepal are waiting to see to believe.

For Modi, his reinvigorated regional relations are an effort to shore up security threats regionally. As South Asian foreign affairs expert Pramod Jaiswal points out, Nepal is a security concern for India. The country does not have a stable government, and until it does will be seen as a security risk. China's rising influence in Nepal may also be of concern. This year, the northern neighbor supplanted India as the largest source of foreign direct investment.

INDO-NEPAL BORDER DISPUTE IN FOCUS AGAIN

The recently concluded convention of Nepal's ruling Maoists — Unified Communist Party of Nepal (Maoist) — would mostly be remembered for the party's strategic policy shift of discarding the path of protracted peoples' war to adopting capitalist revolution. It would also be remembered in lesser measure for party chairman Pushpa Kamal Dahal Prachanda's attempt at using referendum as a tool to resolve Nepal's long standing border dispute with India.

The proposal presented at the convention by Prachanda in his political document was later removed after it met with opposition and ridicule from within the party and outside. Many felt it was illogical to suggest resolution of border disputes through such a method since it required government to government level negotiations between both countries.

Few others compared Prachanda with Kazi Lhendup Dorjee — a key figure in Sikkim's 1975 union with India following a referendum abolishing monarchy and approving the merger. Sensing the mistake Prachanda decided to do away with the suggestion and instead included "revoking unequal treaties and agreements signed in the past" with India in his document.

Border dispute between both countries sprung up after India's independence following discontinuation of annual inspection of border areas by a team comprising officials from India and Nepal to detect encroachment, missing pillars and territories unclearly defined.

To address the issue and clearly demarcate the border, a Joint Technical Committee was set up in 1981. It took more than two decades of work to mark out 98 percent of the border on strip maps. The maps were signed by experts of both nations in 2007. The two most disputed areas, Kalapani and Susta, were however not covered by the JTC as it was felt that problems specific to these pockets can be addressed only through high-level negotiations.

Although more than five years have passed since signing of the strip maps, Nepal is yet to give consent on formalizing them. And unless that happen demarcation of the boundary on the ground can't take place. Nepal's political instability is one reason why the task remains incomplete. But some experts in Kathmandu also question the methods used to delineate the border and claim Nepal lost more than a thousand hectares to India in the process.

There is also the view that Kalapani and Susta are not the only remaining areas of dispute and that both countries need to renegotiate problems at more than 60 different points along the nearly 1,800-km long border. But unlike Prachanda's proposal, these issues can't be addressed by a referendum in one country and both countries need to adopt a pro-active approach to resolve the border dispute before they spiral out of control and affect bilateral relations.

9

The Battle for the Border

The next major development with China and Tibet was when the British called for a conference at Simla in October 1913. The Chinese attended reluctantly, but the Tibetan authorities came quite eagerly as they were now engaged in conflict with their Chinese suzerains. Henry McMahon, then foreign secretary to the 'government of India,' led the British delegation. McMahon was some sort of an expert at drawing boundary lines, having spent two years demarcating the Durand Line at the northwest frontier.

The boundary that followed was the now famous McMahon Line. This boundary now extended British India up to the edge of the Tibetan plateau. It was not really a cartographers delight as it violated several rules of boundary demarcation. But it was an ethnic boundary in the sense that the area, except for the Tawang tract, was non-Tibetan in character.

The Chinese soon repudiated the Simla Convention and thus the McMahon Line. All through this period, the British never challenged Chinese suzerainty over Tibet. The new boundary was not made effective till Olaf Caroe, an ICS officer, urged the British authorities to do so in 1935. Thus, in 1937, the Survey of India for the first time showed the McMahon Line as the official boundary. But confusion still abounded.

In 1938, the Survey of India published a map of Tibet, which showed the Tawang tract as part of that country. Even the first edition of Jawaharlal Nehru's Discovery Of India showed the Indo-Tibetan boundary as running at the foot of the hills. The

Tibetans did not accept this 'annexation' of the Tawang tract and challenged the British attempts to expand their government into this area. But they tacitly accepted the rest of the McMahon demarcation. It is clear that, but for the Tawang tract, there is little basis for the Chinese claim on the whole of Arunachal Pradesh. Even the claim they might have on the Tawang tract is rendered invalid in the sense that it becomes a geographical anachronism and incompatible with India's security interests.

The Japanese thrust towards India in World War II gave urgency to the British need to fix this boundary firmly and securely. Thus, in 1944, J P Mills, the then government's advisor on tribal affairs, established a British administration in the entire belt from Walong in the east to Dirang Dzong in the west. Several posts of the Assam Rifles were established and soon Tibetan government officials were packed off from the Tawang tract also.

This was the state of the Great Game when the British left India. In 1949, the Communists came to power in China and shortly thereafter the People's Republic announced its army would be moving into Tibet. India reacted by sending the Chinese a diplomatic note. Soon after receiving this angry protest, the Chinese occupied Tibet. The Chinese said: 'Tibet is an integral part of China and the problem of Tibet is a domestic problem of China. The Chinese People's Liberation Army must enter Tibet, liberate the Tibetan people and defend the frontiers of China.' India had hoped to persuade the Chinese to desist by offering to take up their case for membership in the UN in place of the Kuomintang Chinese left on Formosa. The Chinese rejected this absurd quid pro quo and said these two issues were unconnected.

The purpose of this laborious recitation of the events of nearly a century-and-a-half of the Great Game is to only show that borders were either never clearly demarcated or established. Lines kept shifting on maps as political contingencies arose. The Indian people were, for this entire period, passive spectators to these cartographic games.

In 1947, the British finally left India. Our choice then was to either call an end to the Great Game or continue playing it with all the intensity and commitment it called for. We did neither.

When the Chinese Communists occupied Tibet, we acquiesced. Neither did we firmly move into the areas claimed by the British as Indian territory, particularly in the western sector. How well we looked after territory we claimed as our own is seen by the fact that, in the early 1950s, the Chinese had built a road connecting Tibet to Sinkiang across the Aksai Chin and we did not have a clue about it for several years.

The Indian government did move into the Tawang tract in force in 1951, overriding Chinese/Tibetan protests. In this sector, at least, it was clear that the Indian government was firm about its control of all the territory claimed by the British. There are several signs that indicate the Chinese too seem to have accepted the McMahon Line as the boundary in this sector.

The situation in the western sector was entirely different. Here no definite British Indian boundary line existed. The only two points accepted by both sides were that the Karakoram Pass and Demchok, the western and eastern ends of this sector, were in Indian territory. Opinions on how the line traversed between the two points differed.

India's boundary was inclined towards the Johnson claim line whereas as the Chinese, having built their road through the Aksai Chin, naturally preferred an alignment closer to the McCartney/ MacDonald line of 1899. The Chinese claim line however went further west and included the Chip Chap valley, Samzungling, Kongka La, Khurnak Fort and Jara La. More importantly, as far as the Great Game was concerned, the Chinese had occupied all this territory by the early 1950s.

This is how matters were by the end of 1952 and by and large how things are today. The Chinese hold all territory, give or take some, within their claim line in Ladakh. In the east, India holds most of the territory below the McMahon line give or take some. These de facto boundaries could have been a basis for a permanent settlement of our boundaries. But we did not pursue it, though there are indications from time to time that the Chinese might want to settle on this basis.

Now the question that arises is: Why did the Government of India not extend its control to the boundaries it claimed in the western sector as it did in the east? This was mostly due to the terrain. The boundary claimed lies beyond two high mountain ranges and is logistically and militarily indefensible. Besides, the Chinese were already in control of much of the area by 1951. The question then is: Why did the government of India not make serious diplomatic or military efforts to assert control over territories it believed was ours?

The answer obviously lies in the fact that, legally, there was not a very good case. Besides, the military price this barren uninhabited windswept desolation would demand did not make it a worthwhile cause. Despite all this, there abounded the zealous spirit with which recently freed nations regarded their inherited boundaries that were often without regard to geography, ethnicity and history. Even in 1954, the most advanced Indian post was at Chushul. Barring a couple of patrols to Lanak La, no attempt was made to show the new flag. Even Lanak La was well south of Aksai Chin and short of the Sinkiang-Tibet highway, which passed east of it at that point.

The main rule of the Game for the previous 150 years was that it be played as quietly and surreptitiously as possible. In the 1950s, these rules still seemed to prevail. The two contesting governments decided to keep the lid on the problems while jockeying around for local advantages. On the surface it was all 'Hindi-Chini bhai-bhai' and the practice of the Panchsheel philosophy. Underneath was the realisation the titles to large tracts of territory under the control of both parties were under dispute. The lid on this roiling cauldron blew away when in March 1959 the Dalai Lama fled to India and was given political asylum.

THE COLLISION OF THE SINO-INDIAN WAR

In many ways, how China and India relate to each other indicates where they see themselves in the international system. Firstly, however, it is necessary to have an understanding of the events leading up to and following the 1962 Sino-Indian War, as this continues to affect the contemporary Sino-Indian relationship.

The major causes of conflict between China and India – namely, the disputed border and the issue of Tibet, including the fourteenth

Dalai Lama's ongoing residency in India – have their roots in the political dealings that went on in the late 1800s and early 1900s between British India, pre-Communist China and feudal Tibet. The major question was whether treaties signed by British India and Tibet demarcating the border – known as the McMahon Line – were valid, given that, according to the Chinese, Tibet was part of China and had no authority to act unilaterally. Disagreements of this nature and the exact location of the border persisted throughout the early twentieth century, further complicated by Indian independence in 1947 (which removed British backing and so altered the balance of power in the region in favour of China) and the Chinese 'liberation' of Tibet in 1950.

1954, marked with a visit to India Chinese by Premier Zhou Enlai in June, and a reciprocal visit by Indian Prime Minister Jawaharlal Nehru to China in October, was a high point in the relationship; it was during the latter visit that the term 'Hindi-Chini bhai-bhai' (Indians and Chinese are brothers) was coined, and denoted a period of rapprochement after decades of strife over the disputed India-Tibet border.

This new-found friendship in theory forged a renewed basis for discussions over the disputed border, though this was tested only two years later. There were (and still are) two contested areas: the north-eastern stretch, which was known under the British as the North-East Frontier Agency (NEFA) and since 1986 has been the Indian state of Arunachal Pradesh (claimed by the Chinese as Southern Tibet), and the western region of Aksai Chin (claimed by the Indians and currently administered by the Chinese), which borders the Indian state of Jammu and Kashmir.

Although up until the mid-50s most of the border tensions had existed over the eastern stretch – and specifically the disputed border known as the McMahon Line – the western region became the focus when in 1956 the Chinese constructed a highway from Xinjiang province to Tibet through the Aksai Chin to allow the rapid movement of troops between the two restive provinces. In spite of disputing the occupation of the territory, India did not actually administer the Aksai Chin in any way, and consequently after the building of the road the region effectively passed into

Chinese hands. Nevertheless, the Aksai Chin continued to be a volatile area – not helped by the fact that the rest of Jammu and Kashmir was the subject of an ongoing and often violent dispute between India and Pakistan – and subsequently provided one of the flashpoints for the 1962 Sino-Indian war.

Matters were further complicated with the Lhasa Revolt of March 1959, an uprising of Tibetans which culminated in the fleeing of the fourteenth Dalai Lama (and subsequently thousands of Tibetan refugees) to India and the systematic crushing of the resistance by Chinese forces. In the northern autumn Chinese and Indian troops clashed along the McMahon Line border. An attempt at resolving the border issue was made during a visit by Premier Zhou Enlai to Delhi from19-25 April 1960, but "the talks...did not resolve the differences that had arisen and the two Prime Ministers decided that officials of the two Governments should examine the factual material in the possession of the two Governments in support of their stands" (Ministry of External Affairs, 1961:1). The committee met three times throughout 1960, with both sides producing reports of the discussions for their respective governments.

The contents of these reports illustrate how intractable the border problem was and indeed still is, with the two sides unable to agree even on the basic tenor of the talks, such as whether the border had ever been officially delimited (no, according to China; yes, according to India). Consequently no resolution was reached at the 1960 talks which, with hindsight, were really the last opportunity to effect an agreement before relations broke down completely.

The Sino-Indian War began on 8 September 1962 when the Chinese crossed into NEFA (now Arunachal Pradesh) and attacked an Indian border post, alleging that the Indians had already violated the McMahon Line. This was the first time the conflict flared along the McMahon Line, though there had been some fighting around the Aksai Chin region, inflamed by Sino-Pakistani border talks which the Indians alleged were aimed at undermining their position in Kashmir. These skirmishes continued throughout September and into October.

On 20 October the Chinese launched a full-scale offensive all along the frontier, from Ladakh to NEFA, arguing that it was a pre-emptive strike against Indian aggression. This was significant because it moved the conflict beyond the disputed areas and into Indian territory, essentially becoming an invasion of India. The Indian force was fatally under-prepared and crumbled before the Chinese onslaught.

The fighting lasted for just over a month, with the Chinese declaring a unilateral ceasefire on 21 November. Statistics released by the Indian government on 29 October had between 2000 and 2500 Indian soldiers killed during the first week of fighting, with 1102 held prisoner, 291 wounded and 5174 missing and presumed dead. On 8 November the Chinese proposed a ceasefire agreement whereby both parties would withdraw twenty kilometres behind the positions held on 7 November, 1959. This meant that the Chinese would withdraw back behind the McMahon Line, but they would maintain control of Indian-claimed territory in Ladakh, including the strategically important Aksai Chin road linking Xinjiang and Tibet. This was initially rejected by the Indians, but after another fortnight of fierce fighting the Chinese surprised everyone by announcing a unilateral ceasefire and the withdrawal of troops from 1 December to the 7 November 1959 positions. The Chinese also added that, provided the Indian government took corresponding measures, the two parties could meet to discuss troop withdrawal and an end to hostilities. Militarily weakened, and with the rest of the world supporting all measures to solve the conflict, India was in no position to argue.

In December 1962 six non-aligned nations (Ceylon, Burma, Cambodia, Indonesia, the United Arab Republic and Ghana) met in Colombo to try to broker a formal peace deal, but their lack of condemnation of the Chinese invasion incensed India. India nevertheless accepted the Colombo proposals, but China rejected them, insisting on a "unilateral implementation" of its 21 November 1962 statement; consequently the talks broke down and nothing was resolved, even in subsequent bilateral meetings.

Sino-Indian relations did not begin to normalise until the mid-1970s; a turning point was the resumption of ambassadorial relations in 1976. Although the two countries retained non-official diplomatic relations throughout the 1960s (with missions headed by a *charge d'affairs* rather than an ambassador), interaction was minimal. In fact, Gautam Das describes the period between 1962-76 as a period of "cold peace" rather than cold war, and notes that "Sino-Indian relations after 1962 are, in substance if not chronology, Sino-Indian relations after 1976 [because very little of note happened in the intervening period]".

Rapprochement continued after the resumption of diplomatic relations, albeit with a few hiccups, but it wasn't until 1988 that the turning point came with Indian Prime Minister Rajiv Gandhi's visit to Beijing. This made him the first Indian Prime Minister to visit China since Nehru in 1954 and marked the end of the impasse on the border issue which had lasted for most of the 1980s; the two sides agreed to maintain peace and stability along the Line of Actual Control (LAC) in Arunachal Pradesh (roughly equivalent to the McMahon Line), and they also agreed to set up a Joint Working Group (JWG) to help defuse the border issue. In addition, India agreed to curtail the anti-China actions of Tibetans in India. According to Das, "the decade that followed the Rajiv Gandhi visit up to the 1998 Indian nuclear explosions (Pokhran-II) has been the most cordial phase of Sino-Indian relations after 1962".

These warm relations continued during the mid-1990s, and were further consolidated by Chinese President Jiang Zemin's visit to India in 1996, where four mutual cooperation agreements were signed, and it appeared that a breakthrough in the tensions had finally occurred.

Unfortunately, this series of small steps forward was followed by a giant leap backwards in 1998. During a visit of the People's Liberation Army (PLA) Senior General Fu Quanyou to New Delhi, the Indian Defence Minister, George Fernandes, publicly stated that he believed China was continuing to carry out border incursions into Indian territory, and later accused China of being India's number one security threat, greater even than Pakistan. This was immediately followed by India's second ever nuclear tests, known as Pokhran II (ibid). The fact that the tests occurred before Fu had even arrived back in Beijing caused a huge loss of face for the Chinese, because they felt that after a decade of overtures to the Indians they had been callously rebuffed and humiliated.

Nevertheless, the overall Chinese reaction to the tests was initially quite controlled, and might have remained so, had India not justified the tests by claiming they were in response to the 'China threat'.

This was articulated in a letter from Indian Prime Minister Vajpayee to US President Bill Clinton, which was printed in the *New York Times* on 13 May (ibid). This was seen as "unwarranted and provocative", and the fact that the issue was given such a public airing caused another immense loss of face for the Chinese; consequently they reacted angrily, cancelling the next meeting of the Joint Working Group on the border issue.

This issue of the 'China threat' still permeates relations today, with more than one Chinese interviewee claiming that the Indian military deliberately promotes China as a threat in order to get increased defence spending, and that 1998 was one of the clearest examples of this (Author interviews with Wang Dehua and anonymous interviewee, 2010).

After the low point of the 1998 tests, relations began once again to normalise, in spite of a brief hiccup over Tibet when 14-year-old Ugyen Thinley Dorje, the 17th Karmapa Lama of the Kagyupa sect of Tibetan Buddhism, fled China for Dharamsala in January 2000.

Nevertheless, in February 2000 India and China concluded an agreement for China's accession to the World Trade Organisation; in March India participated in the first ever Sino-Indian security dialogue in Beijing, and the Joint Working Group sessions resumed in April of the same year. In 2003 an incursion by Chinese troops into Indian territory occurred in Arunachal Pradesh, shortly after Indian Prime Minister Vajpayee's visit to Beijing; Vajpayee put this down to "differences in perceptions" regarding the Line of Actual Control, but some politicians and analysts took it much more seriously. This incident shows that in spite of another gradual thawing of relations, the border question still remains a highly contentious issue in the Sino-Indian relationship. Furthermore, in addition to ongoing Indian concerns about the Sino-Pakistani relationship, China is also disturbed about the growing relationship between India and the USA, fearing that such an alliance will upset the balance of power in the region.

Seen in the light of history, the most recent incidents to affect the Sino-Indian relationship – the 2008 Tibet protests and the subsequent disruption of the Olympic torch relay (including in Delhi); and the border skirmishes and associated negative media coverage throughout 2009 – are unlikely to cause permanent damage to the relationship.

They do, however, highlight the fact that the border issue is still unresolved, and most analysts agree that the Sino-Indian relationship will not be able to move forward in any meaningful way until this question is answered. As well as being rooted in political reality, however, a large element of the Sino-Indian conflict also stems from misplaced perceptions, both of each other's motives and of their own place in the world order.

The concept of 'Chindia' is popular at present but it is based on flawed logic. Although the geo-civilisational aspects, where cultural practices flowed freely across what is now Central Asia to India and China and back again, cannot be denied, China and India are also distinct civilisations with their own histories and cultures and to conflate them is to understate the importance of this in shaping their distinctive governments and policies.

It also minimises the very real animosity which remains between them and deeply influences not only the Sino-Indian relationship but also how they see themselves and how they relate to the wider international community. On a political and strategic front, India and China have followed extremely different developmental trajectories with different outcomes and they also have different aims for their status in the international system. These differences in aims, policy and strategic thought can be seen to be playing out in Central Asia at present.

The 'Chindia' concept is for the most part a Western construct developed as a response to the 'China threat' perception and tied into the former US and ASEAN policy of containment, in which India would play an important role.

This idea of a mutual rise or equating China and India was seized upon by some in India who were attracted by the idea that India has or will soon have the same type of international economic and political clout as China, even when the present reality suggests otherwise. In fact, India should not seek to emulate China because it is unlikely that such a course of action would succeed; in any case the two countries' systems are extremely different.

Rather, India must forge its own path and decide what kind of a role it wants to play internationally, and how it will achieve this. It must also in the immediate-term concentrate on domestic development and remember that 'national security' cannot just be about the military but must also include human, food, environmental and other types of security as well as poverty reduction.

This seems to be the path which the Indian government is beginning to take and it is likely to be far more successful than any which frames the question of India's development in relation to China. Regarding China, we need to rethink the way we examine it in terms of international relations theory in order to avoid overlooking the real issues in Chinese strategic thought because of a desire to fit Chinese development into an established international relations model.

Finally, scholarship – both in China and India and further afield – needs to be developed so that more scholars are educated in the practices and policies of both countries, and communication is facilitated between China and India scholars the world over, rather than operating simply in closed 'China studies' or 'India studies' spheres. This would not only prove beneficial to promoting stability in the Sino-Indian relationship, but would also go some way to ensuring that the two countries can be viewed as separate but parallel entities rather than as 'Chindia'.

BATTLE OF IMPHAL-KOHIMA

By summer of 1943, the British forces were beginning to dominate in the skies with Royal Air Force (RAF) aircraft operating out of India. While Japan had no original plans to invade India, Lieutenant General Renya Mutaguchi of the Japanese 15th Army knew that an offensive into India was the only way he could eliminate the aerial threat. Controlling northeastern India would also create a larger buffer zone between India and Burma. Imphal was the state capital of Manipur in northeastern India and was situated amidst a plain where an invading army from the east must march across. Additionally, a Japanese-controlled northeastern India would also cut off "the Hump" as an aerial supply route into China. As such, it was no surprise that British plans to invade Burma used Imphal as a launch point for ground troops, the same place Mutaguchi also targeted. Mutaguchi's excursion into India was originally rejected by his immediate superiors, but what would eventually become Operation U (U-Go) was approved by Southern Expeditionary Army and the Imperial General Headquarters (IGHQ) in Tokyo, Japan.

Mutaguchi planned to pin-down or destroy the forward-deployed Indian troops with Lieutenant General Motoso Yanagida's 33rd Division, then the 33rd Division will be reinforced by Lieutenant General Masafumi Yamauchi's 15th Division to take Imphal. At the same time, Lieutenant General Kotoku Sato's 31st Division was to attack Kohima, a village on a major road into Imphal, an administrative center of the state of Nagaland, and near the important airfield at Dimapur. Mutaguchi did not receive support from his field generals for his plans; most of them believe the attack plan was too risky.

The city of Imphal was defended by the Indian IV Corps under the command of Lieutenant General Geoffrey Scoones, who reported to Lieutenant General William Slim. As the Japanese troops attacked, Slim and Scoones attempted to move this troops from their forward positions back into the plains near Imphal, forcing the Japanese to fight with a longer supply line, but Scoones had reacted too late; while the Japanese offensive began by crossing the Chindwin River on 8 Mar, Scoones did not give the order to fall back near Imphal until 13 Mar. As a result, the Indian 17th Division allowed its supply dumps to become captured by the Japanese and become encircled. However, the 214th Regiment of the 17th Division successfully counterattacked at Tuitum Saddle on 18 Mar, allowing the division to recover part of the captured supplies and safely retreated to Imphal on 4 Apr 1944. The Japanese followed the withdrawing Indian troops closely. As soon as the Indian 17th Division reached Imphal, the attack began. The Japanese 33rd Division attacked from Bishenpur from the south, though that attack was cautious and slow. From Tamu, Major General Tsunoru Yamamoto, commanding units from both the 15th and 33rd Divisions and two brigades of Indian troops attacked Shenam Saddle near Imphal, and was quickly halted by the Indian troops at this easily-defended junction. From the north, the remainder of the 15th Division attacked and first captured a small supply dump at Kangpokpi then captured Nungshigum Hill which overlooked Imphal's main airfield. The initial attack did not go as well as Mutaguchi originally planned, and the possibly prolonged campaign was now threatened by a long supply line through the Burmese jungles. It was exactly what his field generals warned of. To make matters worse particularly for the Japanese 31st Division, the British 23 LRP Brigade had been seriously disrupting Japanese supply operations behind the lines, making even foraging to the east of Kohima nearly impossible.

The attack on Kohima began around the same time, which was weakly defended by the Assam Regiment and some of the paramilitary Assam Rifles. The Indian 161st Brigade was originally posted at Kohima, but it was moved out of Kohima to Dimapur shortly before the attack. On 3 Apr, the 31st Division attacked Kohima Ridge which overlooked the main supply route between Imphal and Kohima. The siege of Kohima began on 6 Apr. Japanese mortar fire rained down on the Indian troops who were poorly supplied and lacking drinking water. Nevertheless, the Indian troops held, and combat turned into a stalemate.

On 13 Apr, the Indian 5th Division counterattacked at Nungshigum Hill outside of Imphal with support from artillery and M3 Lee tanks. The Japanese had neither anti-tank weapons nor artillery; these heavier guns had been decided against as Mutaguchi planned for a swift campaign, and these guns were simply too bulky to carry through the dense jungle. As a result, the hill was taken back by the Indian troops after dealing heavy casualties on the Japanese.

On 15 Apr, the British 2nd Division which had been in training in southern India arrived at Dimapur near Kohima. The fresh troops relieved the Indian 161st Brigade, who rested for three days before going on a counterattack toward Kohima. As the siege at Kohima listed on about 20 Apr, the incoming troops were shocked by what they witnessed. The once picturesque village was now in ruins, building walls marked with bullet holes and surrounding hills covered by broken trees. "Every inch of ground were disputed in the bloodiest and most desperate hand-to-hand fighting", described historian Frank McLynn.

By 1 May 1944, the Indian troops had a firm hold on the line, and their British commander could entertain the notion of a counter offensive, especially with the arrival of the 33rd Brigade of the Indian 7th Division on 4 May. Although the Japanese line was tough to break, the supply situation had become critical. The Japanese divisions had not been receiving adequate supplies, including food, and the soldiers' health were becoming dangerously poor due to malnutrition. The situation took a worse turn on 12 May when the Indian 114th Brigade arrived near Kohima. Under Montagu Stopford's command as XXXIII Corps, British and Indian forces attacked southward from Kohima toward Imphal. The Japanese troops, despite the difficult conditions they were in, fought back fiercely. Nevertheless, the Japanese troops were drove out of the Kohima region by the end of May; with 38 3.7-inch mountain howitzers, 48 25-pound field guns, and 2 5.5-inch medium guns, the Japanese could hardly hold their line for an extended amount of time. The RAF also stepped up their involvement, bombing and strafing Japanese positions, destroying Japanese morale that had already been faltering.

On 25 May, troops near Kohima reported that unless adequate food supplies had been delivered, the troops there could not last past 1 Jun; in fact, General Sato threatened he would disobey direct orders and withdraw if he did not see supplies flowing in. On 31 May, Japanese troops withdrew from Naga village and fell back southward.

The XXXIII Corps was then joined by IV Corps and attacked the Japanese troops further along the Dimapur-Imphal road on 22

Jun near Milestone 109. When the battle at Milestone 109 was won by the British and Indian troops, the siege of Imphal was lifted.

The Japanese 33rd Division, now under command of Lieutenant General Nobuo Tanaka and freshly reinforced by battalions from 53rd and 54th Divisions, continue to assert pressure on the Indian troops despite the recent setbacks. The 33rd Division nearly broke through the line set by the Indian 17th Division at Bishenpur, but in the end the Japanese suffered such a high casualty that the offensive was called off by the front line generals on 3 Jul 1944. In fact, by this time, many Japanese units were unfit for combat due to various reasons that they had already been disobeying orders to press forward. Reluctantly, Mutaguchi withdrew the remnants of the Japanese 33rd Division from Imphal, India back into Burma. The Japanese defeat at Imphal and Kohima represented the largest defeat in Japanese military history. Of the 65,000 front-line troops, 30,000 were killed, 23,000 were wounded, and 600 were captured; among the 50,000 support troops, there were 15,000 casualties. The Allies only suffered 17,500 casualties in comparison.

The Allied victory at Imphal and Kohima allowed the RAF to continue assert pressure from the skies on Japanese troops in Burma. "The Hump" into China was also allowed to continue because of the successful defense. The RAF also contributed greatly to the battle directly as RAF aircraft delivered most of the supplies the British and Indian forces needed; the RAF flew 19,000 tons of supplies and 12,000 men into the Kohima-Imphal region and flew out 13,000 casualties and 43,000 non-combatants.

Bibliography

Alastair Lamb, Kashmir: *A Disputed Legacy 1846–1990*, Hertingfordbury, Herts: Roxford Books, 1991.

Allen Carlson, *Unifying China, Integrating with the World: Securing Chinese Sovereignty in the Reform Era*, Stanford: Stanford University Press, 2005.

Amitabh Sikdar: *India and China : Strategic Energy Management and Security*, Manas, Delhi, 2009.

Anderson, J.: *Transnational Democracy: Political Spaces and Border Crossings*, Routledge: London and New York, 2002.

Anderson, M. and Bort, E.: *Boundaries and Identities: The Eastern Frontier of the Asia*, Edinburgh: International Social Sciences Institute, University of Edinburgh, 1996.

Anil, K.C.: *Military and Democracy in South Asia : Challenges, Politics and Power*, Sumit Enterprises, Delhi, 2009.

Benjamin, Joseph : *China-Pak Relations : Prospect and Retrospect*, Reference Press, Delhi, 2004.

Bhat, T.P. : *India and China : Trade Complementarities and Competitiveness*, Bookwell, Delhi, 2008.

Chopra, P. N.: *Towards Freedom: Documents on the Movement for Independence in India, 1937*. Delhi: Oxford UP, 1986.

Coakley, J.: *The Territorial Management of Ethnic Conflict*, London: Frank Cass, 2003.

Digumarti Bhaskara Rao: *Military Conversion : Impact on Science and Technology*, Discovery, Delhi, 2003.

Dixit, J.N. : *India and Regional Developments : Through the Prism of Indo-Pak Relations*, Gyan, Delhi, 2004.

Evelyn Goh, *Meeting the China Challenge: The U.S. in Southeast Asian Regional Security Strategies*, DC: East-West Center, 2005.

George Mathew: *Grass Roots Democracy in India and China : The Right to Participate*, Sage, Delhi, 2007.

Ghosh, Ajoy : *Indo-Pak Conflict : Threat to South Asian Security*, Reference Press, Delhi, 2003.

Hodson, H. V.: *The Great Divide: Britain-India-Pakistan*, Karachi, Oxford UP, 1993.

Imtiaz, A.: *State and Foreign Policy: India's Role in South Asia*, New Delhi, Vikas, 1993.

Jagannath P. Panda: *China's Path to Power : Party, Military and the Politics of State Transition*, Pentagon, Delhi, 2010.

Jha, Prem Shankar : *India and China : The Battle Between Soft and Hard Power*, Penguin Books India, Delhi, 2010.

Mary, W.: *Asian Power and Politics: the Cultural Dimensions of Authority*, Cambridge, Belknap Press, 1985.

Nayyar, K K : *National Security : Military Aspects*, Rupa, Delhi, 2003.

Phuskele, Preeti : *India and China : Emerging Superpowers*, ICFAI University, Delhi, 2009.

Prabir De: *India and China in an Era of Globalisation : Essays on Economic Cooperation*, Bookwell, Delhi, 2005.

Seshagiri, K. L. : *Mahatma Gandhi and Comparative Religion*, Motilal Banarsidass, New Delhi, 1978.

Thampi, Madhavi : *India and China in the Colonial World*, Social Science Press, Delhi, 2010.

Wilson, T. M.: *New Borders for a Changing: Cross-border Cooperation and Governance*, London: Frank Cass, 2003.

Index

❑❑❑